THE
LONG REVOLUTION

Sixty Years on the Frontlines
of a New American Theater

THE
LONG REVOLUTION

Sixty Years on the Frontlines
of a New American Theater

ZELDA FICHANDLER

Edited by TODD LONDON

THEATRE COMMUNICATIONS GROUP   NEW YORK   2024

The Long Revolution: Sixty Years on the Frontlines of a New American Theater
is published by Theatre Communications Group, Inc., 520 Eighth Avenue, 20th Floor,
Suite #2000, New York, NY 10018-4156

The publication of *The Long Revolution: Sixty Years on the Frontlines of a New American
Theater*, through TCG Books, is made possible with support by Mellon Foundation.

We would like to offer our special thanks to Furthermore:
a program of the J. M. Kaplan Fund for their support of
this publication.

We would also like to thank the trustees of Arena Stage, past and present, for their
generous sponsorship of this publication. A full acknowledgment appears at the back
of the book.

TCG books are exclusively distributed to the book trade by Consortium Book Sales
and Distribution.

Library of Congress Control Numbers:
2022052436 (print) / 2022052437 (ebook)
ISBN 978-1-55936-975-6 (paperback) / ISBN 978-1-55936-933-6 (ebook)
A catalog record for this book is available from the Library of Congress.

Book design and composition by Lisa Govan
Cover design by Mark Melnick
Cover photograph by George de Vincent, c. 1970

First Edition, January 2024

For my family:
my sons Hal and Mark;
Joyce, sister and friend;
and Matthew and Emily, my grandchildren,
who taught me anew the sheer animal joy of being alive.

And for my students:
You were all my teachers.

What a thing *can* be, it *must* be . . .

—ARISTOTLE

CONTENTS

CONTENTS

FOREWORD

By Nikkole Salter

I 'm writing this from the sunlit living room of my home in New Jersey—close enough that New York City is still a reachable constellation, but far enough away that it is not the center of my orbit—about fifteen minutes away from my local theater, Luna Stage. I thought I'd start with that bit of information, since that is how our beloved Zelda Fichandler began many of her writings featured in this book— where she was at the time—Washington, DC; London; or overlooking Washington Square Park in the West Village.

"Of course she would start that way," I thought. Like every good *director*, like every good *educator*, like every *(r)evolutionary* worth her salt, Mrs. Fichandler understood the importance of context—of environment; of culture; of the widely held beliefs and values of a society that shape perspective, expectation, and, ultimately, determine the borders of possibility for its people.

Mrs. Fichandler's context, then, is of utmost importance if one is to fully appreciate her contribution to the American theater. Her mother emigrated to the United States, a young child of five, in 1905, with her parents and brother. Born Zelda Diamond, in 1924, Mrs. Fichandler's parents likely had high hopes for the daughter they named Zelda. "Zelda" meaning "blessed" or "happy" in Yiddish, and "fight," "battle," even "strong woman" in German. "Diamonds" have symbolized enlightenment, purity, wealth, and indestructibility in the odes of great poets. History further enriches the meaning of her name: When Zelda's grandfather, David Louf emigrated from Russia to America, he was compelled to change his name on his passport to David Diamond—and his second wife's name was Zelda, whom our Zelda was named after. I have been told that "Fichandler," Zelda's married name, means "spiritual," "helper," and "intuitive" (even "animal" or "cattle tender"). Since the practice of naming is intended to describe (or prophesy) the nature of an entity, the very vibration of her name—Zelda Diamond Fichandler—must have created a context of expectation that her young Virgo self could not even have imagined fulfilling, especially during the bust of the Great Depression, followed by the tumult of World War II.

Yet, by the time I met Mrs. Fichandler in my NYU Graduate Acting audition in 2001, despite the many difficulties presented by the world, she *had*, in fact, become the happy and blessed strong woman; the faithful and pure enlightened one; the intuitive helper of generations of theater artists. Luckily, all I knew, as I performed contrasting audition monologues from Shakespeare's *Winter's Tale*, and Phyllis Yvonne Stickney's *Big Momma 'n' em*, was that Mrs. Fichandler was the woman who would tell me if I was "accepted" or not. Throughout my time at NYU she resonated as an unofficial oracle for her students. If her eyes brightened at our propositions, many of us took it as a sign of being on the right path.

I remember telling her, close to my graduation, that I was considering founding my own theater company, just as she had cofounded Arena Stage. I thought she'd be elated. Instead, she looked at me with a mixture of what I perceived to be exhaustion and boredom. Initially, I could not reconcile her response. Mrs. Fichandler was known for being supportive of the artistic and entrepreneurial inclinations of her students. I'd thought she'd be proud to know I wanted to walk in her footsteps.

Perhaps her jaded response came from the decades-long exposure to the conveyer belt of hopeful NYU students. Mrs. Fichandler must have been full of that hope when she was working to launch Arena Stage in 1950—a time of great economic upswing amid rising social tumult. But it was no longer 1950 Washington, DC. It was post-

9/11 New York City. By the time I stood before her with my hope, she already knew how hard it was to start and maintain a theater, and she knew that creating a sustainable business model for a theater committed to new work was nearly impossible. Yet she achieved the impossible by arguing for theater's educational qualities, and by applying the concept of "not for profit" to the theater, thus allowing them to accept tax-free donations like schools and churches.

Mrs. Fichandler also knew how hard it was to move past male dominance in ownership and executive stewardship—because she was a leader, not only of the theater she helped found, but of the regional theater movement. She knew how hard it was to develop audiences—but she cultivated the subscription model that got people invested in the mission of the theater, not just the pleasure of an individual show. She knew how difficult it was to build a coalition of artistic leaders in the field who saw themselves as separate entities—because she helped make sure Arena Stage was a cofounding member of Theatre Communications Group (TCG), which helped unify the collective interests of the burgeoning field. She knew the challenge of lobbying the government and private foundations for their support of our art, without losing the right to freedom of speech—because she did it through the advocacy work at TCG, taking on lawmakers who would censor artists *while* pushing to *increase* the NEA's budget.

Mrs. Fichandler knew how hard it was to keep theater relevant, but she did it by following her impulse to program Howard Sackler's *The Great White Hope* at the peak of the civil rights movement, months before Rev. Dr. Martin Luther King, Jr. delivered his last "Mountaintop" speech. This show—the first to be moved from a regional theater to Broadway—single-handedly validated the work of local artists all over the country, centering their work as stageworthy, and reminding artists that they could (and *should*) grapple with the times in their storytelling.

Our strong woman was certainly a cultural revolutionary, fighting for the dramatic narrative to be an essential part of American life. But even more than an arts general, Mrs. Fichandler was a cultural *evolutionary*—pushing theater and the dramatic form to mature beyond its silos. With her partners, Mrs. Fichandler opened an *integrated* theater in 1950 in Washington, DC—a city whose only theater venue at the time closed rather than desegregate. She helped create a space where marginalized voices were welcome, a space removed from market demands; a place whose purpose was societal enrichment, not entertainment. Mrs. Fichandler created theater that centralized the importance of theater as a service to the public good, not the importance of theater as a service to advertising campaigns and propaganda; and she created homes for artists where they could grow and take risks, rather than being hired hands for one-offs, relegated to the limitations of their previous successes (or failures). She didn't exploit stars for their market share—she *made stars* and added cultural capital and economic value to her community.

In 2004, when she sighed at me, I'm certain Mrs. Fichandler was aware of all the change she had sparked and helped forge to create the nonprofit theater industry. I'm sure she was aware of all the success of TCG and NYU's Graduate Acting Program. As I write this, it is not lost on me that, without her work, the theater sitting fifteen minutes from my house in New Jersey—the one that has commissioned two and produced four of my plays—would not even exist.

Perhaps our blessed strong woman sighed because the context she thought she had helped change—in the context of a post-9/11 America—was revealing itself to have a long way to go. Perhaps she was overcome by the boom of the individualized, on-demand technology of the information age, and she didn't know what that meant for the future of live, in-person, communal dramatic storytelling. Perhaps her sigh was a signal of her understanding of how much my generation of theater makers would have to continue to fight if we dedicated our lives to the theater.

I'll never know what that sigh was about. What I do know now, nearly twenty years later, is that Mrs. Fichandler was coming to the end of her career, and, despite encouragement and support, was actively procrastinating writing her memoir. Maybe our happy and blessed strong woman, our faithful and pure enlightened one, our intuitive helper, our regional theater movement matriarch felt that it was time to imagine the next theater movement, rather than trying to re-create the past.

If she were alive today, perhaps she would tell us that theater, in its original Greek origin simply meant, "to behold." Perhaps she would remind us that everything embodied by humanity was first fashioned in our narrative imagination—and that the theater is a place to view and participate in that narrative creation. Perhaps she'd remind us that theater, at its best, not only allows us to reflect on what is, but also broadens the context of possibilities for what the human experience can be.

Actually, she'd likely not utter a word—she'd *demonstrate* the power of theater, and highlight the responsibility it has—to tell the truth and accept responsibility for its impact.

I have no idea why she sighed that day on the fifth floor of 721 Broadway at NYU. I do know that the commitment she made to change the world of theater became a reality in America. And I know, whether we launch our own theaters or not, we all walk in Mrs. Fichandler's footsteps.

Sigh.

Nikkole Salter is an Obie Award–winning actress, dramatist, educator, and advocate. She is chair of the board of Theatre Communications Group, council member of the Dramatists Guild, board chair of Arts Workers United, and an alumnae and professor at Howard University, where she serves as chair of the Department of Theatre Arts in the Chadwick A. Boseman College of Fine Arts, under the leadership of Dean Phylicia Rashad. www.nikkolesalter.com.

INTRODUCTION

By Todd London

You hold in your hands an origin story for the American theater. If you care about that theater now—whether you're an artist or administrator, funder, patron, or student—Zelda Fichandler's *The Long Revolution* will reveal its mysteries. You can see the crucibles on which our theater was forged—cultural, artistic, organizational, literary, political, educational, and economic. You can track the evolution of the revolution Zelda fomented. It was a revolution of decentralization, getting theaters "out of one center into many." It was also a revolution to overthrow commercialism, to introduce into America's national, post-war culture theater *as art*. It was—*is*—a revolution that, in the nature of all revolutions, can never be complete.

Here, in real time, you can hear a national theater movement *thinking itself to life*.

Some things to know, if you don't, about Zelda Fichandler:

- She cofounded Arena Stage, one of America's first regional theaters, in 1950 and led it for *forty* years.
- With two other women—Margo Jones and Nina Vance— she pioneered a movement to foster American culture by

establishing professional theaters outside of New York and across the land.

- She put the "Resident" in the regional theater movement by keeping the artistic company—a fully salaried, year-round ensemble of actors—at the heart of her national vision.

- Through the power of her example and penetrating Talmudic intellect, she became the principal architect and guiding force behind this nonprofit, art theater movement, as well as its conscience.

- Never acknowledged as a writer, she is, in depth of thought about the art, the peer of almost anyone who has written about the theater.

- In a legally segregated Washington, she was the first to integrate theater audiences. In 1968, she began a process to "fully integrate" Arena Stage, by rebuilding the salaried acting company. When, by her own lights, she failed, she tried again twenty years later. This time she launched a plan to overhaul the entire institution and create a truly "culturally diverse" company of artists, production staff, and administration.

- After running Arena with distinction for forty years, she found her greatest professional joy leading and teaching in the Graduate Acting Program at New York University, which she did for another twenty-five years (seven *while* running Arena).

- Over six decades in the field, she never lost sight of the deepest purposes of theater and our common humanity.

- She was one of the wisest people I—and American theater—have ever known. She was wise because she never stopped learning.

- If you love the theater or live the theater, if you act or direct or write or administer or fund, if you want to know how American culture finds shape and solidity and then challenges itself to change—then Zelda's living history is yours. It is ours.

Through it all, Zelda wrote. She performed a mythic feat. She theorized the revolution, planned it, staged the battles, readied the troops, and rallied the allies. Always in the midst of battle, she redesigned strategy, rebuilt the instruments of engagement and, then, in the quiet of the night—though the night was never quiet—pursued the deepest questions of her struggle: Why do we need change? What does it say about our species, about our *humanness*, that we perform our lives thus? She pondered ambition and retreat, progress, and stasis. Even as the maelstrom raged, she noticed the landscape—the surrounding trees, homes, cities, and fields. She paid close attention to the faces in the blur and to the feelings etched on those faces. She wondered what made them tick.

Of course, the revolution was a theatrical one, the battlefield American culture. As with every revolution, the real prize was hearts and minds.

When, early in this millennium, Zelda retired from her sixty-year run as standard-bearer for the movement she incited, she gathered her notes, thoughts, speeches, memories, theories, and plans around her—they take up too many boxes to count—and started to cull, started to make a book filled with everything she saw and thought and dreamed during that long crusade. (She never cared to include what she *did*. This is no memoir, no "I made this or said that or accomplished all of . . .") Sixty years of words. Volumes and volumes of volubility.

For some reason, despite all she started and made, built and overcame, despite the great thoughts and insights and truths along the way, Zelda couldn't finish that book. *This* book. For some reason, she kept rearranging chapters, adding an essay or speech, then cutting them out again. She tested titles and section headings, thumbing through boxes of forgotten articles and position papers. Through most of her eighties and until her death just shy of ninety-two, she assembled and reassembled it, bringing in helpers (the literary equivalent of dramaturgs), friends, and readers.

She couldn't finish it. And not because the clock ran out, though it did. Maybe she was "Scheherazade-ing," as one colleague called it, trying to keep the night alive by telling story after story. That's not what I believe, though.

I keep hearing Zelda say, "I don't know enough."

"What do you mean?" I ask.

"I don't know enough about *now*, about what's happening now, about what has come of it all, this thing we made, our movement."

That was the main problem, why she couldn't settle on the shape of this book, what to include and what to leave in the archive, why she couldn't write an introduction to her own body of writing. Even after a lifetime in the lead—two lifetimes in institution years—*she didn't know enough*. She needed to hear more from younger people, from the heirs of her efforts. She needed to know what they were making of these Regional-Resident-Repertory "instrumentalities" that she and her comrades bled to bear. She wasn't interested in the past as past, but as seed. And she needed to know what was growing *now*, where she had planted. "We don't know enough to satisfy our intellect," she writes. *She was wise because she never stopped learning.*

I met Zelda many times over a forty-year span. I swear I remember every time. I even remember when I first heard of her, standing with my directing teacher in a college hallway. And I remember the second time—when a girlfriend at that same college auditioned for Arena's apprenticeship program. She recounted what Zelda had said at the audition. ("You're so calm," Zelda reportedly said, surprised at the young actress's unflappability.) I remember hearing my employers talking about her throughout the eighties—in Washington, DC, theaters and in Theatre Communications Group's offices in New York City. They spoke of her with simple awe, always as "Zelda," the way ancients might have spoken of "Moses." And I remember each of the four colleagues who introduced me to her, including in her own theater, where I was assistant directing a holiday reading. These introductions occurred many years apart, because, as you might guess, Zelda did not remember me.

I also remember, during a 1987 artistic director retreat at Storm King Art Center in New York, the first words other than hello she spoke to me. I was there to help facilitate the meeting and write about it for what would become a book, *The Artistic Home*. She was there to be Zelda. She spoke to me exactly twice, challenging me both times. (1) I introduced her to the woman at my side. "She's my wife," I said. "I'm sure she's a lot more than that," quoth Zelda, correct as ever. (2) At some point in the daylong retreat, I posed a question to the table of artistic leaders. She turned the table on me: "What do you think?" I mumbled something like, "I don't think anything. I'm just the writer here." She stared at me hard, as though to remember the face she would soon forget for thirty-seven years, when she would ask me to be the keeper of her legacy project.

Imagine how *not calm*, how utterly *flappable* I was when, around 2013 and out of the blue, she called me. "Todd. This is Zel," she said, as if we'd been to the movies the night before and she'd left her lipstick in my car. "Zel." (What's the diminutive of "Moses"?) She wouldn't recognize me on the street, but, apparently, she'd been reading me for years. She claimed to have spent the past several weeks rereading me. By a quirk of timing, I had two books out that year, my own essay collection twenty-five years in the making, and *An Ideal Theater*, which contained "founding visions" for a century of American theaters of all stripes. I'd quoted Zelda on the flyleaf: "Separately and then together, we forged these theaters . . . we forged a better way, we scratched it out, hacked it, ripped it, tore it, yanked it, clawed it out of the resisting, unyielding nose-thumbing environment." In the introduction to an essay of hers, I called her "the great founding rabbi of the regional theater."

Over the next few months, "Zel" called to speak about my writing and hers. She spoke about the field and how happy she'd been at NYU. She advised me through a professional transition and encouraged me to take a job at the University of Washington. "Todd, this is Zel. I dreamt about you last night. You have to take that job in Seattle. You're a teacher." When Zel tells you where to go, you go there. "You'll be so happy," she said. I wasn't, but I don't blame her.

She asked for my help with the book and had Angie Moy, her assistant and long-time pillar of support, send me pages and files, adding to the boxes my family was packing for the move. Before I left Brooklyn for the Pacific Northwest, she invited me to spend a few days with her in her apartment in the Kalorama neighborhood of Northwest DC.

I'd never been alone with Zelda, even for a minute, and though I was fifty-seven years old, I suddenly felt as if I'd never been alone with anyone. That nervous. I tried on and discarded numerous "outfits," though I don't own "outfits." I worried about our meals together, unsure what to do if she served me bell peppers, which I don't like, or if she found me uncouth or noticed arugula in my teeth. I knew that Zelda suffered intense chronic pain from fibromyalgia, and I wondered how it might manifest. If I shook her hand, would she scream?

They were the nerves you might feel when, in an arranged marriage, you're about to meet your intended for the first time. Like that, but also as though you're sneaking off to have an affair in late life, carting the baggage of years and buzzing with old-timey expectations: Should I bring flowers? Chocolate? Will we hug at the door, sit on the bed together, kiss goodbye? I was in a state and, though I did my best to disguise it, the state lasted for the three days we spent together over papers and lunches, stories and reminiscences, as though we'd known each other for a hundred years (which we had and hadn't).

I was Zelda's guy, by golly, and would remain so, even after her death. Because, when Zelda chooses you . . .

She called me in Seattle at regular intervals over the next eighteen months, and we continued our affair of heart, mind, and book. I would pace the living room, from window to window, looking out at the camellias and Japanese maple, listening, confiding, trying, across the three thousand miles and thirty-three years that separated us, to stay present, to build an honest relationship based on Zelda-esque inquiry, elaboration, and exactitude. Maybe, I thought, she holds the key to becoming a wise elder—how to stay truly alive as an artist and human, how to resist fixity, the backward tides of age. I needed her to teach me.

She sent notes, sometimes scrawled in the margins of Xeroxed essays or speeches she'd uncovered, and letters. "I think of you daily although you haven't heard a word from me . . ." She would talk about progress (or lack thereof) on "The Book."

> I've been in and out of the hospital with complex physical issues. I'm used to pain, but this patch has been and is being harder and has slowed me down by making concentration very difficult and using up time and attention . . .
>
> I write to let you know I'm still here and wrestling and mean to continue as long as I have breath.

In the next sentence her attention would turn to events in the DC theater scene, as if they, for this ninety-year-old matriarch, were the only matters of life and death.

Then, in February 2016, facing a surgery from which she feared she might not fully recover, she called again. "I have an important question to ask you," she said, suddenly tentative. I wish I could remember her exact words, because it was the single most extraordinary conversation of my professional life. She asked whether I would be "willing" to take charge of her papers, if she couldn't continue the work. Would I do her the "kindness" of finishing the book for her. I don't recall what she said, because I knew what she was asking. This I remember: my heart's thunder, face going still, tears pooling. She carried on, as though apologizing for a burdensome request she was laying on me, as though it might be an option to say no.

This time I didn't mumble. I took calming breaths and searched for words beyond the clichés bubbling up: "honor of a lifetime," "humble," "moved," "Oh my god, yes, of course!"

I don't want to leave you with the sense that Zelda, by placing her papers—her baby—into my hands, after her decades of deep consideration and doodling, was acting on instinct or sentiment, though the moment was a deeply emotional passage, as she entrusted this life of writing to my care. It was a dramatic scene, and we played it for real, because it was real. But Zelda was nothing if not strategic. She left little to chance. Practiced in the art of casting, she also made sure her chosen actors followed direction. She had already sought confirmation from mutual friends that I could be trusted to follow through. (I found this out later.) As if trust weren't enough, she sought additional assurances—that they would check up on me and make sure I got the job done. Brilliant revolutionary leader that she was, she possessed just the right blend of Chekhov and Don Corleone.

Here you go, Zel. You made me an offer I couldn't refuse, *and* we made it to Moscow.

You can see, in the breakdown of this collection, the range of Zelda's thinking and the areas of her concern. It's important to know a bit about these subheadings to understand the scope of her thought and the way it fits together.

"Institution as Artwork" leads this collection, as it led her thinking. For Zelda, a theater is more than a place for plays. It is "the enfolding of an idea," an idea that guides and infuses every move that theater makes. Building a theater company is an artistic process, like the making of a production writ large. The nascent theater—which might in time blossom into an institution—must grow organically out of that enfolded idea, never losing its connection to it. One cannot understand her thinking without understanding this: There is no separation between an institution and the artistic impulses that bring it into being, the nonprofit sensibilities that form its business practices, the company of artists at its center. "We wanted theater as an art form," she reminds us, distinguishing her revolutionary objectives from the "Mammon-mindedness" of the Broadway from which she meant to break free. This principle—that *the artistic institution is itself a work of art*—is the ideological DNA of her lifelong, long-life project.

For a thinker like Zelda—and she was nothing if not a thinker—to do a thing right, you have to know *why* you do it. To keep your finger on the theatrical impulse, you have to understand that impulse, what you are *for*, how this particular art distinguishes itself from other arts, what makes theater theater, and what makes it human. When I write that Zelda "never lost sight of the deepest purposes of theater and our common humanity," this is what I mean. What is it about our species that must play? (See "Playing.") How does the theater show us to ourselves? ("Theater and Human Identity.") What is its sociopolitical role? ("Artists Set the Stage.")

And who is at the center of this enterprise? For Zelda, it is the actor, always the actor. A great reader and literary mind, her sweeping director's notes illuminate both text and world. But actors were her heart, as you can feel from her essays on craft and her annual speeches to students and faculty at NYU. Actors and companies of actors. (She even spent three seasons post-Arena as artistic director of The Acting Company.) Why? Because she believed that in an art whose essence was crossing the uncrossable chasm between living beings, "the actor is allowed the ultimate reward—the enduring thrill of human encounter." "To the Players" isn't just the title of a cluster of essays; it's the true north of her artistic compass.

The Long Revolution was the title Zelda and her publisher agreed to early on, though as ever she noodled with other possibilities. The section bearing that name allows us to witness her thinking as it developed, to overhear her question and challenge her own creation, her own ideals. If the encrusted institutionalization of the nonprofit theater distresses you, as it does me, *read Zelda now*. No matter your critique, she got there first, anticipating, for instance, the stranglehold of boards, mission drift, and the "Whiteness" that was baked into our theaters. Never satisfied with the movement she launched, she studied it on the ground and from above at the same time, holding it to the highest standards: Is it doing its human work? Is it bettering our society? Is it truly representative? Is it excellent? "Unless we get it right," she insisted in 1985, echoing her worries from twenty years before, "this 'institution business' is going to kill us."

This refusal to let her baby off easy was nowhere as evident as in the matter of race. A woman of her time and class, with, as she puts it here, "the permissions and restrictions and guilts and opportunities that American society gives to a white upper-middle-class woman," she kept her eyes on what through that lens was the prize—undoing the urban "apartheid" of segregation. She was determined to redeem Arena from its participation in what the Kerner Commission called "two societies, one Black, one White—separate and unequal." Not merely a social problem, this was, as she called it in 1968, "a profound *aesthetic dislocation*," proof to her that the theater she'd built and led was living in "an unreal world," "cut off from its source," that is, its connection to the world and its artistic vitality.

Her essays in "Beyond Black and White" open a window on the promise and limitations of her attempts. She was the first to integrate Washington's audiences in the fifties and to fully integrate her acting company a decade later when Washington, DC, becomes the nation's first minority majority city. For reasons she outlines and others we can only imagine, she was unable to sustain an integrated ensemble. She refused to give up and over the years moved toward what would be, in the late eighties, a holistic, multimillion dollar, organizational overhaul to diversify not just Arena's acting company but the whole place—writers, directors, designers, production staff, and theater administration, including leadership.

In the years after the killings of Breonna Taylor and George Floyd and so many others, years that saw the release of "BIPOC Demands for White American Theater" drafted by the large #WeSeeYou coalition of theater artists of color, it can be useful to scrutinize Zelda's efforts. How did her "permissions" and privileges as a woman of her race and class and time constrain her perspective? How did her activist attempts at inclusion help, and where did they fall short? If willing, why was she unable to dismantle the system she built and evangelized?

On matters of race and throughout the book, I'm moved by the too-human self-portrait of Zelda that emerges: her resolve to defy the history she was handed in the one and only life she got, despite the near certainty of failure. Zelda, prophet of what she called the "fifth freedom—the freedom to fail"—always had a plan for better. Every plan would in some measure fail. She might have had Samuel Beckett's famous dictum taped to her mirror: "Try again. Fail again. Fail better."

Driving all her efforts was Zelda's refusal to separate the beautiful monster she helped create from its cultural context. For her, the making of theater or *a theater* was part and parcel of society as a whole—its economies and policies. It was the permanent plan for better: "The theater's ultimate power [is] to change the environment and man himself." "Creativity and the Public Mind" and "Profit/Nonprofit" both probe this worldly connectedness. Here she tackles governmental funding and its lack, censorship, the pull of commercialism in a capitalistic society. Here she addresses those of us—and I was one she took issue with—who call out her movement for erring on the side of institutional survival over that of artist support.

If you live long enough, you must endure a thousand farewells—to those who leave for other places, who retire, and to those who die. Her collaborators were her company, and the company of artists was her ideal, a model for living. The tributes and eulogies in "The Company You Keep" offer a small sampling of those relationships, of the six-decade ensemble of friends and fellow artists that defined her.

Fittingly, Zelda's collection begins in the middle, thirty-five years into Arena's life, with T. S. Eliot's declaration: "We shall not cease from exploration . . ." And thirty years later, she still hadn't ceased. Only death itself could stop her, and even that hardly stands a chance, given what she set in motion.

And so, we come to this volume's final chapters. "After Words" splices together her acceptance of an award named for her and her comments from the first bestowal of that legacy award. "The Beginning" brings us back to her first major piece of writing, just shy of a decade after Arena's founding. Edited from a lengthy position paper, her vision for "a permanent classical repertory theater in the nation's capital" serves as manifesto of aspiration, the impulse for much of what followed. She returned to that impulse again and again. "And the end of all our exploring," Eliot continues: "Will be to arrive where we started / And know the place for the first time."

Zelda never intended this collection as a summary of the past. Rather, she saw it as an invocation to the future, a destination that interested her more than the places she'd come from. She was always beginning again, circling back and plunging forward. Like Eliot's explorers, she would not cease, not at the Sisyphean start nor the impossible middle, nor at the end, which only signaled new beginnings, about which she would never know enough.

A warning and, just in case, a preemptive apology. Zelda was a capacious reader and a world-class quoter. You'll find many of her favorite, profound quotables in this book, often more than once. She was also, to be frank, a compulsive plagiarist.

Theater is a collaborative form; sometimes it's hard to know whose idea was whose. That's the way Zelda's writing often works: myriad sources get funneled through one distinctive sensibility. Working quickly on many things at once, she wrote more as a speechmaker than essayist, concerned with transmitting orally. She composed like a magpie, reusing old paragraphs, lifting sections from whatever she was reading. Sometimes these lapses (plus the passage of time) make the exact sources and wording uncheckable and, therefore, unknowable, as readers will find throughout. A scholar of mind but not of practice, she acknowledges her sources, but doesn't always pause for the niceties, like pointing out when she's paraphrasing or using the original author's words well after the quotation marks end. This was especially true in speeches, first rehearsal notes, and addresses to students, rarely intended for publication.

I stumbled on this tendency late in the editing process. I hit passages that *just didn't sound like Zelda*. They didn't because they weren't. The *Washington Post* once unwittingly (or carelessly) reprinted a piece in which she'd lifted passages from a scholarly article without attribution. I believe I've uncovered similar thefts—tracking down out-of-print books and obscure sources—and righted my rabbi's copyright wrongs. One can never be sure. And so, the preemptive apology, should anyone be a more obsessive sleuth than I am.

You can be certain, however, that the person Zelda mostly pirated from was Zelda. I can only imagine her, in the days before computer files, leafing through old speeches and grants and papers: "I know I wrote about that somewhere . . ." Then pilfering her own paragraphs, tweaking if there was time and, if there wasn't, just "insert here."

The selections collected in *The Long Revolution* are culled from more than two thousand pages, all worthy of inclusion. I've eliminated all interviews with Zelda—and there were many, often covering the same ground—and all grant proposals and institutional statements that may have been written, in part, by others. If there's motive to focusing on her writing *as writing*, it's my desire that Zelda be given the place she deserves—not just among pioneers and revolutionaries and leaders of art, but also as a theater essayist, critic, and theorist. That said, I've edited heavily, paring sentences and cropping paragraphs. Writing, Zelda had a high-wire ability to pursue every intellectual and verbal digression that occurred to her, aiming for the nuance within the nuance. Her mind was so fine, so thorough and hungry, she never met a thought about a thought she didn't pursue. Her language could drift, but her vision never did. She never missed the gist.

With this caution, one more: the music of Zelda's formulations and the rhythms of her thinking can worm their way into your brain. And heart. For me, the sound of her sentences, read over and over, have become part of my own interior monologue, the way poetry does. Or maybe the way conscience does. Over many years, I've read Zelda to remind myself what I believe in—as a tribal member of the American theater— what's important to me, and why I write and teach and lead the way I do. (I have found this rereading nearly universal among people who knew her.) At this point I don't always know whose voice speaks in my head, mine or Zelda's. It's unnerving, and it's comforting, the way it must be to hear the voices of ancestors, passing down wisdom, passing down aspiration and morality and, above all, passing down questions.

Here, then, are Zelda's questions, the ones that rose up as she marched at the vanguard of a revolution she dreamt and built, rethought and refashioned. We add our questions to hers, and we keep trying to answer them, to make plans, to make plays. Revolutions are never finished and neither, in a sense, are lives. The questions persist.

DEDICATION

(1963)

By Zelda Fichandler

Common wisdom has it that *Homo sapiens* is the top of the line. When we get to where our evolutionary destiny is supposed to take us, there we are: *Homo sapiens*, thinking man, knowing man, judging man. But what if common wisdom is mistaken and wisdom that is *un*common tells us that when we are what we truly can be, we are not *sapiens* but *ludens*, playing man—the animal who knowingly plays.

This, I submit, is where inventions come from—that place of imaginative play where the division between work and play is erased, where what we call work has the joy and ebullience and—yes!—the labor, that we ordinarily give to good, hard play.

My father loved to work. He was an inventor, and he invented many important things. At home, when he was in this study at the back of the hall, he would sing! He would sound like a little baby playing, while he was solving his knotty mathematical problems behind the closed door in the den. And Mother would say, "Be quiet now, Daddy's working." And my sister, Joyce, and I would say, "He's not working, Mommy, he's playing." He left us with that gift, that enormous gift, of making a song of work.

In the late thirties, our father made the first blind-instrument flight and landing from Beltsville, Maryland, to—I believe—Newark,

New Jersey, in a two-man open cockpit plane, hooded to simulate darkness. Not to worry us, all he said was that he'd be home late for dinner and we shouldn't wait.

From him I learned that all things that could be imagined could most probably be done—that flights of the mind could indeed become flights in real time and space.

After World War II, I was trying to get off the ground a flying machine of my own—a theater institution of a certain kind for which there had been no American models. I was awkward with this at first. My husband, Tom Fichandler, and I thought, quite foolishly, that if we just pushed hard enough against the seat belt, we could lift the plane by sheer muscle power! Wrong.

Other lessons from my father came to us to relieve the strain. We remembered: about co-pilots for comradeship and steering; about the wind which would fill the vacuum under the wings and give us lift; about the power of the propeller to get things moving and penetrate the space up ahead.

I honor my father for his hunger for wings. I think if he lived long enough he would have found a way to stand upon the air on his own, without them. And I honor him for showing by his own life what we should honor in ours—our biologic curiosity, our imagination, our courage, our capacity for intimacy, our passion, our will and energy, our persistence and commitment, and—*and*—our interconnectedness.

From "Address on Army Research Laboratory Activation and Harry Diamond Building Dedication," June 1963.

INSTITUTION AS ARTWORK

INSTITUTION AS ARTWORK
(1986)

> We shall not cease from exploration
> And the end of all our exploring
> Will be to arrive where we started
> And know the place for the first time.
> —T. S. ELIOT

I start to write on August 16, 1985, Arena Stage's thirty-fifth birthday. I have brought my notes with me, they are spread out on the big bed in a smallish hotel room on the Strand in London. I have already seen two plays at the National Theatre, one at the RSC, another at Stratford-on-Avon, and I got here just in time to enjoy, though jetlagged, the opening of John Houseman's production of *The Cradle Will Rock* at the newly done-up Old Vic. The rain outside closes in my thoughts of companies, beginnings, economics, governance, the endlessness of the tasks, the nature of growth and change, leadership, the problems ahead, the distance come, signaled by the number thirty-five.

The lines from T. S. Eliot's *Four Quartets* move me. They seem to pierce the exact moment of this birthday and pin it down. They speak not only to me personally, but to the nature and needs of a movement that began over three decades ago and now, middle-aged and in some turmoil, seeks redefinition, seeks to "know the place." I hear them—in a way that is both inspiring and practical—urge all of us who are a part of this movement, first, to get on with it, and, second, to go back to find it.

With curiosity I reread the program note for Arena's opening production, Oliver Goldsmith's *She Stoops to Conquer*. August 16, 1950. I wanted to see what was on our minds then, to test the present against the past:

> Arena Stage plans to bring to its audiences the best of plays both old and new as well as worthwhile original scripts on a permanent, year-round, repertory basis. Local in origin, it was founded in the belief that if drama-hungry playgoers outside of the ten blocks of Broadway are to have a living stage, they must create it for themselves. Arena Stage was financed by Washingtonians—students, teachers, lawyers, doctors, scientists, government workers, housewives—who love theater and who want to see it flourish in the city in which they work and live. Its permanent staff of distinguished actors and technicians, many of whom have come to Arena Stage via the stages of other cities, now all call Washington their home.
>
> Arena Stage invites your participation in the excitement of the first production of Washington's playhouse-in-the-round.

We (Tom Fichandler, my drama professor Edward Mangum, and I) had raised, via a series of meetings with like-minded community members, $15,000 for stock in a regular profit-making corporation, set up a Voting Trust arrangement to be sure we retained artistic control, collected a cadre of actors and helpers through auditions and interviews and from among friends, and converted an old movie house in a slum area of Washington to a 247-seat theater-in-the-round. (We wanted the symbolic intimacy of that form and to save money on scenery.) With our "investors," we scraped the chewing gum off the seats, hung the lights, laid the carpet, painted the walls, scrubbed the johns, and on a budget of $800 a week set out to achieve our goals. I ran the publicity campaign to open the theater, designed the sets that were built in the alley, helped in the box office, directed seven out of seventeen shows we did that first year, slept many nights on the carpeted stage floor and, along with Mangum, made $65 a week. The actors made $55, and from there the pay scaled to zero.

We put on fifty-five productions—nonstop, without a break—in the five years at that first location, had many successes and sometimes played to under a dozen people. On several occasions we had a bank balance of under $100. We ended the five-year period with $25,000 more than we started with. The rest, as they say, is history.

A recent interviewer asked me what made me think it would work and I said, truthfully, "I was young, I had no doubts, I was sure people would respond. Believe me, we didn't do any marketing surveys." In the early fifties, I read Margo Jones's book called *Theatre-in-the-Round*, in which she outlined her dream of a nation with forty (sic!) resident, professional companies performing new plays and classics, and I knew that she, the mother of us all, could not be dreaming in vain.

This is not only "My Story." It is the story of several of us who began theaters way back there when. Most importantly, it is the story of our heritage, even those of us who began life later, on a grander scale. I do think we were the only theater to experience life—for seven years—as a so-to-speak "profit organization," an experience I have never regretted, and as the only theater to pay its own way on box office income alone for fifteen years. That gives me a special edge when I have to explain to newcomers why our theaters have to be nonprofit.

When I read our initial program remarks—to be called in a later, more evolved time a "mission statement"—I am astonished that they prefigured most of the potential as well as the pitfalls that our movement was (is) to achieve and would encounter. Most of the themes and, implicitly, counter-themes are there: "audiences," "local in origin," "plays old and new and original scripts," "permanent," "repertory," "outside of Broadway," "create it themselves," "financed by the community," "where they live and work," "permanent staff," "distinguished actors and technicians," "Washington their home," "participation," "excitement."

When I reach back through the years to our initial organizing principles and the labor of the earliest years, I find some real wisdom there: The need for artistic control. The need to take responsibility for one's own vision. The value of an ongoing collective. The centrality of an acting company. The fundament of contact between play and play-goer, of a continuing dialogue with the audience. Each individual theater being a part of a whole theater. The ever-presence of budgetary tension and of the success/failure seesaw. The primitive yet sophisticated power of selflessness and faith in the dream. In our innocence, in our knowing-yet-not-knowing—Eliot's "Quick now, here, now, always— / A condition of complete simplicity / (Costing not less than everything)"—we sketched in with fairy-tale boldness the outline of the whole story, the principal characters and the underlying themes.

How far we have come! We should allow ourselves our amazement and our pride, if only for a moment. The size of the achievement is not diminished for me even here in London, across the bridge from the National Theatre with its three stages, its five companies each with about seventeen actors, its elaborate and for the most part splendiferous physical productions held in repertory and brought back at will, its heavy subsidies and affordable ticket prices, its bars and buffets and bookstalls, its intense and responsive audience queued up in the hopes of a securing a returned ticket at the last moment.

Progress is a snail that jumps. Our growth has seemed to us so very slow, as fretfully, exhaustedly, we have waited for the next transformation to occur, either to us (private foundation support in 1957, the coming of the NEA in 1966) or, aggressively, by our own hands (building theaters, devising subscription plans, forming companies). But in objective truth, ours has been the fastest-growing art form in history.

Thirty-five years ago there was Broadway and the Road. Today, there are more than 250 theaters (What would Margo think?) of varying shapes and sizes and styles, and our national theater no longer operates within ten blocks of Broadway but across five thousand miles of melting-pot America. While the level of work and the extent of enterprise and courage vary greatly from theater to theater, and no single theater as yet stands as a pinnacle of artistic achievement, the overall sense is of individuality, energy, quest, and growth. Our many theaters now offer more employment weeks to actors than does Broadway, gradually year-by-year realigning work patterns away from New York and changing the way actors can lead their lives and make their living. Community after community has had its hunger for live theater responded to or even awakened for the first time. Taste has been elevated, discrimination sharpened, life enriched by being made into art. People have come to want their theaters and will pay money—in taxes, at the box office, and in contributions—to have them. A career in the theater, though hardly a sure thing, has come to seem plausible (even noble, to certain enlightened parents). In these few decades the theater as a profession has lost some—not all, but certainly some—of its historic aura of aberration, dropout-ness, illogic.

The proof has been in the pudding: Most of the gifted actors in the country have come the resident-theater route and could not have evolved without the continuity and stretching that years of on-the-boards experience provided. Many come back from films and television to stretch and test themselves more against the demands of a classic role and a breathing audience. And where would our writers, directors, and designers be, without these congeries of work places, these sites for experimentation and development? Would we even *have* this enviable pool of American talent without these places? Where would these artists have gone to see their work evolve, to become who they are? For Broadway has been priced out of the market for risk-taking and now, irony of ironies, takes its dependence on regional theater "product" and talent for granted so much that it points the finger at us when we don't come up with enough of it.

I clipped a front-page article from the *New York Times*, headlined, "Broadway Economic Season Is Called Worst in a Decade," to keep as a sign of the times. One producer, asked to explain the slump, cites the high cost of road tryouts of musicals and, then, the failure of the noncommercial theaters—"which have been able to provide Broadway with a stream of notable plays"—to do the same in the area of musicals, Broadway's staple moneymaker. "'The nonprofit theaters have never paid attention to developing musicals,'" Mr. Sabinson said [then executive director of The Broadway League]. "'There's no place for young directors, young songwriters, young singers to learn.' In addition, few noncommercial theaters can afford the stagecraft demanded of contemporary Broadway musicals." Do you hear the gigantic turnaround, the wad of social history stuffed into that complaint??

The achievements that I list have been listed before. I list them again on this birthday as a surround for other thoughts. And as an admonition (to myself, first of all) that we not take for granted the *fact* of it, the very *existence* of it, and the transformation this movement has made in our cultural landscape. Our theatrical world will never be the same. We committed a revolution that is irreversible, and attention should be paid to that.

Particularly remarkable to me is that it took place without models. We had no teachers except the environment, our own mistakes, and each other. We *did* have each other (Mac Lowry[1] put us together twenty-five years ago and TCG has kept us there). And we had some crucial gleanings from the outside. I recall how astonished I was in the mid-fifties by the craft level at the Shakespeare Festival in Stratford, Ontario. Our production standards were influenced by my visit there. We learned much from the Berliner Ensemble's trip to London in the mid-sixties—both about the repertory actor (Ekkehard Schall as both Coriolanus and Arturo Ui) and about the physical aesthetic—Brecht's "Reality is concrete." I can still visualize the long, silent moment at the beginning of the Moscow Art Theatre's production of *The Cherry Orchard* as the family, back from Paris, re-embraces the house. As a director and producer, I was opened to a new level of possible stage behavior. It changed our work.

But chiefly, and especially in our organizational forms and institutional development, we had no models. We taught ourselves out of our own impulses, which, made into deeds, showed us what to do next to stay alive and progress. It has been a revolution made of many and diverse feelings and viewpoints, all discharged more-or-less simultaneously—in the eye of history, thirty-five years is but a blink—a kind of collective artwork, like a quilt, a "something" truly surprising, truly unique. As we grapple with our current problems, we should not forget where we started nor diminish what we made.

We read about (and experience) "artistic deficits," a term that first appeared in a report by the National Endowment for the Arts last year. An artistic deficit represents the distance between what one wants to and should do in one's theater, and what one can afford to do. It is the shadow between intention and reality. The term has come into wide acceptance very rapidly. It seems to explain our feel-

1. W. McNeil Lowry, director of arts and humanities at the Ford Foundation and later its vice president.

ings of dissatisfaction and longing for something better. It names what ails us.

It is true that our theaters are underfunded and our artists under-paid. It is true that in order to remain solvent some theaters pull in their horns in terms of predictability of repertoire, size of casts and production costs, and channel funds into fundraising rather than onto the stage. And the art itself suffers and we fail to meet our own standards, and, feeling that it is time for a ripening, we rail against our fate, asking, "If not now, when?!?"

The current episode of our national story, told in numbers, is discouraging indeed. With expenses up seventy-one percent over the past five years and, despite record attendance and box office income, a doubling of the economic deficit last year alone, is it any wonder that we have this sense of our reach forever exceeding our grasp, that we seek to find our salvation somewhere in that interlocking system of economic/artistic deficit?

Without minimizing the seriousness of our economic situation and its direct effect on our power to produce art at the highest level, I think we must look into other areas of our being, where the prob-lems may be less immediate, less visible, but potentially even more corrosive. For while poverty of means can, of course, lead to poverty of ends—and often does—still, courage within can sometimes pre-vail over negative forces without—passion over penny-pinching and "four boards" over an extravagant set. Artistic deficits have been with us from the beginning. They seem more painful today because we are older and feel we should be *There* by now. But what if there is no *There*—at least in our lifetime???

Be that as it may, no theater can ultimately survive the dry rot of institutionalization, the absence of versatile and committed actors, timid and visionless leaders, or a troubled, unresolved relationship with its forces of governance. Let's speak about these four hazards of our middle years.

What our early, innocent "mission statement" omits is any ref-erence to the fact that we were about to create an "institution" or, indeed, that such a mechanism might be necessary to do the things we intended to do. We simply didn't think about it. I suppose we knew about institutions (schools, prisons, families, museums), but we didn't think we were one. We thought we were a theater, something else again. Who could have imagined thirty-five years ago how elaborated all this would become—that one day we would live in our own building, make five-year plans(!), have a budget hovering around $7,000,000, write grant applications, and hardly know ourselves for all the baggage we had collected.

At the time, we proceeded very simply and directly: "What needs to be done?" was followed by doing it, preferably by someone who knew how, but, if necessary, by someone who learned it as he/she went along. Not that we were naive. We were tough and smart and painstaking, and we would not be stopped. We set up a box office and ran it well, informed and enticed a public, paid our bills, and wrote our contracts, selected and hired actors and directors and designers, put together the exact repertoire we wanted and made a myriad of difficult decisions—both artistic and managerial. But out of poverty and from the vantage point of our early evolution, we saw a simpler connection between needs and filling them. And from these needs to "each according to his ability" seemed a logical and direct route. We couldn't yet project such evolved concepts as job descriptions or even discrete jobs—departments of this, that, and the other, tables of organization, etc. While this was a hectic, often misshapen and, in the end, impermanent way of doing things, it did, I must confess, hold its own kind of magic.

Our primary concern was never in question, which way the arrows of energy were pointed. The work on the stage was central, and we lived, breathed, and slept (no, we rarely slept!) with that in mind. There were no communication problems—all you had to do was stick your head out and yell. Although everyone suffered overwhelming fatigue for about the first ten years, we felt that we could hold the whole animal in the palm of our hands and touch it directly. I remember the sensation of knowing—both empirically and philosophically—everything at once: the sentence and the story, the pebble and the beach, every corner of our little world.

When I speak of "institution as artwork," my clearest image comes from these earliest years when things were most frantic and yet most whole. They serve as a reference point for maintaining a sense of unity within the theater as it is today—175 people, 3 stages, the divesting/sharing/delegating that is essential for running a large, theatrical institution.

Unless we get it right, this "institution business" is going to kill us. Something began to feel uncomfortable around the end of the sixties, but by that time the thing had already happened to us. By the time we looked up and noticed, it had been done to us: We had been institutionalized. No, I'm not saying that right. I exaggerate the degree of passivity involved. In point of fact, we were not force-fed. We wanted what we got. We just didn't realize where it was taking us.

We vigorously, implacably tracked down our subscribers, making a kind of fetish of the yearly subscription brochure. We feverishly raised money for new buildings and, using ingenuity, skill and new knowledge, built them with zealous alacrity. We developed and engaged administrators. PR people and business managers. We added the concept of production managers as artistic leaders got more involved in fundraising and the like, and, still later, we added associate directors, literary managers, and dramaturgs as theaters grew and artistic directors got still more involved in fundraising and the like. We created development departments to meet economic deficits. Later they often grew as large or larger than the artistic staff. In general, we poured a lot of money away from art and into making more money in order to make art. Recently, we computerized. Computer technology, someone said at a staff meeting, holds all our operations together. Is he right?

A few months ago the artistic director of a large regional theater wistfully, ironically remarked to me, "They wouldn't even notice if I disappeared. The administrative machine would go on grinding. No one would stop to see that there was nothing in the grinder."

But I am speaking too negatively. Our institutional structures are necessary to us. Compartmentalization, specialization, clear and clean procedures and good personnel policies, a strong middle as well as top management structure, the best of promotional and development techniques, budgets that define and defend values and provide guidelines for growth as well as survival are all absolutely essential to us. It isn't 1950 anymore, and our budgets aren't $800 a week. We have heard other voices and lived in other rooms since that time. You can't go home again, and no one wants to.

On the other hand, we don't want the tail wagging the dog or— worst case—the tail *becoming* the dog. We do want our institutions to organize themselves around the spiritual/aesthetic life they exist to nurture and not to make that life subservient to the demands of institutional paraphernalia.

A theater is the enclosing, the enfolding of an idea—a vision—something imagined that has the possibility of finding concrete embodiment. It is simultaneously an imaginative act and a place. When the institutional machine ceases to support the imaginative act and begins to encroach upon the place; when it constricts rather than releases the flow of creative energy by its labyrinthine demands, its busyness; when the accumulation of resources, the dissemination of information, and the marketing of the "product" take more focus and absorb more power than what we are making and the conditions under which we make it, then the institution must be dismantled and reconceived along better lines.

An institution cannot have a life of its own, be a thing in itself. Its life is derived from the animating Idea, and each and every one of its actions must flow from this Idea and contain a piece of it. When we say that "the business of art is art and not business" we don't mean that there is no business in making art (surely there is). We mean that the function and purpose of the business is not *itself*, but the making of this art. If we fail to get this crystal clear, the institutions we've created will become blind mechanisms instead of sentient organisms (the trend is already clear in a number of theaters). They will eventually petrify and crumble due to the absence of living tissue. An active recollection of our origins can help us to "know the place" in a new way.

> And all shall be well and
> All manner of thing shall be well
> When the tongues of flames are in-folded
> Into the crowned knot of fire
> And the fire and the rose are one.

I write now from New York. My apartment overlooks Washington Square. From the windows facing east I can just see Broadway where the new building for the Tisch School of the Arts is located. I currently chair the graduate department of acting there. I have had a longstanding interest in the American actor: the growth and development of the professional actor and the training of the young actor. I am interested in their inner technique (how to produce living behavior), their physical technique (voice, speech, movement), and, no less, in their mind and psyche, including how they see themselves and the part they are to play in shaping the American theater, for worse or, hopefully, for better. I'm interested in the connections among these three aspects and grateful for the fresh outlook this new post is providing me.

"See that the players are well bestowed." Indeed, we must. The actor stands at the center of the art of theater and always has. Before there were literary forms, when there were only rituals and embodied myths, it was the actor—the en-actor—who performed the deeds, represented the human situation and stood in for those who, like himself, were seeking to find out why. The theater is and always will be a special place—a differentiated, imagined, moral place—that society sets aside in order to examine all that fascinates it and all that it seeks to understand. We are endlessly curious about our world and especially about ourselves. It seems a biologic necessity, a means of survival, that we ask the questions and act out even what is unanswerable. A society without a theater is a society in disintegration.

Theater=*Teatron*: a place for seeing. Albert Camus wrote, "If the world were clear, art would not exist. Art helps us pierce the opacity of the world." In the struggle for his own truth, in his attempt to peel away the life-mask, the actor lets us see ourselves. By being himself while walking in the footsteps of another, by showing himself while still being faithful to the truth of another, the actor teaches us who we are. The theater can make do without anything but the actor.

So why do we deal with actors in so desultory a fashion? The theater of our beginning took for granted that the actor came first and, therefore, that the company came first, because a company is the natural habitat of the actor. No one taught us that. It was simply organic knowledge, and we acted on it. Perhaps it came from what we knew of the Berliner Ensemble, the Moscow Art Theatre, Shakespeare's company or Molière's, or from our own idealistic attempts—Eva Le Gallienne's Civic Repertory Theatre and the Group Theatre of the thirties, for example.

In the early years of the fifties we chose plays that suited our particular company, assigned roles with the growth and development of our individual actors in mind, cast to the furthest, not the nearest, limits of an actor's talents, and looked upon these companies as our greatest asset. The fact that young actors played older characters and someone who "just wasn't the right type for the role" played it anyway proved itself out. At least for us at Arena. And not only were major talents developed by these choices, but later, when actors moved on to other work, the whole American theater became enriched.

The output of a theater is always more than the sum of its parts. Its level of expressiveness (I prefer this phrase to "professional standards") depends most of all on releasing the energy and creativity of a whole group, on shaping and emanating a collective consciousness—"the spirit of the collective"—as well as, more specifically, an interpretation, a viewpoint toward any production. Since a play is its own world and since the chief ingredient of any world (fictive or real) is the pattern and timbre of its human interrelationships, the interior meanings of the play stand a better chance of being revealed by a group whose members know each other, relate well to each other, think and play well together, approaching their tasks in a mutually understood way with a common vocabulary. That is to say, by an acting company.

At the same time, the individual actor always develops best within a continuing group. It astonishes me to see the flowering that takes place when failures can be outlived, successes don't get blown out of proportion, continuity is assured and quick results deemphasized, when offbeat casting sometimes happens to benefit the actor not the management, and friendly faces permit experimentation, a "what-the-hell" attitude toward work that everyone knows is really serious.

Despite the advantages to the actor (and therefore the art) of continuous, creative work, in our long middle years all kinds of justifications cropped up for the virtual abandonment of the company idea: The audience got tired of the same faces; actors wouldn't stay, because the lure of TV and film was too overpowering; limited casting options shortchanged productions; it was cheaper to job in actors for each production, while money was needed to build up the administrative machine and raise funds for sheer survival. All these justifications had some truth to them. (The Devil can cite Scripture.) But whenever a real commitment was made to the idea of company and to the individual actor, actors stayed. (Christopher Morley once said, "There is only one success—to be able to spend your life in your own way." Many actors agree.) And because they stayed, the work of our theater gathered momentum and opened up, expanded beyond itself.

I said that the theater can make do without anything but the actor. I don't want to retract that statement, but I confess it is more ideological than practically true. In the complex theater world we live in, someone has to chart the course and steer the ship. We frequently call the person who does that "artistic director." This title can send a shudder through the body of any gifted, sensitive, insightful, responsive, politically minded, knowledgeable, curious, growing, searching, young (or middle-aged?) director who is the right candidate for the job, but who really wants to spend time with actors evolving the life of a play, rather than dissipating physical and psychic energy planning season after season, gathering up and retaining artists, supervising the work and developing the talents of others, informing, educating, exhorting and stimulating a board, and representing a theater to its own members, its community, its world. Gather together a group of artistic directors, and you will have a group of weary, tormented humans who suffer from the Jimmy Durante syndrome: "Did you ever have the feeling that you wanted to go and yet you wanted to stay and yet you wanted to go . . . ?"

Stay, some of us do. Although there has been of late a fever of movement into and out of theaters. It was not this way in the old days. In the old days, the theater *was* its artistic director. The artistic director, propelled by a vision of burning intensity, brought the theater into being, assembled the meager economic and physical resources (in our case the theater was, for months, a $1.98 cardboard file-box), persuaded into existence a small board, and collected a group of artists ready to set out on a journey of undetermined length to a vaguely determined destination. The artistic director had no contract as such, except with him/herself, and that was unwritten and, therefore, binding, more-or-less until death do us part. "Poetry attaches its emotion to the idea; the idea is the fact," wrote Matthew Arnold. In that sense, our theaters were poetic.

There are still a few theaters left of that original kind. But the more typical situation is that a second or third generation of leadership heads the theater, and that he or she was brought there by a board of directors and has been commissioned, as it were, to create an artwork for the community. Commissions are a viable way to bring artworks into being—history shows us that—but for many reasons the analogy breaks down in the instance of theaters/institutions. In the first place, the new artistic director doesn't begin with a clean canvas. There is as least a sketch, maybe even an elaborate design inherited from the past, and numerous clear-cut expectations as to pattern and shape. Since an artwork has to start from an internal impulse, a personally held view of some portion of reality, the commissioned artist begins the labor at a disadvantage.

In the second place, any artist needs a clear run on the artwork and needs to follow her own nose as it develops. Renewing a contract every two or three years, "evaluations" by the board as the artwork progresses, input coming from all over the place (e.g., a publicity department memo sent to an artistic director, criticizing the proposed list of plays and suggesting alternate titles, better suited to seasonal needs, group sales, and the look of the brochure), and kibitzing along the unending route to completing this piece of art—About subscribers: don't lose them. About money: take in more, spend less. About repertoire: be daring, but hang on to audiences. About failures: by all means have them, but only two out of eight. None of this is conducive to a sure hand or the free play of instinct necessary to the creative process. In the third place (which may be the first place), the board, despite its care and concern, might have selected someone from the wrong genre altogether. They may have picked an action painter when what they meant to have was an abstract expressionist or a representational landscape artist. After a while, the divergences become obvious to one party or to both, and separation, usually very painful, becomes the only way out.

I am describing the nature of things, how things are. The pressures are real on both sides. However, since the artist is primary to the artwork—which is to say, we can't have a theater without an artistic director and, indeed, the theater derives its life from within him or her—it seems that we should scrutinize with great care and revamp this "commissioning" process where necessary. There is no going back to our beginnings. Because of current economic pressures, I doubt there will be many new theaters starting from scratch with the old insistence, the old do-or-die. And because of the very fertility of the field, born out of the success of the movement over the past decades, there are so many seductive opportunities out there that turnover in leadership is bound to remain the prevailing mode and a persistent problem. The closest we can come to perpetuating our personal visions—those of us who came down on the side of "feeling that you wanted to stay"—is to train our successors from within the institution we are still making.

I received a letter from a distinguished management consultant firm outlining the criteria for selecting an artistic director for one of our major theaters:

1. Appropriate scale of work
2. Commitment to, and experience with, classics
3. Ability to develop a resident ensemble of artists
4. Long-range planning and vision and ability to lead the board
5. A personality and style suitable to institutional leadership, especially as it relates to developing the ensemble and community support.

These are excellent criteria and I wish with all my heart that an available visionary will leap forward to take up the challenge. I hope it is not too forward of me to add to five points, to flesh them out.

With this man or woman, young or older, American or from the world at large, I would like to share these suggestions, born from my own long journey. People have more power over their own lives and the lives of others than they think, but this power is not necessarily theirs. It comes from the idea that inhabits them. The world has more cracks in it than substance; more-or-less everything and everybody constantly slips through them. If you marshal your ideas clearly, know as much as you can know about what you want, your foothold will be strong. Until you are sure enough, put up with the pangs of aloneness. If you have a friend or two with whom you can share your doubts, you are blessed. Your doubts may be the most creative thing about you, but boards, foundations, and the community at large will not be smitten by them. Know your position inside and out; when it is ripe, share it.

Also, know your territory. Incorporate into your vision deep, experiential knowledge of its tastes, hungers, presences and absences, past, dreams, pocketbooks, proclivities and, of course, its trustees—your theater's board, especially the president. If this knowledge, when incorporated, despoils the vision, go somewhere else or do something else. There won't be time to make profound change. The long run doesn't exist anymore.

Hang on to your obsession for dear life. If they pry it loose from you with their caution and precautions, you have lost and become a functionary. In order to lead you have to be a leader, which is to say, someone obsessed with a vision that propels you over and under all obstacles and through the inevitable periods of despair and fatigue. If "other considerations" begin to tip the scales away from the permeating vision (except, perhaps, in the very, very short term), the battle has been lost. You just haven't gotten word.

Be a genius. If you aren't a genius, try harder. Nobody would dare encroach upon Picasso, Frank Lloyd Wright, Stanislavsky, or Balanchine. If you try and still can't be a genius, be a strong, committed working artist. If your work is original enough, *yours* enough, it is unassailable. But even this won't be sufficient. You must also stand firm with it. You must hold to your point of view, your way of seeing things, and compromise only in the scheme, in the details. If you permit open spaces around the center of the impulse, other forces will rush in and occupy them.

Antithetically, you must make your own all the conditions and circumstances that others see. They are real. The constrictions of budget must be felt as your constrictions; only then will you not resent them, while retaining the power to burst them. The recalcitrance of the audience; the difficulty of assembling a repertoire that satisfies both you, your fellow artists, and your audiences; the limits of time for rehearsal and contemplation; the unending institutional demands made on you—you must feel these as coming not from outside yourself but from within. Otherwise they will deplete you to the point of powerlessness. Claim the place, with all its problems, as your own. Face up to the fact that you don't have the years to prove yourself; the world is moving too fast, and things cost too much. You have to deliver the goods—produce—in the present tense.

And, if you possibly can, arrive with collaborators, artistic associates with whom you have worked before and who share your vision. The job is now too complex to be a one-person show. Learn to plan. Live in the moment, as if you are an actor onstage, and plan as if you were the director of an opera company. Rub your belly while you pat your head. These things being subscribed to, you may, by degrees, dwindle into . . . an artistic director.

Given an inclination to take it on, plus the requisite touch of fire, artistic leadership can be taught and learned. It's no longer a mystery.

I empathize with the burdens placed on the shoulders of theater trustees who volunteer their time and concern, often at the expense of their own work and private pleasure, for an endeavor that cannot stand at the center of their lives as it does ours whose profession this is. I salute and thank them. The demand, again and yet again, for more and more money for expanding artistic need must be wearying indeed. Holding in one's hands the very definition of an institution through the choice of an artistic or managing director must be awesome.

Underneath the responsibilities of raising money and finding new leaders, and affecting them, lie other matters. The relationship between staff and trustee must be creatively probed, and questions of attitude and feeling illuminated if we are to improve upon what exists. A deeper understanding of our separate positions might lighten the burden on both staff and trustees. I make these remarks in the spirit of exploration and not final wisdom. I, too, am in changing waters.

Arena does not have a "money board," and, given a choice, I prefer it this way. The board, many of its members hardworking and deeply caring, has limited fundraising capacities in a city notorious for its lack of philanthropic yield. The theater's development department has always borne the main responsibility for closing the deficit gap. We chafe at this a little and wish the board could do more, and so do they. But both Tom Fichandler and I believe that a theater in this society is most artistically free in this society when it can earn as much as possible by its own devices—box office, special events, interest on reserves and investments, royalties, and the like.

Tom and I have been the sole leaders from the beginning, so the question of continuity has not weighed upon the board. Indeed, we both feel it our responsibility to provide choices for our own successors, in order to maintain the Arena tradition to which both board and staff subscribe. We have been, if anything, over-assiduous in sharing our "ideas, beliefs, visions." If nothing else, I am a talker. If talking can do it, the board knows what Arena stands for, what it needs and means to do, and how much it will cost. Where, then, is the rub?

In 1959, Jacques Barzun wrote, in *The House of Intellect*:

> Many directors of corporate foundations and some univer-
> sity trustees handle money for research and education not as
> if they were engaged in a nonprofit enterprise, but as if they
> were engaged in an enterprise that was failing to make a profit.
>
> In other words, they do not see where the actual profit
> lies. It being intellectual, and they not, it is to them invisible.

Replace the terms "corporate foundations" and "universities," and note that Barzun says "many" and "some" (we all have trustees who *are* intellectual), and his statement is worth pondering. However much it has been hammered at, however much it is cerebrally *understood* that "not-for-profit" is a benign, affirmative idea and not a negative, death-dealing one, we have decades of empirical proof that it has not been accepted—viscerally accepted—by boards. *Not* for profit sounds less defining than to be *for* something, but it is: something more transcendent than economic profit and in another category altogether, a mode of human transaction entirely other than the one about money. Can this attitude ever be dug out from the subconscious of our governors—lawyers, doctors, accountants, builders, businessmen, whose days are lived elsewhere and in another way. To paraphrase King James: As a man *lives*, so is he.

I would be overjoyed to find a trustee (am I not sending out strong enough signals?) who would position himself on the other side of some issue, so that we could switch and have a fresh look at things. I often take his position; why is he not able to take mine? I wait expectantly, hopefully, for that Special One who will plead with me to consider lowering ticket prices or raising salaries of underpaid technicians or middle managers, who will prod me to expand our playwrights' wing or advertising budget, to take the company on tour or spend more on the art. But the pressures never surprise. The tug-of-war is played over and over again in just the same way: art against money, how much nonprofit is too much, us against them, our eyes raised up in aspiration, theirs cast down to the bottom line in anxiety and dismay. They stand for us and for our dreams. In combat over the Good, they often join us. So why will they not embrace the First Principle: *that it is the Art that makes the Money*? Does it feel to them, in the deepest places of their hearts, that—when all is said and done—nonprofit really costs too much??

We use the term "partnership." Can we truly be partners across this philosophical divide?

A board tends to think more of the future of the institution and to be terrified of its death. A theater tends to think more of its present and that it will only die when it is ready to and should. This is another great philosophical as well as psychological divide. The board wants to squirrel away resources against the winter. The theater wants to use them now, thinking that if they are used well, there is a chance of perennial spring. The board's way of thinking is contradictory to the world's oldest wisdom, which teaches that, unless we are fully alive in this very instant, there is no life at all. I say to our board that risk-taking is not a line item in the budget but a style, an attitude toward living. No one hears me, and that makes me sad. Perhaps I am not saying it well enough.

A 1965 Rockefeller panel report on *The Performing Arts: Problems and Prospects* states:

> Good business brains and performances are essential to the successful operation of these organizations, but more than these are required, for the problems are unique. Artistic judgments defying business calculations enter at every step. Bottom-line thinking doesn't always get to the bottom of things. An artistic director lives in dread of getting out of touch with his/her subconscious sources. An institution is a work of art: Feats of deliberation strategy, craft and cunning derive from powerful, unconscious motives . . . If boards of trustees could offer up their trust, especially on key forward moves and, of course, totally on artistic choices, perhaps the great divide would narrow.

Or as Bertolt Brecht tells us in *The Caucasian Chalk Circle*:

> Everything should belong to whoever is best for it—
> Children to the motherly, so that they shall thrive.
> Wagons to good drivers, to be well driven.
> And the valley to those who will water it and make it fruitful.

The board must be accountable to the community for the honesty and integrity of its theater, for the perpetuation of its leadership, for its overall policies in the broadest sense and for resources of all kinds, including funds, to assist it in its stability and growth. But "the sand takes lines unknown." The board must also support the elusiveness of the creative enterprise. If there is to be a partnership, it must be one of the spirit as well as of the pocketbook.

How we, at thirty-five, resolve these four questions—the one about institutions, the one about artists and especially actors, the one about artistic leadership and the one about staff trustee relationships—will determine how we will look five years from now. After forty, someone said, a man is responsible for his own face.

From *Theatre Profiles 7*, published by Theatre Communications Group, 1986.

THE OPEN STAGE
(1967)

P ast the lobby one enters the auditorium through a long, low-ceilinged link. Suddenly the space, quite unexpectedly—almost shockingly—opens up.

It is a high, vaulted room with a ribbed ceiling pierced by innumerable sources of lighting. The stage cube is not small: thirty feet by thirty-six and twenty-four feet to the bottom of a large catwalk—a brooding, dark gray metal machine larger than the stage rectangle, bisected several times in both directions. Hundreds more lighting instruments hang on the catwalk rails. All the machinery of light and sound is exposed.

Four concrete tunnels for the movement of actors and scenery intersect the stage at the corners of the rectangle. Because of geometric laws they are not of a direct diagonal. The four tiers for audience seating are steeply banked—over sixteen inches for each row. There are eight rows. Behind the tiers is the circulation aisle from which the audience is seated downward. Behind the circulation aisle and above it by several steps is a ring of boxes. The auditorium seats 800.

This vision is always direct to the stage, to the very feet of the actors, with no heads in the way. The floor pattern is perceivable from every seat. The stage space is totally trapped. The cube of usable acting area extends from below the stage level to the catwalk above. Objects can be flown in and out between the sections of the catwalk as high as to the grid forty feet above the stage.

The theater was built in 1961 on the basis of eleven years of experience with what is called an "arena" stage at two other locations. The name of our company is Arena Stage—by virtue of historic accident. At the time we began in 1950, the District of Columbia Building Code defined a theater as a place of public assembly, giving regular performances, which had a proscenium arch, a fire curtain, and smoke pockets, where the audience area had no steps. In order to get a permit to open we had to demonstrate, in writing and in public hearing, that we were, indeed, not a "theater" but an "arena"—much like a boxing arena, a circus arena, or the ritual hillside theater of ancient Greece. By compiled erudition and strained analogy we got our permit—with the proviso that we could not use the word "theater" in our advertising or, indeed, in our name. And that is how we became Arena Stage. (The code, incidentally, has since been changed to include us as a legitimate sister of the proscenium.)

But the echoes of association remain. We are, for example, much more of an "arena" than we are a "theater-in-the-round." Theater-in-the-round has overtones of improvisation—the reconversion of gymnasia, abandoned warehouses and movie theaters where there is an air of make-shift and make-do; bad sightlines—the rake of the seats is usually not more than six inches per row, so one can see the actors only from the waist up; inadequate lighting (poor angles, insufficient sources and instruments) although lighting is the heart of this particular form; and intimacy or the quality of eavesdropping. Intimacy is talked about as a good thing, a desirable thing, but usually implies: (1) that there is no separation of audience and play, no isolation in space of the *event* from the people gathered to witness it; (2) insufficient acting area in which to release the life of the play in choreographic terms; and (3) the audience crawling over the set to get in and out of their seats, i.e., no separation of the traffic of the stage world from the traffic of the real one.

The arena stage has less in common with the three-quarter thrust or platform stage than people suppose. They share the fact that neither is a proscenium stage. In both, the stage has pushed itself forward from behind the proscenium arch, wiping out the imaginary fourth wall. Both gather the audience more or less around them and deal with the change of time and place as a succession of dramatic events, rather than in terms of literal scenic description.

The three-quarter and the total-arena form also share the Brechtian dictum, via Hegel, that "truth is concrete." Cabinetmakers, not only stage carpenters; sculptors, not only painters; and workers in real stuff—be it leather, metal, hair or woolens—are what we need.

But there are significant and fundamental differences between the arena and the platform stage. The arena playing area, for example, is totally neutral. With no back wall and no permanent stage platform, "place," a new plastic and physical "world," may be created for each production. This has certain budgetary disadvantages, but it makes for infinite possibilities. The stage can be small or large. With light, it can alternately expand and contract within a production. It can be sunken or raised. Platforms can be built up into one or all four of the tunnels or into none of them. The space may be used as *one* place. Or, because of the capacity of light to define numberless areas *within a totally neutral cube*, it may be used as an *infinite number* of places.

This is all a matter of light combined with form—even the simplest of forms. In *The Caucasian Chalk Circle*, when Grusha crosses the bridge over a deep gorge, a rope was tied to the railing of one tier and then to the railing diagonally opposite. A transverse beam of light became, for the moment, the "stage" and, in combination with the rope, the "footbridge." When Grusha tripped and almost "fell," the audience gasped, so strong was the illusion of isolation of place. Floor, ceiling, and walls disappeared, and the physical world became, for that instant, precisely what emotional reality made of it.

The three-quarter platform stage acquires a dominant axis for composition and movement from its back wall, the architectural memory of the proscenium stage. As a result, the dynamic thrust seems to run from the back wall toward the tongue of the stage. The strong position becomes the point where most people can see the face of the actor. This tends to be somewhere rather upstage and facing downstage.

The arena, on the other hand, has no one fixed reference point architecturally. It is a space comprising countless points of primary focus—the focus can be anywhere—wherever you want to put it. Combined with total control of light, the possibilities become literally infinite.

Since it has no back, front or sides, the arena becomes a highly democratic form for the audience, it is true that the individual witnesses the stage life from one particular point of view, depending on whether he sits north, south, east, or west. But kinesthetically and emotionally, one has fundamentally the same experience wherever he is sitting.

I have not found this to be true with the platform stage. I have noticed that the plays in this form have been designed, sculpted, directed, and acted more or less from the front, the aesthetic weight of the rear wall finally prevailing. When I have sat on the sides I have not merely seen the play differently, I have seen the sides of the play. The experience of the play—intellectually and sensually—has been weakened. Surely this perception is borne out in the pricing policy of such theaters: The most expensive seats splay out from the tongue of the stage; the cheaper seats edge around the stage toward the wall at the back.

The laws governing stage space insist on the utmost contact between, and interpretation of, the forces in conflict. The dynamics of movement and relationship in the arena form are based on principles of collision and withdrawal, attraction and repulsion, as if one were watching moving bodies on a slide under a microscope. One perceives the positive and negative charges attracting and repelling each other within a totally free field where the current is "on" all over the place and equally potent everywhere. This gives the dramatic event an enormous sense of aliveness, of spontaneity, of irresistible pulls—"reality" in the fullest sense of the word. The audience impact appears to increase in direct proportion to the depth and volatility of this stage life.

A younger reviewer on a local college newspaper wrote about our production of *The Crucible*:

> The word "arena" originally signified a sandy place and especially the gladiator ring. Something of this ancient and grim sense has gotten itself into Arena's current production of Arthur Miller's *The Crucible*, a sense of the stage as a pit where a ferocious struggle is taking place. Ming Cho Lee's set is a large square platform of unpainted, rough boards lifted a foot or so from the floor of the building. This is exactly right,

for the elevation is just enough to call our attention to the depth of the pit itself and to allow us to look down from a great height on a terrible contest, on a terrible *agon*. We are distanced but involved.

Milton Katselas, the director, exploits what the staging gives him. His players enact a tortured set of movements on a platform hovering just above a bottomless well of darkness, and they vainly struggle to evade or to wrestle with invincible emanations from the darkness beneath their feet.[1]

I have been unable to get this young man a job on one of the major Washington papers, but I applaud his description. Not intimacy. Involvement. Not being "part of the action" but being a witness to it. Not eavesdropping, but attending the event and really looking at it. Not gawking but watching. Aroused, alert, emotionally involved, but watching. And learning. For truth is specific. And truth is sculptural. And truth is mobile—ever-shifting, ever-changing, presenting ever-differing faces of itself. The first law of relationship is self-containment. In the arena, the audience and play are separated. But one surrounds the other, envelops the other. And when the art "happens" the impact and connection that can be achieved *between* them is simply not achievable in any other form.

1. I haven't been able to identify the author of this student review. [T.L.]

From introductory remarks at a panel on "The Open Stage," given at the International Theatre Institute Conference in New York City, June 1967.

GROUNDBREAKING CEREMONY

(AUGUST 28, 1968)[1]

I want to call to your attention the power of the human imagination. Do not ever underestimate it. Yesterday I was told my role in today's proceedings. I was to take up a shovel and dig it here into what Shakespeare called "the proud and receiving earth."

Everyone took great pains to reassure me. For at our last groundbreaking, some eight years minus two months ago, the earth was proud but not receiving. At the climax of much distinguished oratory, I took up the shovel and jammed it downward. I hit rock. Or I hit concrete, or, whatever I hit, the ground would not yield. At any rate my sense of drama was thwarted, and the laugh I got was not in the script.

Last night I dreamt about today. I dreamt hard and intensely and all night long. And look! Lo and behold! A hole there is—a mile long and plenty deep enough! Such is the stuff our dreams are made of.

Our dreams. This building is one of these dreams.

But times change swiftly, more swiftly than we can keep up with. The last time around I said that "a building is the enclosing of an idea." I think I said it again only a short time ago. It seemed a good

1. Written as Arena broke ground on its STAGE II, later renamed Kreeger Theater after donor David Lloyd Kreeger. According to Arena's in-house history, *The Arena Adventure: The First 40 Years*, the groundbreaking took place September 10, 1968, not August 28.

enough thought at the time. For it emphasized that it takes a heap of living to make a house a home, and that a building should not be an empty vessel, a form with nothing real to fill it.

But now, of a sudden, this seems too pallid a way to put it—that a building is the enclosing of an idea. The sense of *enclosing* is somehow wrong. Its connotations are too personal, too hidden-away, too much at rest. What about putting it this way? That a building is a place where ideas can be, not enclosed, but *EXPLODED*. A building is a crucible where ideas can be fired up, tested out, and then thrust strongly upward.

There are many challenges and, yes, obstacles to what we want to do here. And it will take real explosive force to make them happen. We have passed the edge of our ability to support ourselves at the box office. Yet the country spends $35,000,000 a day on the war in Vietnam and has appropriated to the National Foundation for the Arts and Humanities $3,500,000 for the entire year.

We have the most original and potent program in the country for the development of teachers and the young through theatrical means. And we confront a school system where so-called "cultural" activities are cut from the budget as unessential, like dangling paragraphs at the end of a news story.

We live in a city and a country where the confrontation between Black and white people permeates our experience every day of our lives. And we have yet to draw this confrontation into the gut of our art.

We are a nation with uneasy values, seeking new ones, not having found them yet. Our playwrights, too, are breaking up the old forms but have not yet found their tongues. Improvisation, more often than not, substitutes for articulate creation.

There is much to do. And swiftly. There is a great sense of urgency about all this. There is not all the time in the world.

We want to enclose our working space. And then we want to explode the notions that fill our hearts and minds.

I am glad to have had help, from you all—and from the silent ministers of the night—with the digging of this hole!

WHY THEATER?

THEATER AND HUMAN IDENTITY
(1 9 9 4)

Theater speaks to all the Big Questions that the child asks: What is Death? Where will I go when I die? Who am I? Where do I stop and you begin? What is God? What is the meaning of life? How can I get what I want? Why am I being punished? Why did my balloon burst? Where did Mommy disappear to? Will she come back? Why must I give up my secrets? Will somebody always be there to love me? Will my nightmares come true? If I think it, will it happen? All the Big Questions of life.

By the time she is an adult, the child has learned to ask the smaller questions and, most likely, to ask them of science. But the child who lives on in us asks the Big Questions that only art can answer.

"All the world's a stage, / And all the men and women merely players," Shakespeare tells us. And we are "guilty creatures sitting at a play." No, we are guilty creatures sitting *in* a play. We are personages in our own drama. The art of theater, the dramatic experience, starts just here, within the subjective experience of each one of us.

I start with this very moment, as theater does. And since I know myself somewhat better than I know any one of you, I start with myself, myself as a character. What is my sense of reality at the moment? Who am I?—as if that were answerable! How did I come to be this way? Wordsworth said, "Trailing clouds of glory do we come / From God, who is our home." Not many of us buy that anymore.

I hold these pages in my hands. It's 10 o'clock. I need new glasses; I feel annoyed about that. I want to do a good job, to get my thoughts over to you in a clear and meaningful way. Perhaps I should have worn my other shoes. I spiral out a little.

I am a teacher, a director. I head up some things. I have accomplished some things, and I have a sense of that. My NYC apartment on Washington Square hangs in the sky and gives me a great sense of space. My house in DC's Cleveland Park is full of a family's memories, sometimes sad to be in. I have certain friends, certain relationships, certain cups and saucers, certain pieces of art, certain chairs, certain pots and pans, an 82-year-old housekeeper. I, too, am getting older. I spiral out a bit more. It's 1994, and I have the permissions and restrictions and guilts and opportunities that American society gives to a white upper-middle-class woman: I can wear a pantsuit instead of a hoop skirt and go somewhere unaccompanied and earn my own money and have the illusion that I am free.

I spiral out even more. Justice Blackmun has just resigned. I am happy with the return of the Big Band sound. I wonder if Jane Alexander [as head of the NEA] will make any difference in the sorry story of funding in the arts in America. Hillary Clinton didn't report $6,498 of profit in her 1980 commodity account, one out of four children live in poverty, 25% of people live alone, homicide is the number one cause of death among Black males aged 18 to 24, and there are more Black youths in jail than in school. I think the short baby-doll dresses they are showing for spring are foolish—even for those young enough to wear them. I read the news from the former Yugoslavia, and I think of Freud's comment about "the narcissism of small differences," as each group struggles to find its identity. Tuberculosis is coming back in frightening numbers. My closest colleague died of AIDS this year at age 42. I have lost a lot of my friends to AIDS. What is it to be, then, a mastectomy or a lumpectomy and radiation?

I have memories that some of you may share and memories that are just mine. These memories are as much a part of me as bulletins from my present. I remember America's entry into World War II. I remember Stalingrad and marking it with pins on the map in my dorm room. I heard Roosevelt's voice: ". . . the only thing we have to fear is fear itself." I lost a chemistry prize—I was first in a class of five hundred, but it was designated for the top *man* in the class. I remember "togetherness"—*McCall's* slogan and the ruling ethic for mothers of the fifties; my friends moved to the suburbs then, but I remained urban. I remember signs in Washington that kept out Black people. I remember the riots after the assassination of Martin Luther King. I have seen milk bottles give way to plastic and now some glass coming back. My few leftover pieces of Russel Wright china have become collector's items. TV sets have become more prevalent than indoor plumbing, but I remember life without TV, and it wasn't so bad. I bedded down dozens of young people during the four marches in Washington in the sixties and saw two sons through the hippie drug culture. Now the hippies have children of their own and struggle to equal the living standards of their parents and probably won't, but I remember it as it was.

I remember Tommy Dorsey and Glenn Miller and progressive jazz and abstract expressionism, pop art, action painting. I remember a time when there was only Broadway and a few touring shows, before the more than three hundred theater companies America now has. I remember long skirts, short skirts, bouffant skirts, knitted skirts, and I wore slacks before it was fashionable. I remember when it was chic to smoke.

Who would I be without these memories and a million more? Who would be the "I"?

I share with you a biologic past, a past derived from our evolution from the one-celled animal and plant to the thinking, language-bearing, culture-producing animal, species *Homo sapiens*. I think we are more defined by the origins of our species than by anything else; it is these origins that give us what is called our "human nature." My capacity for thought and language came late in the evolutionary climb; these are our jewels and our instruments of survival. The thin layer of consciousness provided us by nature is what is most precious, most human, in us. It also gives us access to that other part of our reality: our fantasies and dreams, our imagination, our deepest creativity—access to the dark yet fertile, dangerous yet rich, unfathomable realm of the subconscious.

Our feelings, our emotions, come from this earlier part, from way back to the limbic alligator brain. We try to use this earlier self in a constructive way so as not to blow up ourselves and, along with us, the world. And with its help we create the riches of civilization: law, ethics, religion, social rituals and, the peak of all, works of art. If we lose touch with this early self, we are deprived of our natural abundance.

Watch the child, before she has been too stamped with culture. She is endlessly curious, for curiosity is her way of learning about the world and thriving in it. Learning is to a child as a long neck is to a giraffe—a way to reach the topmost leaves. Motion, action, a life geared to the pulse beat and the heartbeat, to internal rhythms, to seeking and moving and finding and grasping and knowing—all are natural to her. She is highly responsive to stimuli; they now say that a baby one month old can identify its mother's voice out of a cacophony of other voices. The child's products and inventions show an easy connection with subconscious life, though control and intentionality—what we call craft—have not yet been achieved. The barrier between outward and inner reality hasn't yet risen to block the imagination or make strict contrasts between what is "real" and what is "merely fantasy." No wonder all those Big Questions that the theater deals with come so naturally to her.

We are here, and we face each other. We each have the density of this particular moment, our shared cultural past, varying according to how old we are and where we have lived, our shared biologic past, which we have in common with everyone everywhere. And we have, last of all, our personal histories—our individual psychobiographies, the narratives of our life. Each of you has a psychobiography, and I'd love to know them, for no one of them is uninteresting. "Tell me the story of your life, and I'll tell you mine." It's the opening gambit toward understanding, toward intimacy. I'll go first.

My parents emigrated as infants from a shtetl in Eastern Europe. My grandfather, an Orthodox Jew, slept on a feather bed on the stove in a dilapidated house next to a dump in a suburb of Boston, ate large white turnips, thinly sliced and sprinkled with salt, and by the kitchen window read learnedly from the holy scriptures and, so, was exempted from labor. My grandmother, unhappily married in the Old Country by arrangement, rose with the sun. She, with my four uncles (one of whom later committed suicide), ran their small dairy business, until it was wiped out by the milk trusts. She milked the few cows, pasteurized and bottled and delivered the milk in a cart drawn by horses, all before school time.

My father, a brilliant inventor and scientist, originated, among other things, blind-instrument landing and flying devices still used in world aviation today. He took the first blind flight in an open two-man cockpit plane from Beltsville, Maryland, to Newark, New Jersey, and made history. He read the newspaper at the dinner table and seemed too busy to make himself known to me. My mother was . . . My sister was . . . I felt so and so about this and this . . . And when that thing happened, it made me want to do that and that, and make people feel such and such about me, and so I did thus and thus, but it didn't make me feel that, so I kept trying and hoping I would find this and that, and so on and so on. We each have our personal events and wantings, which are etched into our bodies and into our souls—no, which *are* our bodies and our souls. Eventually we die, usually from the disease that represents the sum total of the way we have lived and what has happened to us. Until then we experience our life as a story, repressing for as long as we can its inevitably. The maker of theater is the one who tells the story.

"We are such stuff / As dreams are made on, and our little life / Is rounded with a sleep." We are the dreamer; we dream the dream. And we are restless to know our dream, to see our dream palpably before us, and so we created, before recorded history, over the rim of history, the art of theater.

De Quincey wrote that art was *idem in alio*, the same thing in another place or form. The art of theater, the most innovative of all the arts, derives from life, weaves itself from the very stuff of life that I have shared with you about me and that you might share with me about you. Our adventures in life, our feelings in the course of it, our habits, the outside and inside forces that push against us and that we push back against, the events that change us and the ones we change, how we get what we want or don't, and what we do about it when we don't, the artifacts that we live with, the social and cultural events that form the thread we trace from birth to death—these provide the living substance for the art of the theater, the *idem* (the "same thing") of which De Quincey speaks.

The theater, using those coded symbols for thought, feeling, and action that we call language, and its particular artistic means—costumes, lights, sets and, chiefly, the actor—is a way to give "another form" to our existence as human creatures on our planet. So that we may better understand it, more clearly recall it, more surely control it.

Sigmund Freud likened the analysis of the psyche to "a reclamation project as vast as draining the Zuyder Zee." Well, the theater lives in an adjacent territory: the unfathomable, the unknowable, the uncontrollable, the dimly remembered. The theater form—De Quincey's *in alio*—helps us to experience our own experiences, puts our life in front of us so we can see it.

How exactly does the theater do this? Listen to this.

> HE: Have we any Burgundy in the wine cellar?
> SHE: I wasn't aware we even had a wine cellar.
> HE: You're never aware of anything. Well, we must get some in
>   for our silver wedding anniversary.
> SHE: Do you actually mean to celebrate it?
> HE: Naturally.
> SHE: I'd rather attend a funeral.
> HE: Mine, of course.
> SHE: Yours or mine. Either one would do.[1]

That bit of loving dialogue is between Edgar the Captain and Alice his wife of some twenty-five years, locked up in a fortress on an island off the coast of Sweden. Locked up in a prison house, the love-hate ambivalence that is their marriage. The play is by August Strindberg, considered to be the father of modern psychological drama. Written in 1901, it is called *The Dance of Death*, and I bring it up to illustrate a point.

"We have met the enemy and he is us," said Pogo, in the pages of the *Washington Post* some years ago. Edgar and Alice are, of course, us. Or projections, created in the playwright's mind and then embodied by actors, so that these projections may live—may talk and walk around in front of us—and, so, recall us to ourselves. If Edgar and Alice were not us, or, at least, part of us, pieces of us hidden away from ourselves, tucked away in corners (for surely there are nasty little places in us we are not anxious to admit to)—if Edgar and Alice were not us, then we would be in a strange land and not in a theater at all, where what we see seems so recognizable.

1. Translation by Bill Coco and Peter Stormare.

The enemy is us. In us. We see ourselves. Face-to-face and no place to hide. Right in front of us, the life-size package. And we are changed somehow in the encounter. We lose a little bit of ourselves or gain a little bit back. We learn.

The enemy. Also the friend. We see him there too. The deep, human core of us, the base of our common humanity. A part of us that, unfortunately, we are too often ashamed of and, so, hide away in still other secret places.

I keep an old photograph to remind me of the origins of the dramatic experience. In a Vietnamese village gas bombs had been thrown into holes and huts to drive any remaining Viet Cong out of hiding. One child, about two years old, routed out with his older sister, sits on her lap looking up at a large Black Marine. The side of the child's face is dirty with smoke and soot; he has been crying. He looks up with an expression of bewilderment, not knowing what to make of such a world.

The Black American Marine, commanding, weird somehow in his battle uniform, looks down at the child. He has exactly the same expression: bewilderment, eyes wide open as he stares at the boy, mouth slightly ajar. Is the Marine recalling that he too had once as a child been driven out from where he had been playing? That he was once a child in a world at which he could only look up and out, a world that no child could fathom? Did he see himself as this tiny Vietnamese child?

"Sometimes I feel like a motherless child," the song goes. "A long way from my home."[2] We all feel this way sometimes. And so we do what is called "identify with" or "empathize with" or "feel compassion for" the pains of others. We have this capacity born out of the knowledge of our own pain. It is, I think, our saving grace.

We are given, by virtue of our birth as humans, this capacity to identify with people moving about on a stage, people who are really us and who go through their actions on our behalf, in our stead, and suffer or exult in our place. We hurt, laugh, feel frustration or rage or pity or terror, as they feel them. For such is our ability, and such is our need.

The theatrical experience is made of this kind of enactment. Our substitutes—inventions of the mind—are given concrete life and

2. Traditional spiritual.

show us our own faces. And since the proper study for man is man himself, they do us deep, deep good.

Of course, theater is not real in the way that life is real. The actors put on their characters as one puts on a suit of clothes. Inside every character there is an actor who never stops being himself, however much he may fool you into thinking that he is really the character. When you wound an actor onstage, he only pretends to die. Tomorrow he will be there again, safe and sound. The actor's anger is real, but it is real with a difference. His passion is not really a passion at all, but an action. That is to say, the actor rules his emotional life and is not ruled by it, except when he is acting badly. When he is acting well, he is really angry, but he is angry "on purpose," at exactly the moment he wishes to be angry and to the degree that he wishes to be. More or less. After all, we're all human—even actors.

And nothing we think of as "real" is at stake in what the actors do. Only the outcome of the play is at stake—and how deeply the audience can be made to respond, to listen, to laugh, to cry. That is to say that *only the entire world of the imagination is at stake.* And yet, at the same time, nothing is at stake. For is not the theater only a game?

The difference between this world of fantasy and the real world is a significant one. It marks the thin edge between the theater and what we call "real life." In the theater we always have a plan of some kind, and we have agreed upon this plan before you come in. It is not too rigid a plan, and you (the audience) can change it a little, but not very much. (Unless, of course, there is a fire in the theater.) For we are in the saddle. Like gods, we know how things are going to turn out. We are in our own hands, sculpting experience according to our will, according to what the playwright has charted for us, and according to the choices we make through a long rehearsal period. We lead you where we mean to. Trick you at the very moment we have chosen. Tease you on schedule and by any means we like. We play *upon* you, hoping you will play along and play back. If you can't or won't play along and back, you've given us a very bad night. "What's the matter with them out there?" we ask each other.

It is, indeed, a very sophisticated art.

The rules of the Art-hyphen-Game require that the witnesses and those who act out the ritual pretty much agree beforehand just what will go on, and how it will be done, and what will be gotten out of it. We are in cahoots, the actors and the audience. The degree of surprise, of suspense, is very slight when you come to think about it. When the rules are broken—like when an actor really gets hurt in a sword fight, or when the scenery collapses—everything is messed up and the magic game is spoiled.

As a matter of fact, the magic event is ruined quite easily. When the audience is uncooperative or lazy, too full, too drunk, too tired, too polite, or too *turned off*, it is ruined. When the actions enacted mean nothing to the witnesses but boredom, it's ruined. When the theater and the community aren't tuned in to one another, it's ruined.

No wonder Broadway has become the scene for *Cats*, *Cats*, and more *Cats*, *Kiss of the Spider Woman*, *Tommy*, and a $12,000,000-production of Disney's *Beauty and the Beast*, and the serious investigative play has been pushed out. However, at $65–$75 a ticket, Broadway is hardly the place for a community and its conscience and curiosity to meet across the footlights.

Where are we then? What's wrong with us? How can the theater help? Who needs it? What has it got to say to drive-by shootings, HIV-positive babies, and a dehumanization and rage born out of deprivation? The theater can't cure cancer or AIDS, but it can, in its own way, speak to that central disease of disconnection that artists have recognized since the turn of the twentieth century.

I ask what theater can do. William James wrote that "feeling is everything," which doesn't mean there is *only* feeling, but that everything starts there.

I think about that term: "turned off." There is the Disease of the "Turn-Off" and its opposite: "turned on." To be "turned on" refers to a feeling of spontaneity, of aliveness, openness, and involvement, of availability to sensation, expansion, awareness, joy. It describes aspects of our fullest humanity, and yet the term comes from the machine. It is no accident that we not only "turn on" ourselves but that we also "turn on" our electricity, our cars, TVs, and computers. We turn them off when we are through with them or when they get in the way.

A whole new language has grown up around that new wonderful tool, the computer. William Safire, writing about this development in his "On Language" column in the *New York Times*, quotes from an article about cybersex in which Janis O., a person conducting an online human sexuality forum, says, "There is nobody in my offline life that I would feel comfortable exploring sexual submission issues with." Online, then, carries a sense of being connected and turned on; offline means "not now, not here." When a person removes to an online life, she avoids the dangers of direct human contact.

We describe our humanity in words which derive from mechanization, from the technological process. Man invented the machine, and now the machine reinvents man. And who is made in the Image of whom? It is no exaggeration to say that many people today experience their life as a kind of machine, without moral competence or consequence. For many Americans, their experience of themselves or of life is a mechanical one—compartmentalized, programmed, short-circuited, detached, and second-hand. For others, the semiautomatic is an extension of their own arms.

The theater is in a position of a strange complexity. As a social form it inevitably shares the ills of the society it lives within. As an art, it must stand outside of this society and be chastiser, humanizer, redeemer, lightning rod, sentinel, and rebel. According to its ability and its nature, it must help others to find their own cure.

I think of a story about nine-year-old Joey, a patient at the Sonia Shankman Orthogenic School, a therapeutic treatment center for the psychologically damned, founded by Dr. Bruno Bettelheim in 1944 on the campus of the University of Chicago. This audience will know more about it than I do, but I believe it restored a good percentage of its patients to life, primarily by means of a "one-to-one confrontation" technique: "One cannot help another in his ascent from hell unless one has first joined him there," said Dr. Bettelheim. And further: "What we also have to demonstrate is that together we can make a go of it, even down there—something that he alone at this point cannot do. Hence at the heart of our work is not any particular knowledge or procedure as such, but an inner attitude to life and to those caught up in its struggle, even as we are."[3]

How effective this "inner attitude" can be is seen in the treatment of Joey, autistic nine-year-old Joey, who was convinced that he was

3. Taken from Bruno Bettelheim's *The Empty Fortress: Infantile Autism and the Birth of the Self* (New York: The Free Press, 1967).

run by machines. So controlling was this belief that Joey carried with him an elaborate life-support system made of radio tubes, light bulbs, and a "breathing machine." At meals, he ran imaginary wires from a wall socket to himself so that his food would be digested. His bed was rigged up with batteries, a loudspeaker, and other improvised equipment to keep him alive while he slept.

Joey was allowed to play out this fantasy for years while Bettelheim and the counselors explored his individual history. Gradually, as he realized that he was not going to die, that he was an individual in his own right, Joey was able to substitute a "real" life for a mechanical life. After eleven years, he returned home and entered high school.

Part of the function of the dramatic experience is and has always been to arm people with the knowledge that God gave to Job, that their own right hand can save them. To awaken them to the life that is in them, so that they can dispense with all forms of tyranny, including the tyranny of habit that makes them unable to substitute a real life for a mechanical one. To give them the courage of their own sensations and the knowledge that feeling is primary to action and that action is moral and right only when it is welded to feeling and emerges from it. To communicate that inner attitude of life of which Bettelheim speaks—that humanity is one, that we are all caught up in the struggle and that drama is the enactment of this struggle and part of it, part of its releasing and part of its healing. To speak, not to man as he will be, not to posterity, but to him as he is, to speak for the now, for the moment in which we are alive. To make a demonstration of life.

There is a Burmese saying that "the fish dwell in the depths of the water, and the eagles in the sides of Heaven; the one, though high, may be reached with the arrow, and the other, though deep, with the hook; but the heart of man at a foot's distance cannot be known." We who work in the theater in a serious way try to know that heart nonetheless, using, in place of arrow and hook, the tools and means of our theatrical art.

I think that you and I come together in that thought.

Address to the Washington School of Psychiatry, April 24, 1994.

43

ARTISTS SET THE STAGE

(1974)

A rena Stage had a love affair with the Soviet Union last fall. That there was a love affair in both Moscow and Leningrad is simply no denying. That it could not be a love affair pure and simple is also a truth. Indeed, the truth is rarely pure and never simple.

For me the experience was highly charged and deeply important and not easy to sift through or sort out. The experiential sense, the taste and feel of it, was a kind of love and appreciation that we had never before received in our twenty-three-year history. I was not in any way prepared for the waves of it, for the continuum of it, much less for the documentation of it—in press, from theater people, from the audience.

It was almost more than one could take, this daily bombardment of love. One lady in Moscow saw every performance, wrote us impressionistic poetry in her minimal English, brought flowers to the curtain calls, and one night brought a garland of large gold coins covering chocolate disks which she put around my neck. The stagehand, Vladimir, studying to be a drama critic at the Theatre Institute in Moscow, saw us off at the train from Moscow to Leningrad, met the train on its return, and came to wave goodbye at the Moscow Airport. Each time he brought flowers and records and notes of admiration and affection: "Your technicians have taught us how to sweat blood," he wrote.

A young woman from Radio Moscow who interviewed me said she had stood in line every day for a month trying to get tickets, but the box office opened for unannounced hours and closed by whim. A toothless babushka made an appointment to give me a book of prints of old Russian icons and to say, "Everywhere I look on the stage I see the actors living. I see life in every corner." She pinched my cheeks and said she was glad that I was married and had children as well as a professional life. Three young directing students engaged me in conversation for nearly an hour after the open dress rehearsal we held to accommodate some of the theater people who couldn't get tickets. They asked me how I had made the crowds in *Inherit the Wind* so individualized and so alive, and they invited me to lecture to their directing class at Moscow University.

The audiences stomped and clapped rhythmically and shouted bravos at the curtain call, standing up in all five tiers of the theater, calling the actors back again and again. The press bestowed the mantle of Chekhov and Stanislavsky upon us; a higher compliment they did not have to give. *Pravda* acknowledged our "serious and humane art." *Izvestia* noted our "broad and diverse artistic methods" and the actors' "capacity for transformation from one character to another," as shown in the two contrasting productions. The press was astonished in general to find out that a theatrical company of this kind even existed in America. They had thought of American theater as musical comedy and slick commercial plays put on on a hit-and-run basis, for profit. But here was a company who spoke to them about the universality of man's fate and about—as *Pravda* summarized *Inherit the Wind*—"the triumph of reason over folly."

And then there was radio, and taped scenes and interviews for television. And beside all this, the endless autographs on the streets, the flowers and gifts, the embraces and hand kissing, and the thanks and misty eyes and fervent pleas to come back. After a few days, we hardly knew ourselves.

REALITIES OF DÉTENTE

At the same time, of course, in the back of our minds it was not possible to forget that we were part of a larger phenomenon called "détente." Further, détente itself was not primarily about love but about bread, and about the fact that war, by some awesome developments in technology, was ruling itself out as a viable instrument of policy.

In the midst of the love affair, the Yom Kippur War started. I first learned about it from a member of our company who had heard it from a Soviet Jew he had been in contact with, who had heard it from the Voice of America. At the outset of the attack, the Soviet media, from all I could tell, did not report about it or about Soviet airlifts of military goods to the Middle East. So, there was our love affair!

At a midday reception at Spaso House, the U.S. ambassador's residence in Moscow, Mr. Voronkov, the Soviet Deputy Minister of Culture, thanked the Arena Stage troupe for "presenting your art of realism." "By coming here and performing," he said, "you have made a new contribution to developing cultural relations between our two countries. You have provided a new stimulus to relations." He offered a toast: "To the friendship of our peoples, to the friendship between artists of the two countries and to the furthered continued success of Arena Stage." At the very same time, Soviet Jews were attempting to send messages to Senator Henry M. Jackson to convey their appreciation for his sponsorship of a measure linking most-favored-nation trade benefits to the right to emigrate.

Madame Furtseva, USSR Minister of Culture, leaving her box seat under the American flag, appeared backstage at intermission one evening to thank the company for coming to the Soviet Union, and to invite us back to a list of other cities. At about the same time, Representative Hansen, Republican of Idaho, read into the Congressional Record from the House floor commendations for Arena Stage for bringing to the Soviet Union a play about freedom of speech, *Inherit the Wind*. He reminded House members of the harassment of Russian writer Aleksandr Solzhenitsyn and others that made the performance of such a play in Moscow so unfortunately timely.

A passionate love affair and a complex one.

Oleg Tabakov, the director of the Sovremennik Theatre in Moscow, perhaps the Soviet company that most resembles our own in temperament and style, summed it up movingly at an historic party their company gave ours, lasting until 3:00 A.M. Oleg made a speech in which he explained that artists cannot really do anything, only politicians can do things. Artists can only point out what has to be done and set the stage for the feelings needed to bring them about. He quoted Carl Sandburg in Russian: "What has been, already has been. But the future is in our hands." *We* said, "We shall never forget this evening." He said, "It is not enough not to forget. Something has to come of your not forgetting." He then noted that the children in the room were not sleepy or bored, even though it was very late. Because, as he said, children know when something important is happening.

ANOTHER MEANING OF LOVE

Pinned to the bulletin board over my desk is Hegel's comment:

> Love is a little moment in the life of lovers; and love remains an inner subjective experience leaving the macrocosm of history untouched. Human history cannot be grasped as the unfolding of human love.

This admonition for objective action, rightly taken, has been useful to me in the past. It has urged me to make decisions I thought were right rather that those that might make me popular. It has kept me from setting too much stock by what is called, whatever it may mean, "success." It has kept my nose to the grindstone, my principles essentially private, and my eye upon the sparrow.

And now in interviews, press and television, in conversations with friends, I am asked, "Tell the truth, now, aren't artists really better diplomats than politicians?" And I want to say to those who cheer and hope: "Yes, of course. All that is true. I agree with you. But surely the ambiguous, confused relations between the USSR and the U.S. remind us that a love poem is not enough. Between the poem and the action stand the thorns."

The thorns: time, for one, and oil, wheat, emigration restrictions, Sakharov versus the Communist Party, the case of Aleksandr Solzhenitsyn, the battle lines at the Suez Canal at the time of the October 22nd ceasefire. It would not be accurate to say that we transcended uneasy political considerations, for the stages of the Moscow Art Theatre and the Pushkin on which we played were at every moment set upon the larger stage of *realpolitik*, and we all knew that. "Human history cannot be grasped as the unfolding of human love."

But if we didn't transcend politics, we circumvented or cut through it. And what we cut through *to* is something basic, imperative, tough, and real. Man's attempt is for union, for being one with the objects of the world. Among these objects is, first, his fellow man. Man, the discontented animal, seeks the life proper to its species; his history consists of the forward-moving search for a lost, prehistoric time when he was, without effort or anxiety, a part of all around him.

In this search, art plays a unique role. It makes objective and transferable our deepest human impulses and yearnings. There are times when you meet another human being, and you simply show something you have made. It pleases him. In such meetings we are at our best. The optimistic in life takes over, and we are, for a moment, fully human and most alive. At that moment what we too lightly call "cultural exchange" is taking place.

We played on a very large stage—larger than the Moscow Art or the Pushkin—a stage set by the two great powers of our contemporary life. The conflicts and divisions between them is not the final point. Surely, we didn't alter the course of history of these two great powers with fourteen performances. But the things we made and shared caused important feelings, in them and in us. If those who have political power, as we do not, exercise their insight, intelligence, leadership, and will—if they, as Walter Lippmann once posed as the final requirement of diplomacy, *Keep Talking!*—then we may have set in motion uniquely important reverberations.

This "love affair" could turn out to be more than a passing fancy. We fervently hope it shall.

Published in the International Educational and Cultural Exchange newsletter, 1974, revised from, and with inclusions from a speech to the National Press Club in November 1973.

TO THE PLAYERS

THE LYING GAME

(2005)

Stella Adler once quoted her father Jacob, patriarch of the Yiddish theater, on the reasons why someone wants to become an actor: "You don't want to get up early, you don't want to work, and you're afraid to steal."

But seriously, why does someone want to become an actor? To enter that arena with the lions and subject oneself to rejection on a regular basis? To chance the masochism of love for a profession that makes no promise to love you back? To risk a life of temping and maybe even poverty? To postpone having a committed relationship or raising a family? Why in the world would you even dream of becoming an actor, let alone audition for a graduate acting program—running up a debt that not only means you'll go without steak dinners and dental work, but that could define your choices until you're middle-aged?

If you're in such a program, I'm sure your mother asked you these very same questions. I hope you didn't get angry when she did. And I hope you didn't respond, "I wouldn't even consider, simply can't imagine, would rather die than be a lawyer or a doctor or anything but an actor! Why, ever since I was in the third grade—remember when we went to see *The Sound of Music*, how excited I was? . . ."

That's not enough; that won't see you through. You have to really understand the nature of your commitment, the depth of it, and its sustainability under pressure.

Let's say you've chosen—you insist on it to defy the odds and become an artist at all costs, financial as well as psychic. In an act of strong will, and after a period of ambivalence, I'm sure, you've decided to make your way in a crowded, competitive, inhospitable profession. I congratulate you for that leap and offer some words of advice.

At Tisch School of the Arts, where I teach, we ask our students to hang on stubbornly to the "why" of their presence there. There are periods of not knowing how one thing relates to another. An actor in training must live in that state. In moments of doubt or fatigue or tedium, when you are doing repetitions for a voice class or memorizing lines or rehearsing a scene at a god-awful time of night, when you think that you'll never live up to expectations, repeat the mantra of your commitment, and stay the course.

Since you know why you are on this path and how urgent it is for you, please give your teachers your trust; the longer you withhold it, the longer will the changes within you be delayed. Do your best to be open and vulnerable. Surrender cynicism. If you experience fear or shame, thrust through it. If you enjoy the work, that's a real bonus. You should expect to feel joy.

Adopt an attitude of curiosity that will lead you into the work rather than away from it. In your training, you will be bombarded with many new things to do and new ways to do the things you've always done. There's juggling and the trapeze, simulating punches and slaps and fighting with daggers and swords. There's researching the world that gave birth to a particular play. There's breathing in a new way and learning muscular relaxation. (A word of caution: Never confuse relaxation with nap time—in class, rehearsal or, Thespis forbid, on the stage!—or with being anything other than alert, poised to act, to do, even if you're just sitting quietly in a chair. The basic law of our technique is that something inside of us is always in motion.)

The hardest thing may turn out to be not what we traditionally think of as "working"—not physical or even intellectual effort—but rather, the act of surrendering, of allowing things to happen to you instead of lunging after them. Numberless demands are made on us, even before we're old enough to internalize them. Clean your plate, or you can't go out to play. You have seven minutes to finish the test. Big boys don't cry.

It takes time to dissolve the restrictions of an educational system where answers are either right or wrong and where uniqueness can be perceived as disruptive. Be patient as you discover the ways in which you are not replaceable by anyone else.

In thinking about my own life, I've decided my greatest talent has been in receiving criticism, incorporating it into my "attend-to" list and moving on. I learned somehow that criticism is a gift, or at least a commodity that can be very useful (and, after all, comes free). If you are defensive or too frightened to listen, or if you mistakenly think it is easy for others to find the precise way to move your work forward without demolishing your sense of self, you are holding back your own progress. If you see how everything contributes to your becoming an artist—from fixing your slouch, to ridding yourself of speech regionalisms, to gaining flexibility and daring within your very psyche—perhaps you will come to welcome critical evaluations as a demonstration of interest in you and of a desire to help you claim and evolve your talent.

I return to my first question: Why would someone want to be an actor? The response to this is crucial. It is the reason I've been besotted with the theater for most of my life.

If I had the gift of being an actor, I would have bent my will, energy, time, and money to become the very best one I could be. I chose instead to produce, direct, teach and, especially, to create structures that make it possible for others to live their lives as actors. Actors are the very center of the theatrical experience, for only a human being can embody another human being. It's to see what can happen to a human in this time between two darknesses—and, imaginatively, what could happen to one's own self—that audiences need the living experience of theater.

Each of us is given but one life: the life of a fly measured against eternity. That life might seem to us free, in terms of choice and possibility. In limited ways it is, but in major ways it is quite determined. Chromosomes decide our sex, the color of our skin and eyes, our bone structure, our predisposition to certain talents and tastes and even to the illnesses that ultimately will whisk us away. The one life we have is determined, too, by how the knobs of inherited characteristics are turned by the culture into which we happen to be born.

Do we want to be hemmed in by one fate? For a creature with high imagination, naturally empathetic, curious and daring, is one life enough? The possibilities of other lives within us propel some to be part of the maddening, glorious world of theater.

The ultimate companion of mankind should be com-passion, "feeling with." If you were a Jew, could you find a way to play a Palestinian suicide bomber? It would depend on how far you could stretch that ability to *feel with*. Would you choose to play him or her as a crazy? An uncultured bandit? You could, surely. Or you could play him as someone who has not received from life what he expected, who has seen atrocity, who looks at this singular act of terror as an "instant of courage." If you chose to play him this way, you would find support in Mahmoud Darwish's "Psalm 11": "Nothing remains for me / but to inhabit your voice that is my voice."

I don't know if you would want to undertake this role. But if you did, if you chose to enter the character's own point of view, you might open the minds in the audience to a different—and perhaps to them dangerous—way of looking at a reality they think they already know. You might give them sight into an alien soul. *Tikkun olam*: in Hebrew, "to repair the world." We are the only animal who strives to do that. In my view, that is the mission of the actor.

Another "why": The actor is allowed the ultimate reward— the enduring thrill of human encounter. There is ebullient joy in performing as an acting company, as part of an organic whole that would not be the same without you, nor you without it. The company is the actor's natural habitat. A cast can be assembled for a single production and work out well, and a company can be brought together for administrative and economic reasons. But neither of these systems provides the creative advantages of a company that evolves from the same aesthetic root, in which all play by the same rules. Without common training, the words "acting company" are misapplied.

If professional actors are members of a company, they've learned to live within the same world in any given production. They've mastered the technique of give-and-take. They are comfortable with the notion of spontaneity within form (or form to support spontaneity; it can be stated either way). The sense of competition—"this is *my* performance; don't get in the way of it"—gives way to the collective will.

You're onstage—the Ides of March scene from *Julius Caesar*. Here comes Caesar, Cassius and Brutus, Metellus Cimber, Cinna the Poet. You know your relationship to them, what will transpire for the next twelve minutes. Most important, you know who's inside the togas and under the helmets: It's Sanjit and Bill, Harry, Peter, and Mano.[1] They're the ones you've eaten lunch with, criticized in class, taken to the emergency room. Now you're playing a game together—the profound, physical, fun game of acting. Afterward, maybe you'll go out for a beer. You're from the same tribe; you have elders to learn from, as younger artists will learn from you. An acting company avoids and civilizes the barbaric one-shot method of the Broadway theater, which sees the actor as another commodity from which to grow rich and remains oblivious to him as an evolving artist, as important to society as a teacher, doctor, or spiritual leader.

The following is *my* "why" for sustaining a life in the theater for half a century: the audience—my friends and neighbors; visitors of different colors; the despairing who lead tight, circumscribed lives; the rich and comfortable who, in the dark, may experience guilt, and the rich and comfortable whose hunger can never be assuaged; the wide-eyed children in their one good dress; the lonely one in a single seat; the Masons in their funny hats; the cognizant and the non-knowing; the old who can forget about dying for a few hours; the egoists; the damned; the teenagers who, under their bravado and with rings in every part of their anatomy, yearn to be useful. The Audience, the terminus of all our work. God bless them all.

They enter into a conspiracy of belief with us, and it would not be moral to betray them. I called what we do a game, and I don't take it back. But it's a game with stakes higher than any other game I know. It's not about getting the shuttlecock over the net or having your foot on the plate. This quirky game is also an elaborate deception, prepared over months and years. We must admit theater is a lying game; actors lie to play it. But these lies are designed to trap the truth, and the more convincing they are, the deeper the truth exposed.

---

1. Sanjit De Silva, Bill Heck, Harry Barandes, Peter McCain, and Manoel Felciano, all Zelda's students at NYU at the time she was writing.

The audience eggs us on: *Lie like mad, and give us your golden truth*. The Prologue from *Henry V* urges us, "Think when we talk of horses that you see them / Printing their proud hoofs i' th' receiving earth / For 'tis your thoughts that now must deck our kings." Yes, we'll imagine with you. Give it to us, we'll give it back; play with us, we'll play along.

A conspiracy of belief, I said, and we mustn't disappoint. We have to believe in the imaginative world with everything we've got. But, I remind you, that belief has to stop just short of falling into the orchestra pit, or, as Medea, howling in anguish on the street outside the theater after you've killed your children, drawing the police with your cries and jeopardizing tomorrow's sold-out matinee, just short of formless excess. If the actor can contain herself just below the level of the truth, she has an opportunity to reach a supra-truth and move us to understand the un-understandable—that a woman's feelings of rage and abandonment could be so ravenous as to lead her to destroy what she loves. Theater fabricates everything from the storm's roar to the lark's song, from the actor's laugh to her nightly flood of tears. The actor opens us to a new understanding of ourselves. What could be more important than that?

How actually one does this is, of course, the matter of actors' training. All technique serves spontaneous life. A famous Hungarian bassist said the same thing: "One must work one's fingers again and again so that one is able to say the things of one's heart."

Or, take the stunning conclusion of Arthur Miller's *On Politics and the Art of Acting*:

> However dull or morally delinquent an artist may be, in his moment of creation, when his work pierces to the truth, he cannot dissimulate, he cannot fake it. Tolstoy once remarked that what we work for in a work of art is the revelation of the artist's soul, a glimpse of God. You can't fake that.

Published in *American Theatre*, January 2005.

TO THE ACTORS AND FACULTY
(1999)

It has been said that theater is life in a smaller room, which is to say a number of things. First, that the enterprise of theater derives from life, from reality, this reality, ours, as it is *now*: from how we occupy ourselves day to day, what we strive for—and win and lose—over the arc of time. "The smaller room" implies that to share with others the experience of our reality, we need to provide a form, a glass to hold the water.

Life tends to be deconstructed—to lie about in fragments. Motives are often hidden from view and the connection between events difficult to perceive. In this smaller room, we connect the dots, compress the actions—leaving out the boring parts—give meaning and a through line, tell a story. Real, live people with breath, muscles, thoughts, and needs perform for real live people with breath, muscles, thoughts, and needs. A conspiracy of belief, a riveting of attention, creates in this smaller room an energy, an electricity, that contrasts—alas—to the inattention we pay to our own lives.

I take my job here very seriously. I can't think of anything more important to do. Before this, I contributed to that culturally critical movement, beginning roughly mid-century, of getting theater to be— like libraries, schools, churches, symphony orchestras, museums, and garbage collection(!)—out of one center into many, wherever in the U.S. people work and live. From the launch of this idea until now, some 1,200 theaters—large and very small—have come into being. These theaters will be very important to your artistic development; they originated, in fact, to contain you.

I came here from there because of you. My acting company was getting older; younger actors trained to perform in a broad repertory of classics, and new plays were becoming more and more rare. I came in 1984 and left Arena Stage in the spring of 1991, so for a while I worked nine or ten days a week. That was okay though, because it was only one job really: to bring the actors to the center of our art, so that the audience could see through them back into the world and, by seeing, grow into a higher awareness of life.

Each of us on the Earth today is but a temporary trustee in an infinitely long evolutionary process. It behooves us, therefore, in the time of our lives, to move that process along, to help in the climb up, to take sides in the struggle to be fully human. What better thing is there to do with one's life, after all?

There is a Burmese saying that speaks to me:

The fish dwell in the depths of the waters,
The eagle on the sides of Heaven.
The one, though high, can be reached with an arrow,
The other, though deep, with a hook.
But the heart of man, at a foot's distance,
Cannot be known.

Theater—in its arrogance and *hubris*, in its insatiable curiosity and deep compassion, aims to cross that foot or, at least, to close the distance. Only through you—the en-actors, the doers, the possessed ones, acting out our stories—in *this* moment, *this* space, here now, can the mysteries be unveiled. You, my friends, are the teachers of your generation, and *teacher* training is what you came to get.

Since, of course, your venue will be not the classroom or the lecture hall, you will be teaching not through books, blackboards or "how-to" demonstrations, but by the way you behave upon that magic platform, within that sacred space. *For behavior is the real language of the actor.* What you do is who you are—even as it is in life. First the deed, then the words for it, out of those is born the character.

Words, of course, are the pinnacle of human achievement. Our awe-inspiring language instinct, together with the miraculous she-nanigans of the evolving brain, made possible Shakespeare, Shaw, August Wilson, and other poets of exquisite sensibility and insight.

Human beings make about 160 different sounds. This, say the linguists, is the elemental sum of all the world's languages. English, one of the more complicated vocal systems, has about 55 of these sounds. Norwegian has 75. The San (Bushmen) language of the south-ern Africa Kalahari have more than 145. Colonists despised the very sound of San voices and, in their campaigns against these great vocal acrobats, sought to eradicate their languages. As if the tribe's mind was itself the enemy. Clearly, language is a political instrument—in the hands of liberators or oppressors, as the case may be. When a Native American tribal language is wiped out—when children are no longer taught to speak it—the tribe loses connection to its ancestors and, as a result, its culture.

Language is a very important part of the curriculum here; how-ever, as I have mentioned, behavior is, even more, what we're about. What we *do* sometimes speaks so loud that it's hard to hear what we're saying! All of us—every culture on the Earth, every race, every tribe, every family, members of every social class, *every mother's son*—belong to the same species of animal: human. This species acquired language only a blink-of-the-eye ago, a mere 10,000 years ago. For millions of years we had to get along without it, grunting and groan-ing, gesticulating, grabbing, mounting or grooming The Other, bar-ing our teeth—*displaying* not *saying* what we wanted and meant to get. We functioned and survived without language. It took a long time for our brains and speech organs to develop this other, extremely economical and effective means of getting what we want—*speaking.* (And, then, still later, came the truly extraordinary ability to set down in permanent form what we thought and said.)

We know that what comes soonest lies the deepest within us. Which is why our childhood, when we are most anarchic and closest to our animal heritage, assumes such a large role in determining who we turn out to be. There are enormous implications for actor training in the fact that human behavior came before speech in our evolution. What we *did*, what we manifested *physically* to satisfy our needs—for food, sex, alliances against the enemy, social prestige, for having fun between the arduous tasks of survival—is what kept us evolving as a successful human animal, until we made the leap into our higher powers.

The point for you as citizen/actors is that *talk* is a kind of press agent for your inner life. It's a civilized, biologically advanced way to get for the character what he wants or wants to get across. Sometimes it happens that the press agent gets lax or terse (Harold Pinter?) or is sly or fearful and, so, tries to conceal the wants *behind* or *under* the words—which is where we get the word *subtext*: under the text. But anyone who remains alert and attends to a character's behavior will figure things out, anyone who listens to the tone of voice rather than to just the words. Language can lie, but the body never lies. The body has a millions-of-years' habit of telling the truth. The body of the actor must be trained—which usually means *freed* from the restrictions acquired while growing up—to reveal physically the truth that lies within. "Why do you stay in prison," the poet Rumi asks, "when the door is so wide open?" Why, indeed!

Sigmund Freud described consciousness as thin, surface tension on the top of a glass of water. But he described the *sub*conscious—the place of dreams, improvisation and play, Freud's own territory, and that of Stanislavsky, Chekhov, the Impressionists and Einstein, too—as deep as the Zuyder Zee. We summon the innocent "let's pretend" of childhood to release the riches of imagination and transformation deep inside. To become an actor/artist, we must let the goblins of our soul out to play.

After evolutionary heritage and genetics, culture is the third powerful determinant of our identity, so strong that it acquires the force of instinct. Your baby brain was born unfinished and underwent in early life important physiological changes as it interacted with the environment and found out what your particular culture held for you—your mother or mothering figure being the most important part of that culture. And everyone thinks that his or her culture is the best, because it is what she knows. Peace among cultures is only possible if we can recognize the Other as different, and valuable, and irresistibly interesting in that difference.

What makes theater so powerful is that, through it, we discover experience *beneath* the expressions of culture—*beneath* the shape of language, standards of honor, the relationship to ancestors and between men and women, what clothes are worn, how food is prepared, what music is listened to—beneath all this, past these differences, we discover the universal human situation: who we really are after all is said and done. It is precisely because every important piece of theater comes from and imbeds a specific culture that it can instruct us about our underlying, indissoluble connections to each other. It seems to be a contradiction, but it isn't.

My final thought for you is of *company*. You will be trained as a member of the company that is your class. We hope that this will inspire you to join companies when you graduate or, since there are not many out there to join, that you will create them on your own.

The family unit—nuclear or extended—exists in every known society. A family indoctrinates the young into its culture, nurtures and protects them, and helps them master the skills of living. The acting company provides a parallel function in the society of the theater. The individual artist grows greater within the embrace of consistent fellowship, building in concert one performance upon the other, steadily ascending in psychic awareness and technical skill. Actors can explore large moments of drama more fully when they are not afraid of their own vulnerability or of being unmasked in front of each other. Acting is, in many ways, a physical sport. As the team is strong, so is the player strong; as the player is strong, so the team.

A play concerns itself first of all with a web of human relationships, the interactions of a particular small society, usually—not surprisingly—a family. For two or three hours this society-in-miniature stands for a larger society that, in turn, stands for the human situation in general. Actors can best help each other embody those relationships when they share an artistic process and know and respect one another. Actors with a common goal and common standards, participants in a collective consciousness, can dare together.

As Aristotle put it, "What a thing *can* be, it *must* be, whether it be a horse or a man." My dream for you is that you will be what you can be. I'm here with you in this smaller room in the hope that these ideas can live within you, not abstractly, but incorporated—made into *corpus*, into body. By living them out concretely onstage, you can show the people with you in the room who they are to themselves and to each other. By daring to peel from yourself what Ibsen called the life mask, you challenge their capacity for truth. And a mind, once stretched, never returns to its original dimensions. What a noble calling you've had the courage to choose! I'm committed to you. I salute you.

Remarks to the students and faculty at NYU's Graduate Acting Program, for the school year beginning September 3, 1999.

TO THE FACULTY AND STUDENTS
(2001)

Let me speak about the relationship among playwright, actor, and audience, for theater is rooted in that triangle. The theater is a public space, and playwrights are, essentially, social artists. The forms they use to tell their stories are to a large degree culturally determined. Even Shakespeare, the greatest artist the world has known, inherited his dramatic form from the Elizabethan playwrights around him; he might not have been Shakespeare had there not been a Thomas Kyd or Christopher Marlowe to loan him a verse form that suited the magnitude of his imagination. The expansiveness of the age of Elizabeth, the shape of the playhouse, and the rowdy, curious audience melded with his own unique genius, and out of this melding came *Hamlet*, *Macbeth*, *King Lear*.

One can see in the plays of our time the influence of film and television and of the economic parameters of the theater: many short scenes rarely sustained for even fifteen minutes, few long speeches of significant architecture, small casts that focus on interpersonal relationships rather than large political or social themes. Of course, there are always the form-givers, artists who see things in a new way and break the mold.

In whatever form the playwright casts her story, as she bends over the accumulating pages in her study, there is always the imagined presence of an audience. She never forgets that the characters, the actions they take, the consequences of these actions, and the words the characters use to get what they must have—all are to be tested in public, in front of living, breathing people, who will believe or not, laugh or not, applaud or—God forbid!—sit on their hands.

August Wilson says: "When I was writing *Joe Turner's Come and Gone*, I realized that someone was gonna stand up onstage and say the words, whatever the hell they were. That's when I realized I had a responsibility to the words. I couldn't have the character say any old thing. There couldn't be any mistakes." Society is in the room with him, in his mind's eye, waiting to see what he has to show them this time. This expectant audience, in various guises (not all of them benevolent), pass through his dreams and keep him on the edge as he moves through his working days.

The playwright has other expectations, as well. There will be actors, who by opening night will hopefully have discovered, *un*covered the feelings, actions and meanings for which the words are clues. They will make what may appear to be unnatural forms of speech entirely natural. Through the instrument of their bodies, voices, and intelligence, and by means of the thoughts and feelings they loan to the characters they play, they will make the blueprint of the script into a palpable, living thing.

Sitting in the theater on opening night, the audience has no direct contact with the playwright (who by now hovers nervously in the back of the theater or has sneaked away to the nearest bar), but breathes the same air with the actors, lives in real time with them, journeys with them to a destination that must never feel certain. Maybe the theater will burn down, or there will be a bomb scare, or maybe tonight, just tonight, Juliet's potion will not work, and she'll be magically united with her Romeo. Who is to know? Theater is a living art.

The public has gifts of its own to contribute to the theatrical event. First among these contributions is empathy, the ability to identify with the joys and pains of others. Some suggest we empathize through the knowledge of our own feelings of pain and joy; some suggest empathy is hardwired in us, an evolutionary advantage. Both are true, and if we look around, we see people who still have the gift, and those who have lost it. We hope that our audiences still have it.

Because one crying infant in a hospital nursery can trigger the whole pack into loud wails, the act of theater is possible. Because tots of one or two years instinctively offer their bottles to sobbing comrades, we can receive the glories of Shakespeare! Because empathy is contagious, a large audience is more intelligent and responsive than a tiny one. Together, they get things more quickly and on a deeper level. You can tell that an audience is following when everyone laughs at the same time. A soft murmuring laugh of recognition, coming from everywhere, is one of the most beautiful sounds an audience has to offer.

Of course, if the story is unconvincing or illogical, if the acting comes at them only from the neck up—from talking heads—the collective boredom can be deafening. Programs rustle, feet shuffle, clothes rub against seats as the bored squirm. Suddenly everyone has a cough; a wave of wristwatch checking passes through the hall; pocketbooks open—lipsticks and mirrors urgently retrieved—and snap shut again. These noises come on suddenly. As I say, it's a living art. And that, of course, is its wonder.

Along with empathy, the audience gives to the theater its imaginative power. All of us are born artists: We all can, when young, see things that aren't there, believe in what logic defies—a tooth fairy or magical friend. Any child can crawl under a table and—presto—it's a cave! Or give you a plastic ice-cream cone and only be satisfied when you really lick it. Some grown-ups hold on to this capacity for enchantment, and some desire a life other than their own, if only for a few hours. No life contains all possibilities; the theater does.

These creative people constitute a talented audience. A few chairs become a room if the actors use them as one. In *Henry V*, the Prologue invites them to "think when we talk of horses, that you see them / Printing their proud hoofs i' th' receiving earth." Their silent response: "Yes, we can do that, we want to do that, let's do that! We will piece out your imperfections with our thoughts, as you ask. It is indeed our thoughts that now may deck your kings." In this way, the experience of theater is different from that of film. Film shows us, even fantasy, before our eyes; it doesn't call upon our imagination to complete the experience.

The audience also gives to us its attention, the most precious gift of all. To attend is a form of prayer; a form of loving. When you attend to something, you affirm its value. Life itself has a way of going unobserved, getting lost in a clutter of miscellany and familiarity, the narrowing of sight by habit. But clear a space, any kind of space—let some people gather around it in a natural way and have a person cross that space for no other reason but to fetch his coat. People will grow quiet and absorbed, wondering what is happening and what will happen next. We are born to seek out stories; it's a biological given. We experience our own life as a story and, on the path to intimacy with another, what we want to know is *their* story.

Because theater shows us people like ourselves acting out stories, because we attend and are moved, while others, in turn, are moved by our being moved, it's quite possible for a fire of emotional contagion to break out in the theater! No wonder plays have caused riots or raised the ire of governments, national and local, whose power derives from legislating *their* version of the truth. Theater has a terrible and wonderful power to reach people's minds through their hearts and—maybe—change them. Who knows what exquisite mischief can come from a changed mind?

The stage is a place of expanded meaning. Living is shaped into art and resonates outward, back to life again. You see, then, why the actors must act as if the imaginary circumstances are real—that is, must act well—bringing their own real thoughts and feelings, transposed, to the characters they play. For if they only *pretend*, the audience will spend their precious empathy, imagination, attention on something that is less than life. If on the other hand the actor *makes believe* (makes *belief*), which is different than mere pretend, then life is sharpened, clarified, brought to a higher level of perception.

Theater is an art of experience. The playwright in her study sets her experience down in words, a kind of code. The actors break that code, and we enter their experience—and understand. So that we can see, see *into*. And, having seen into the experience of life itself and into the experience of others, we are changed and will never be the same.

Excerpted from opening remarks, NYU Graduate Acting Program, September 7, 2001.

TO THE ACTORS ON
THE ANNIVERSARY OF 9/11
(2002)

Sometimes it happens. Sometimes there is carnage and a Trojan horse—the disassembling of human bodies; the separation of sons and daughters from their father, from their mother, of parents from their children, friend from friend, wife from husband, lover from lover. Sometimes a person at work will grab the hand of a colleague and together they will fly through the air to certain death, rather than suffocate in the inferno of the 100th floor.

I often think that Wordsworth's lines, as he muses on the birds and flowers and "budding twigs" in early spring, make bitter, ironic, indisputable sense:

If such be Nature's holy plan,
Have I not reason to lament
What man has made of man?

Sometimes carnage happens, though not since the Civil War at Antietam has it happened to us. And since it did, a year ago today, we have been required to enter our maturity as a nation and join the rest of the world, where carnage has been happening and happening and yet again happening through the centuries and millennia and to this very day: Bosnia, Croatia, Romania, the Congo, Zimbabwe, Chechnya, Afghanistan, Indonesia, Iran, Iraq, Israel, and Palestine.

In 1993, at the World Trade Center with its prelude attack, we had a warning of what more might be coming, had we only been able to hear that warning. We were too occupied elsewhere, especially with domestic matters. It was the economy, stupid. One president and another found it politically disadvantageous to attend to the rest of the world in a forceful way. There wasn't enough at stake for us to become engaged *soon* enough, *deeply* enough. And surely, America would be safe, as she has always been safe, from enmity across the seas. Our watchdog agencies—the FBI and CIA—had very few Arabic translators; the stack of intercepted secret documents that might have clued us in was too high, too dense for so few.

I want to think that nothing could have been done to stop the well-educated, fanatic young men bent on suicide and heavenly virgins. Sometimes it happens that nothing could have been done. I am not comforted by that thought, though I hope the people who lost loved ones will be comforted.

Today is our *yahrzeit*—literally, the "year's time"—the anniversary of our Death by Fire. There will continue to be a *yahrzeit* each year, I imagine, as there is for a private family death. Today 9/11 is being retraced, revisited, re-memorialized in the press, on TV, in concert halls, in the theater—in poetry, song, drama, essays, on occasions for collective worship and recollection. The Towers will fall again, and people will leap from them again, holding hands; heroes will again rush into the holocaust to die or be permanently disabled, and our grief and bewilderment, our helplessness and loss will return, raw and, perhaps again, unmanageable. Is this a good thing? I don't know.

It's for each of us to decide how we want to remember the last 9/11. Quietly with friends or family, in the embrace of the collective—there's a candlelight vigil at Washington Square tonight—or in front of a TV, or at church, or privately, alone. I'll have dinner with a friend. Then I'll light a candle tonight—the custom on *yahrzeit*—in my apartment by myself. Focused on that point of illumination, I'll try to connect meaningfully to the people in my own life whom I have lost, who have given me my particular story.

My brilliant father, who taught me that work is play, and died of a heart attack at age forty-eight; my mother, who lived as an emotional and psychological shadow after that; my husband's father and mother, theatrical figures, larger than life; my husband, father of my children, partner in the creation of Arena Stage; Alan Schneider, my closest creative partner; Richard Bauer, a truly great actor who was a mainstay of our acting company for thirty years; Nora Dunfee, Master Teacher of Text here; Troup Mathews, whose soul is imprinted on the school and on every student who studied with him; and, alas, others.

Grieving for them, I'll be able to grieve for still others I don't know, in a true and personal way. For it's through knowing our own feelings that we can know the feelings of one another. The capacity for empathy, for compassion, is born in us, but it is kept alive by staying in touch, first of all, with our own hearts. Since this is true of the human being in general, it is doubly true of the artist and, especially, of the artist/actor. I will grieve and then, hopefully, I'll be able to rejoice that my dead were once in my life, that they are forever a part of me, that I am still in relationship with them.

We live this day in a tension between the political and the personal. They tell us that we are at war, but not when it will end and how. Is this a phantom war, to stifle dissent and concentrate power at the top, where business interests and governance meet? A hundred children were born this year after the death of their fathers. One woman, with three little children to raise alone, the last one five months old, says, "The whole year was September 11th. At the beginning, I sat on the floor in a corner and sobbed. I thought I would never get through it. Looking back on the year, I'm aware that we did get through it, and I'm proud of that, and now, finally, we can move on to September 12th." Another woman, having organized the anniversary celebration for other mothers, says, "Thank God, we're more than our losses." In that thought I find comfort and a tentative way out of mourning.

I'm thankful for this community and for the privilege of working. Art begins with the empty space: "What do I do? What do I say now?" I'm eager to confront that empty space with you.

Opening remarks, NYU Graduate Acting Program, September 11, 2002.

PLAYING

(2005)

I don't like the word "training" as applied to what we do here. I associate *training* with received information—like the birds who chew up the food and mouth-to-mouth feed their babies with what has already been half digested. I associate *training* with the military, with computer programming or secretarial school, or even with nursing or doctoring, even though these fields involve deeply human skills. You will acquire skills here—all the skills you will need to have a rich, productive career in the theater—but here's the difference: This faculty will not only teach you those skills; they will, on a very deep level, educate you—*e-ducere*, to bring forth, to coax forth. What they will coax forth is not some skill, external to you, but you yourself, the *you* in your personal history, your psychobiography, your physicality, your present state, your nowness. They will bring that *you* forth in all seriousness and in the spirit of play. For this is a play school, and all the skills we teach fall within that overarching idea of play.

The species of humans is not only *Homo sapiens*—thinking man—but *Homo ludens*—playing man. The child's is the first voice of our inner knowing, and the first language of this knowing is play. In this light, Donald Winnicott, the brilliant psychiatrist, defined the aim of psychological healing as "bringing the patient from a state of not being able to play into a state of being able to play." He said, "It is in playing and only in playing that the individual child or adult is able to be creative and to use the whole personality, and it is only in being creative that the individual discovers the self." To transform, actors must be their own unique, special, distinctive—*and free*—selves. Playing and freedom are aspects of each other.

My understanding of this idea has been deepened by the book *Free Play: Improvisation in Life and Art*, by Stephen Nachmanovitch, a violinist, composer, poet, teacher, and computer artist. I have drawn heavily on this extraordinary book for my remarks today, and will summarize and paraphrase as I go.

We improvise every day. We talk and listen, we draw on a set of building blocks (vocabulary) and certain rules for combining them (grammar), given to us by our culture and, especially, by our mothers or primary caregivers. But the sentences we make with these have never been said before and will never be said again. Every conversation is a form of jazz.

The activity of instantaneous creation is as ordinary as breathing. Whether we are creating high art or a meal, writing a poem or organizing a political rally, we are also improvising, moving with the flow of time and with our own evolving consciousness. In improvisation, there is only one time: *Now*. Memory (the past) and desire (the future) are fused with intuition (the present), so that the iron is always hot. On the stage, we try to reproduce that aliveness, to live in real time.

The creative moment, that flash feeling of lightness and energy and rightness we sometimes feel in daily life, can come and go. We can get stuck. Through technique, we can learn to stretch out the momentary flashes we've known simply as part of being human, and extend them into a work of art.

Stephen Nachmanovitch writes of two musicians improvising together:

> I play with my partner; we listen to each other . . . we connect with what we hear. He doesn't know where I'm going, I don't know where he's going, yet we anticipate, sense, lead, and follow each other. There is no agreed-on structure or measure, but once we have played for five seconds there is a structure, because we've started something. We open each

> other's minds like an infinite series of Chinese boxes. A mys-
> terious kind of information flows back and forth, quicker
> than any signal we might give by sight or sound. The work
> comes from neither one artist nor the other, even though
> our own idiosyncrasies and styles, the symptoms of our
> original natures, still exert their natural pull. Nor does the
> work come from a compromise or halfway point (averages
> are always boring!), but from a third place that isn't neces-
> sarily like what either one of us would do individually. What
> comes is a revelation to both of us. There is a third, totally
> new style that pulls on us. It is as though we have become a
> group organism that has its own nature and its own way of
> being, from a unique and unpredictable place . . .

I point to his phrase, "the symptoms of our original natures, still exert their natural pull." We look on your growth both as a member of an ensemble and as a distinct individual. Your uniqueness is our special treasure; we train to that uniqueness. The art that each of you create will have your signature on it, at the same time as it meets the creativity of others to form an artistic whole.

When I told an artist, whose painting I had just bought, how much I loved his work, he replied shyly in his native Mandarin, which was translated for me: "I am so complimented, for of course the brush mark is the man." The brush mark is the man. Who you are is what you will create; what you create tells us about who you are. We each have something in us, about us, that Nachmanovitch calls our "origi-nal nature." As we grow up, we also accommodate to the habits of our culture, family, physical environment, the style and technology of the time, the people who influence us. But somehow, even when we are grown and integrated with our world, everything we do and are—our handwriting, our voice, the way we handle a violin bow, lob a ball over a net or walk across a stage, the colors we choose to paint with, the language we use—are symptomatic of our original nature. They all show the imprint of our deeper style or character.

A few words about form as it relates to play: It is sometimes thought that in an improvisation—an artistic form of play—we can do anything—*galumphing* it is called in *Alice in Wonderland*. Galumph-ing has its place—just letting go, romping as puppies, children, and baby baboons do. But true improvisation has rules—implied structure—even though they are rules that grow from within the improvisation itself as it unfolds. The freedom of our improvisation is the opposite of "just anything." Why? Because, as Nachmanovitch writes, "We carry around the rules inherent in our organisms. Our body-mind is a highly organized and structured affair, interconnected [as any] organism that has evolved over hundreds of millions of years. [Improvisers don't] operate out of a formless vacuum, but from three billion years of organic evolution, encoded somewhere in us . . . As our playing, writing, speaking, drawing, dancing unfolds, the inner unconscious logic of our being begins to show through and mold the material." Trust me: Everything you need to become an artist is already within you; the body has a wisdom that is deep and strong. You know so much more than you know you know.

It's your task to learn how to release those unique patterns of your body-mind, so that they are usable in the process of creating other characters, characters *like* you and at the same time *unlike* you. You are in charge of this releasing—you have to decide to surrender to the process—but we can help you. You might recall Michelangelo's idea that the statue is buried in the stone and that the task of the artist is to release the artwork buried there. The pattern is in you in the same way that it is in the stone.

Some words about *practice*. Nachmanovitch puts it this way: "Unless you have been thoroughly drenched in perspiration, you cannot expect to see a palace of pearls on a blade of grass." Meaning you're going to have to work hard. The most frustrating, agonizing part of creative work is the gap between what we feel and what we can express, between the what and the how. In this gap the would-be artist *feels* most deeply, but *is* most inarticulate.

Laziness will not make an artist of you. You don't practice *for* something—a good evaluation or good role—but to deepen the art in yourself. We don't practice the scales to make music later, but to make music of the scales. The exercise of technique is not boring or tedious or uncreative in and of itself; it is we who manufacture the boredom. You must practice with this awareness. You must *decide* to perceive it necessary to practice in the spirit of imaginative play.

Alas, reality is contradictory and inconsistent; it's all a matter of balance. On one hand, it's dangerous to separate practice from "the real thing." On the other hand, if we judge ourselves too harshly, we will not have space to experiment. Our practice resonates between two poles—getting things right on our instrument and "just playing" to explore without fear of judgment. Each of you will locate your own balance.

I have two grandchildren, as most of you know since they are currently my primary teachers, and I refer often to what I'm learning from them. Matthew at nine is methodical, successful at school, obedient, careful to look before he leaps. He learned the names of fifty-three countries of Africa overnight and is obsessed with, and a rabid player of, baseball. His parents help him release the playful, irreverent clown inside, and even encourage him to break a few rules. Emily, seven, is playful, loves animals and all of nature. Gentle and self-generating, she wanders easily into the world of her imaginings, narrates her dreams, invents recipes, and cooks and serves them up. She has endless, improvisational conversations with me and has to be eased into doing her homework, practicing her piano, wearing socks that match, and being ready for the school bus in the morning. Which are each of you? Know it for yourself, and keep yourself in balance. As an adult, take good care of the child in you. Give him or her what is needed to flower.

To create, we need to learn both technique and freedom. To this end we practice until our skills become unconscious. When skill hides in the unconscious, it is able to *reveal* the unconscious, where the bottomless reservoir of our humanity lives, waiting to be tapped. *By touching this layer of our being, the artist who is consummate separates himself from the artist who is merely competent.* If you want to be a consummate artist, practice your skills as a form of play until you surprise yourself into this most dense and fertile terrain of mankind's evolution. From this place, you will be able to speak to all of mankind, even across cultures. For this is the place where we are all one.

Shall we speak about the hazards and doubts that stand in the way of our expressivity—that gap between what we desire to express and how we achieve that desire? What stands in the way of releasing the sculpture that lives in the stone? As adults, we are all afraid to make mistakes. We hate to be wrong, to be foolish, de-valued. I've struggled with this fear all my life. But because I've both succeeded and failed so many times in public, I've learned that success and failure are two sides of the same coin. Eventually the words have lost their power—somewhat. I'd rather succeed, but most of all I want to keep on doing and learning. It can take a long time to discover the creativity—the direction-finder—that lives inside failure.

Nachmanovitch is also good on mistakes, which he compares to "the irritating grains in the oyster that become pearls." He quotes musician Miles Davis: "Do not fear mistakes. There are none." I don't know whether I believe him, but it's good advice. He also quotes the head of IBM: "Good judgment comes from experience. Experience comes from bad judgment." The renowned director Alan Schneider, from whom I learned so much, said, "I look for accidents in rehearsal. I set them up. They teach me what is really happening in the scene, better than all my planning could." And on: Freud illuminated the fascinating way in which slips of the tongue reveal unconscious material. Since the unconscious is the artist's bread and butter, slips of all kinds are priceless treasures from beyond and within.

What else holds us back? What may cause the stops and starts in your movement forward? The seesaw of the artist's, "Yes, I can/No I can't," "Help me/Leave me alone," "Tell me what I'm doing wrong/ Just tell me what's right." Self-doubt writes a little supertitle to every impulse we have: "But on the other hand, maybe not." Driving a car is usually performed unconsciously, without thinking. If you let self-doubt intrude on each of the thousands of actions and decisions you make in a minute of driving, you'd panic and never get anywhere. You can't let it stand between you and the ability to play either. William Blake: "If the sun and moon should doubt, they'd immediately go out."

As you grow, you will learn more about integrating mistakes and pain and disappointment into your personhood. You will learn to use that knowledge—the empathy it instills—in your work. You will learn to keep moving toward your creative self. How shall you overcome self-doubt and remember how to play? That's a question school puts before you.

In packing to come back to New York at summer's end, I decided to bring an old purple linen jacket. I reached into a pocket and pulled out an outdated address card from a playwright friend. On the back it said, "Ring the bells that still can ring. Forget your perfect offering. There is a crack in everything. That's how the light gets in." Lyrics from Leonard Cohen's song "Anthem."

That's the good news. Play with it.

Opening remarks, NYU Graduate Acting Program, September 2005.

A DIRECTOR'S NOTES

I work for months in finding what I call in Russian (there is no comparable English word) *zamissel*. It means "the pervading sense." *Missel* means "thought" and *za* is an intensive prefix. It's the thought that binds together all elements or the idea. The *zamissel* accounts for the whole—explains every action, every breath, every pulse, every second of the life of the play. It's like looking at a tree. The sap is in every leaf and it's also in the roots. I can spend months looking for the exact *zamissel* or idea or super-objective that will set a play in motion, unlock its hidden conflict.[1]

—Z.F.

1. Quoted from an interview with Arthur Bartow, *The Director's Voice: Twenty-One Interviews* (New York: Theatre Communications Group, 1988).

THE THREE SISTERS
BY ANTON CHEKHOV
(1983)

What about this play? It can be looked on in so many ways. For the most part, audiences and critics have agreed with the one critic who, on seeing the famous Katharine Cornell, Judith Anderson, Ruth Gordon production in 1942, remarked that she "could not see much sense in three adults spending four acts in *not* going to Moscow when all the time they had the price of a railroad ticket." Of course, that was not the point and was never the point. *Real* students of Chekhov have always known that the cry, "To Moscow," had very little to do with geography and very much to do with the yearnings of the human heart to find its own desire.

The world has caught up with Chekhov's sensibility since 1942 and, now, all of a sudden, his plays seem to have a startling, refreshing contemporaneity. They always had it, but it was hidden by another time, another historic mood, another angle of viewing life. Just as we have rediscovered Shakespeare as our contemporary (as if he had ever been anything but!), so Chekhov has in recent years become more accessible. His plays evoke the very response my mother spoke aloud when she first saw his work at Arena: "My god, isn't it just like life!"

"Life," Chekhov said, "is an insoluble problem." At the end of the first act of *The Seagull*, Dorn—one of the many doctors in Chekhov's plays (no doubt since Chekhov himself was one)—is trying to comfort the distraught and unhappy Masha. All he can find to say is, "But what can I do, my child? Tell me what can I do? What?" *What can I do?* This question is a leitmotif that runs through all of Chekhov's plays and ties him to our own age with its fear of nuclear war (as Chekhov's folk feared the Industrial Revolution), its international terrors, its economic displacements, and most of all with the pervading awareness of our smallness in a gigantic universe, our sense that we have lost control of our lives. "What can we do?" Indeed.

But what could we ever do? Life has always been lonely, and love has always been misplaced.

Chris Durang, the irreverent, says it perfectly in *Beyond Therapy*, now playing in the Kreeger.[1] In the words of Charlotte, the mad psychiatrist, talking about Chekhov's *The Seagull*:

> Masha loves Konstantin, but Konstantin only loves Nina. Nina doesn't love Konstantin, but falls in love with Trigorin. Trigorin doesn't love Nina, but sort of loves Madame Arkadina, who doesn't love anyone but herself. And Medviedenko loves Masha, but she only loves Konstantin, which is where we started out. And then at the end of the play, Konstantin kills himself!

Yes. Love is misplaced. And time passes and wears away our dreams. We hang on to our illusions by our fingernails—surely by next fall we'll be in Moscow! But they are snatched from us. We search for meanings. "For love alone did nature put us in this world," says another doctor, Chebutykin. Is *that* it? "We will work, and the time will come when everyone will know why all this is, what these sufferings are for." Is *that* it? What is the meaning of our lives?

Chekhov wrote to his actress-wife Olga Knipper, for whom he created the role of Masha in *The Three Sisters*, "You worry too much about the eternal verities. You ask 'what is life?' That is just the same thing as asking 'what is a carrot?' A carrot is a carrot, and nothing more is known about it." Chekhov's way is not to understand what a carrot is but simply to show us the carrot. Let us take it from there.

---

1. Arena's second theater, a 514-seat modified thrust stage.

If life cannot be known—in the sense of being decoded, penetrated, wrapped up in a solution, or even responded to in a total way—it can at least be shown and seen. We can know it by seeing it, by looking at it, not in its meaning but in its *is-ness*. If it can't be deciphered, at least it can be described, uncovered, opened to the light of day. And good can come of this. "Man will only become better when you make him see what he is like," wrote dear Anton.

It was this incomparable ability to show us what we are like that makes Chekhov, finally, not the dramatist of doom and gloom he's been cast as, that makes his plays comedies not tragedies. In our "is-ness" are we not foolish, absurd, funny creatures, railing and straining against a basically irrational, inexplicable universe?

This ability also gives the plays their mysterious quality of affirmation: If we can't get to Moscow, at least we can keep fanning the dream. If Masha and Vershinin had an affair, at least the Army is departing now (and Vershinin with it); at least Masha's husband, Kulygin, can put on his funny face, and his marriage to Masha can somehow soldier on. If the Baron is killed in a duel, perhaps he will live on in the trees, still part of the life that continues after him. And Vershinin will philosophize and complain at the next military post. And Andrei will rock the carriage and hope that his child's life will be better. And Natasha will find her place in the new rising bourgeoisie. And because life is never predictable, old Anfisa will end up with her heart's desire—her own bed in her own apartment! At government expense! And the three sisters will huddle together, in love and support, and sing their song of hope and faith. And life will go on, questions still unanswered, solutions as yet unfound. Will they ever be?

The Three Sisters—like all of Chekhov's plays—is an actor's play. Only through the soul of the actor can the distance be shown between aspiration and failure, urgency and passivity, self-love and self-hate, breaking free and settling for, the dream and its extinction, between resistance and acceptance—the distance that defines Chekhov's art and, indeed, human experience itself.

And they are actors' plays because an actor is a doer. Though not always perceived as such, Chekhov's dramatic art consists of layers of commonplace detail wrapped around large and significant *doings*, around extremely climactic events.

"Let the things that happen onstage," Chekhov writes, "be just as complex and yet just as simple as they are in life. For instance, people are having a meal at a table, just having a meal, but at the same time their happiness is being created, or their lives are being smashed up." The placid surface of daily routine masks the artist's controlled manipulation of human events, their development and crisis. Characters seem to exist in isolated pockets; they are in fact parts of a tight network of interlocking motives and emotions. Dialogue seems to meander aimlessly—the need for a cup of tea, the future of mankind, the season in Moscow—even as character is revealed and action propelled.

In *My Life in Art*, Stanislavsky movingly describes how he stumbled upon the deepest truth of Chekhov's work while producing *The Three Sisters*:

> We worked with spirit. We rehearsed the play, everything was clear, comprehensive, true, but the play did not live; it was hollow, it seemed tiresome and long. There was something missing. How torturing it is to seek this something without knowing what it is. All was ready, it was necessary to advertise the production, but if it were to be allowed on the stage in the form in which it had congealed, we were faced with certain failure. And then what would happen to Anton Pavlovich? And what would happen to the Theatre? . . .
>
> At one of our torturing rehearsals the actors stopped in the middle of the play, ceased to act, seeing no sense in their work and feeling that we were standing in one place and not moving forward. At such times the distrust of the actors in the stage director and in each other reaches its greatest height and threatens to cause demoralization and the disappearance of energy. This took place late at night. Two or three electric lights burned dimly. We sat in the corners, hardly able to restrain our tears, silent, in the semi-gloom. Our hearts beat with anxiety and the helplessness of our position.

The despair of work gone badly leads to a sudden accident of understanding:

Some one was nervously scratching the bench on which he sat with his fingernails. The sound was like that of a mouse . . . Apparently the sound of a scratching mouse, which must have had some meaning for me at an early period of my life, in conjunction with the darkness and the condition and the mood of the entire night, together with the helplessness and depression, reminded me of something important, deep, and bright that I had experienced somewhere and at some time. A spiritual spring was touched and I at last understood the nature of the something that was missing. I had known it before also, but I had known it with my mind and not my emotions.

Stanislavsky sees, in this instant of unleashed memory, that the play is not vague, formless, and actionless, but rather highly organized and theatrical, rooted in the characters' search for "life, joy, laughter, courage." Beneath the surface of trivial routine, he found people who "like Chekhov himself . . . want to live and not to die." He writes: "I came to life and knew what it was I had to show the actors . . . And they also came to life."

People who want to live and not to die—like Chekhov, like Chekhov's characters, like you and I, that is what we will try to show in this production.

Opening remarks, first rehearsal, Arena Stage, December 9, 1983.

A DOLL HOUSE BY HENRIK IBSEN

(1990)

It's taken a long time for Arena Stage to get around to this play, which, written in 1879, has come to be regarded as the first truly great realistic drama of modern times. As *Brand* and *Peer Gynt* established Henrik Ibsen's name in Scandinavia, so the story of Nora Helmer, Ibsen's favorite character, winged his fame to all the corners of the Earth. It isn't that Arena's audiences are not attracted to Ibsen. *Enemy of the People*, which I directed in 1975, and Lucian Pintilie's amazing *The Wild Duck* in 1986 sold to capacity. Actors love to do Ibsen, for he wrote great characters with an eye to the meaning behind the meaning, the life underneath the words. Actors can get their teeth into his plays.

No, the fault is mine. I must confess that I have skirted and, indeed, mistaken the life of this great play, my own life being out of sync with it, its psychologic appearing either too soon or too late for me. Halo Wines[1] handed me a Sunday, July 13, 1975 *Washington Post* clipping, in which, I am ashamed to admit, I'm quoted calling *A Doll House* "a rather silly play . . . I don't see how a woman could leave her children and still experience herself as free."

1. Longtime Arena company member.

The French critic Sarcey had much the same reaction, summing up the play as "an enjoyable comedy, apart from its denouement." For a German production Ibsen was forced to concoct a happy ending. "I would never leave *my* children!" declared Hedwig Niemann-Raabe as Nora. But that was in the nineteenth century, after all, before Betty Friedan and Simone de Beauvoir wrote their books and launched us on our modern way. Shouldn't I have thought more progressively? (I must confess that, in the same article, I described Hedda Gabler shooting herself as "a personal idiosyncrasy, which has nothing to say to women at large." And I mused that Ibsen had mixed it up: Nora should've shot herself, and Hedda should have slammed the door!)

Well, one grows and changes. That is the kernel, the root meaning of the play we are about to do. So, I must be forgiven for my earlier self, just as I try to forgive the earlier selves of all with whom I live and work, knowing "what fools we mortals be." Also, times change. As they change, works of art acquire new meanings or reveal meanings that were there but unseen.

The play is called in Norwegian *Et Dukkehjem*, *A Dollhome* or *A Doll House*, but not *A Doll's House*, as it is usually translated. The difference is important, for Ibsen titled it with clear intention. The point is not that Nora is a doll and that the house belongs to her, but that the house is a house *for* dolls. By implication, then, all the people who live in it partake of the aspect of miniaturization, of doll-ness. Not just Nora but all of them. If that isn't clear in the beginning of the play, it becomes totally clear in the climactic confrontation at the end, where Nora, having come upon this truth, spells it out.

There is a word for house in Norwegian, but Ibsen uses the word for home instead—a "doll home." He coined this word, and it entered the language, new minted. When new-thinking people came to use it, they knew exactly what it identified—a cozy, bourgeois home for cozy, bourgeois people in cozy, bourgeois relationships, patterned on the cozy, bourgeois expectations of the day. While promising no mysterious depths or intense spiritual entanglements, the doll home compensates by guaranteeing no disruption, no catastrophe, surely no abandoned husbands and children!

The title, then, is ironic, sardonic. Who'd think that little Nora would walk out in the end? Surely not Torvald! For aren't the Helmers an ideal couple? Isn't Nora an adorable "trophy wife," well-bred and educated (for a woman), and a wonderful mother—sexy to boot? Don't they have wonderful, intelligent, healthy children? And isn't it Christmas, the happiest time of the year? And isn't he, Torvald, coming up in the world, a big raise and a promotion in the offing? Hasn't he been hard-working, faithful, dependable? Isn't he attractive and also sexy? Don't they play well and dance well together? Don't they "love each other"? Of course. God is in his Heaven; all's right with the world.

Only something has happened. Nora had the occasion, some years before the play opens, to break out of the social mold, to use herself, not as a dependent of her father or a co-dependent with her husband but as an independent human being, and now the fat is in the fire. The rules got changed, the roles got jarred, the relationship shifted without Torvald knowing it, and with Nora knowing it only subconsciously, without seeking to know it.

The play deals with the trauma of Nora's awakening to personhood and with the consequent breaking apart of the doll home. The house breaks; they all fall down. No cozy, bourgeois soul or relationship will ever be the same again. No wonder *A Doll House* exploded like a bomb into contemporary life, pronouncing a death sentence on accepted social ethics.

Who is to blame that the house falls down? What happens to Nora after she leaves? What does it mean to leave a home? How are we to feel about all of this? Who are we rooting for? Is this a "feminist" play? "To be a poet means essentially to see," wrote Ibsen about his chosen vocation. What does he see in this story about Nora? Ibsen was an artist, not a journalist; the truth turned and twisted under his pen. Fittingly, his final, deathbed words were, "On the contrary."

But let's address the questions a little, for they are fascinating.

In the seventies I saw two productions of *A Doll House*, one with Claire Bloom and one with Liv Ullmann. I had the chance to talk about the play with Liv Ullmann at the Norwegian Embassy a couple of months ago. She reminded me that, at key moments in her production, the audience hissed and mocked Torvald (Sam Waterston) and applauded Nora as a militant liberated woman, giving him his comeuppance. Sam, she said, injured his leg and had to perform on crutches for a while. He hoped that his disability would engender some sympathy—poor, beleaguered Torvald—but, no, the sensibility of the times was such that he couldn't win, crutches or no. The audience reaction persisted throughout the run.

The play reads to me now another way. It is about Nora's awakening, yes, and we root for her struggle to end her sleep at whatever cost. But we now see Torvald as victim of his own history, too, for he is as he has been made—pitiful, foolish, chauvinist. His struggle for personhood, at the end, has barely begun. He has destroyed a marriage he didn't know how to construct in the first place, and lost much of what he wants, what he's been taught he deserves. The road ahead is long and torturous.

The play cannot shock today's audience as it did Ibsen's, circa 1879. (Party invitations would arrive with the injunction that *A Doll House* not be discussed at dinner!) But it sounds a deep, contemporary note: That freedom is a thing of interconnectedness, that neither you nor I can be free until both of us are free.

It raises contemporary questions: Can Torvald give over his received wisdom for a real self? What will be available to Nora after she leaves? What was there for her to do when she threw over her profession as wife and mother? Work in a flower shop? Become a secretary or seamstress? How would she live without income or alimony (she walked out, after all)?

Her radiant courage must have overwhelmed the first audiences, even those who believed in a Life After Domesticity. In "The *Doll House* Backlash: Criticism, Feminism, and Ibsen,"[2] Ibsen scholar Joan Templeton quotes essayist Richard Pearce, who, as late as 1970, writes that "the audience can see most clearly how Nora is exchanging a practical doll's role for an impractical one." She goes on to note how this condescension echoes that of Victorians, like Edward Dowden:

> Inquiries should be set on foot to ascertain whether a manuscript may not lurk in some house in Christiania [Oslo] entitled *Nora Helmer's Reflections in Solitude*; it would be a document of singular interest, and probably would conclude with the words, "Tomorrow I return to Torvald; have been exactly one week away; shall insist on a free woman's right to unlimited macaroons as test of his reform."

2. *PMLA* 104, no. 1 (January 1989): 28–40.

Have we answered the question yet today: Where does the woman go after she leaves? With her briefcase or without? Without her children? What if with them? What if she "has it all": briefcase, children, nanny, daycare, Torvald, furniture, dinner party? In her book *On Her Own: Growing Up in the Shadow of the American Dream* sociologist Ruth Sidel quotes a woman she labels "Neotraditionalist":

> I want to be smart. I want to be somebody. I want to make money. I want to be a successful lawyer, but my personal life comes first. I want to be a lovely wife, do my husband's shirts, take Chinese cooking lessons, and have two children. I want my children to be angels and I want to have a great relationship with my husband. I want to be thin and gorgeous and have a spectacular Bloomingdale's wardrobe. I want to have a briefcase in my hands. I want to look good and feel good and be happy in what I'm doing. Happiness comes first.

Can a woman have it all? Can anyone have it all? Ibsen has a way of setting questions in motion that will never stop trying to be answered.

The stage for Ingmar Bergman's current production of *A Doll House* in Stockholm is a coffin/prison with high windows with bars on them, a theatrical image of oppressiveness and joylessness. "Neither air nor light nor sound from the outside could penetrate this closed, hermetically sealed realm of fixed social values and conventions," one critic observed. I find this choice interesting, and I would love to see that production, but I view the play differently.

I see the Helmers as having a good marriage, within the expectations of bourgeois life, and a happy home, where objects are lit with memory and the beauty of use. The season's joy permeates the home. It is Christmas, and there are toys and decorations, a party coming up. There is also the undertow—as for all of us at holidays—the tensions and incompletions, the disrupting waves of feeling under the joy. The undertow pulls Nora away, and she goes with it.

Neither Ibsen nor his wife Suzannah had the gift of making the place they lived homey. Un-homey-ness was characteristic of Ibsen, and yet his plays are often permeated with a sense of home. More than fifty years ago, Gunnar Heiberg, a distinguished director of Ibsen's plays, pointed out how important it is that *A Doll House* conveys the feeling that a home is being broken up. Nora's sense of loss, the enormity of what she is giving up, seems to me an essential chord in this play.

> *A Doll House* is no more about women's rights than Shakespeare's *Richard II* is about the divine right of kings, or *Ghosts* is about syphilis . . . Its theme is the need of every individual to find out the kind of person he or she is and to strive to become that person.

So writes Michael Meyer in his biography of Ibsen. Removing "the woman question" from *A Doll House* is part of a recent, corrective effort to free Ibsen from his reputation as a writer of thesis plays, a wrongheaded notion usually blamed on George Bernard Shaw. Ibsen, it is now fashionable to explain, did not stoop to "issues." He was a poet of the truth of the human soul, unsullied by the topical taint.

In Richard Gilman's phrase, *A Doll House* is "pitched beyond sexual difference." Ibsen, explains Robert Brustein, "was completely indifferent to [the woman question], except as a metaphor for individual freedom." Discussing the relation of *A Doll House* to feminism, Halvdan Koht, author of the definitive Norwegian Ibsen life, says in summary, "Little by little the topical controversy died away; what remained was the work of art, with its demand for truth in every human relation." [Templeton]

Well, yes and no.

Surely it can't be true that the *Uncle Tom's Cabin* of the women's rights movement is not about women after all? That—angel-like—Nora has no sex? Or that Ibsen meant for her to be Everyman? We must be wary of thinking that "women's rights," and other human-rights struggles based on biological or social identity, are subjects too limited to be the stuff of art. We must stay free of viewing feminism as a precondition for uninteresting characters in flat-heeled shoes, appropriate not for literature but for propaganda pamphlets.

Do we think that what happens to a woman is significant only to the extent that it can happen to a man as well—i.e., that the universal is male? This would mean that Nora's journey from dollhood to self-awareness has essentially nothing to do with her identity as a nineteenth-century married woman, married woman, or woman.

Remove the "woman problem" from *A Doll House*, give Nora Helmer the same rights as Torvald Helmer, let him consider her his spiritual and intellectual equal, emancipate her from the dollhouse—we would then have a central character in a state of being, not in a condition of becoming. We would have no conflict, no central action. We would have no play.

In 1890, eleven years after Betty Hennings as Nora first slammed the shaky door in Copenhagen's Royal Theatre, Havelock Ellis summarized what *A Doll House* meant to the progressives of Ibsen's day:

> The great wave of emancipation which is now sweeping across the civilized world means nominally nothing more than that women should have the right to education, freedom to work, and political enfranchisement—nothing in short but the bare ordinary rights of an adult human creature in a civilized state.

Profoundly disturbing then, *A Doll House* remains so still, because it is the plea for woman as a human being, not more nor less than a man, that Ibsen made.

The play's characters are organized around the theme of love, beginning with the document Nora forges out of love for her husband. Ibsen regarded loving, the right to love, as the highest human value, higher even than the law. He saw that, in order to love, one has to be self-determining, free of the structures of constraining society. One has to be who one is. The contradictions contained in this idea—the struggles it implies for a socially responsible person—he never resolved. How could he have resolved a living issue incapable of resolution?

Ibsen, we are told, was a lonely man. In that sense his work transcends the issues of his time and grapples with the confusion and terror of living in the world, man or woman, with the existential aloneness of simply being. Templeton tells the story of a Scandinavian lady and her lover appearing in Rome, where Ibsen was then living. Having found her marriage unsatisfactory, she had left her husband and children. Norwegians in Rome condemned her action as unnatural. Ibsen, when asked his opinion, said; "It is not unnatural, but it is unusual." When the lady sought him out at a public function, Ibsen treated her coolly. When she complained that she had only behaved as Nora had, he replied: "But my Nora went alone."

A Norwegian poet wrote of his native land: "Everywhere people are separated by fjord and mountain and sea, and in that way every mind becomes a separate kingdom, all its own."

First rehearsal remarks, January 23, 1990. This essay, edited, was published in the *Washington Post* a month later.

THE TRUE WORD:
THE CRUCIBLE BY ARTHUR MILLER
(2005)

"When a scholar dies," goes the Yiddish proverb, "everyone is his relative." So it is with Arthur Miller. The whole world grieves because the whole world is implicated. When we scheduled *The Crucible* as the culminating production of our 2005 graduating class, and I invited my close friend and colleague Tazewell Thompson to direct it, we had no thought that in dedicating our production to Miller's immeasurable, seventy-year creative achievement, we would also be mourning him. It's very painful for me to accept that his voice of rabbinical righteousness is quiet now, that we are left with what has already been said.

If I were asked to name the one playwright who best represented the face of Arena Stage as it grew from a small, struggling enterprise to a three-theater complex with a national and international identity—always centered around a community of artists as it brought forth roughly four hundred productions—the name of Arthur Miller would spill from my mouth before it even passed through my brain. Though he only came to visit and stayed only briefly, though he was never in residence, Arthur Miller was our resident playwright.

Just as the world has so completely absorbed what he taught us about mortality and guilt, duty and community, so, during my forty seasons as artistic director, did he sound our dominant themes, the bass notes of our repertory. He showed us how we wanted to reach out to our audiences, what we wanted to speak about with them, how we hoped to change the world with our theater, and how, as artists, we wanted to live with each other on the stage. Arena Stage did nine Arthur Miller productions, including three separate productions of *The Crucible*, all of these highlights of our history.

Miller was an actor's playwright. In Mel Gussow's *Conversations with Miller*, there is a fascinating interchange on this subject:

> MG: Do you ever think what your legacy would be?
> AM *(Quickly)*: Some good parts for actors.
> MG: "Some good parts for actors"?
> AM: This is not said speciously. I look at the plays that I've done, that is those plays that continue to have their life, and if you look hard enough you're going to find that you've got pretty good parts for actors . . . I think Willy Loman is going to be around for a long time because that's a challenge. You can do it a number of different ways, and it takes a big actor to do it.

Gussow presses him:

> MG: Do you want your epitaph to be: "He gave good parts to actors"?
> AM: I wouldn't mind! There are lesser things you can do with your life. I would hope that there would be more seen in them, that they are an image of some kind of the human circumstance.

Gussow continues to press him until Miller admits that there is "another element, of course," which he's "too modest to say what it is." He is persuaded to.

> AM: My plays are dealing with essential dilemmas of what it means to be human. I would hope they are.

Miller wrote parts for actors because he wrote about the deepest places in the human heart, and only actors can bring us information from there.

In *Conversations with Miller*, Arthur salutes a Russian phrase: "The true word." The phrase, he explains, refers to "the quote-unquote truth . . . they want in the theater, an expression of some kind of an insight that would tell them how to live, not how to amuse themselves." Unfortunately, Miller's work was not born into the Theater-of-the-True-Word he wanted. Except for a few years when the newly founded Lincoln Center was his artistic home, his work was born into Broadway—with its economic pressures, boom-or-bust psychology, and artistic discontinuity. The true word about Miller's work remained to be discovered in the theaters that grew up all around the U.S., in England—especially in the subsidized National Theatre of Great Britain—in China, and in other countries with a tradition of theater as an investigation of life.

The Crucible first opened at the Martin Beck on January 22, 1953 to mixed reviews. It was listed as a failure in *Variety*, the trade magazine that charts such matters, and was, like many of his plays, criticized for being "objective," "coldly intellectual," "polemical," "lacking in humor." (*Death of a Salesman* was of course the critical exception.) The *true word* of the play, as I remember it, was buried under a rather stiff formality and a falsely elevated vocal tone (an American take on Greek drama?), the actors mostly facing downstage, not talking to each other much. Of course, it was seen as a play about blacklisting, as a modern parallel to the Salem witch hunts of 1692—the nine-month firestorm that hanged sixteen, crushed one man to death and caused three more to die in jail, one an infant.

America was just emerging from its own firestorm—a Red Hunt led by the House Committee on Un-American Activities and, in the Senate, Joe McCarthy—with its own count of ruined careers, broken friendships, and suicides. Political analogies were easy to jump to. In both places and times, there was the dead weight of fear, the sense of a danger that must have seemed equally real. For us at the time, Western Europe seemed ready to become Red, China was lost, Italian and German fascism was seen as the final manifestation of capitalism. As in Salem, the Devil had to be somewhere.

But beyond politics, what was the pith of the play? In 1954, Arena Stage presented the first out-of-New-York production. Our tiny 247-seat arena overflowed with success; *The Crucible* pushed us to look for a larger home. The production was reviewed as superior to the original but was also framed by political issues.[1] We captured well the sense of a terrified community out of control. I can still hear Olive Dunbar's voice as Elizabeth crying through her strength as the drums rolled: "He hath his goodness now. God forbid I take it from him." The tears still come. But had we found the true word? I don't recall.

In the mid-sixties we wanted to approach the play again—to generate the same heat in a larger (temporary) space, the audience steeply seated around a central raised stage, as if in an operating theater. Michael Higgins, who had played John Proctor Off-Broadway, was also ours. Michael wrote to Miller to ask if he had any new thoughts on the play. I've found a copy of Miller's reply:

> . . . . as for new thoughts on *The Crucible* . . . I wouldn't so far as to call them new, just older ones which the years have reinforced. Now that McCarthyism is only a word to a large part of the audience, the play seems closer to what I had envisioned in the first place: There is a wider reference— to the human tendency to lay conscience on the altar of Authority—and perhaps this comes through more evidently now. At bottom, I suppose I was trying to assert that there is almost a biology of human ethics and that people literally die when it is violated—all in order to further define what a man is. Now that the journalism is out of the way, maybe this comes to the fore . . .

I happened upon my own version of these "new thoughts" in preparation to direct our next *Crucible* twenty years later, in the fall of 1987. I started my investigation of the text as if it were a new play, never before produced, never produced by us.

It hit me that the play, though rooted in a specific time and place, is not about that time and place. Nor is it about that other time and place—the McCarthy hearings. John Proctor, the company and I realized, is no hero. He falls without thought into his decision, pushed by

---

1. During our 1954 production, we were visited by the FBI, taking notes from actors and staff about my husband (Tom Fichandler, the theater's executive director) and me—"Whose side were we on?" We were a young, small, poor theater and surprised at the attention and nothing came of it at the time. It was the beginning of a dossier for Tom and me, which I suspect grew fatter over the years. [Z.F.]

the pre-thinking "biology of human ethics." Proctor is as surprised as anyone to discover the size of who he is, by the sacrifice he stumbles into making. He is surprised, even, by the sound of his own voice:

> Because it is my name! Because I cannot have another in my life! Because I lie and sign myself to lies! Because I am not worth the dust on my feet of them that hang! How may I live without my name? I have given you my soul; leave me my name!

Conscience, then, is a private, quiet corner of the human soul. It is ours alone. Elizabeth knows better than to demean her husband by entering there. Private conscience before the needs of the community? Yes. One dies, but the self will not die. And somewhere in this is the meaning of freedom.

Since the company and I had never thought this way before, not to mention *lived* this way, we chanced upon an understanding of the play's mythic substructure and were deeply changed. I believe that many others, seeing the play this way, were changed as well. When we performed at the Jerusalem Theatre Festival, for example, the response of the Israeli public was overwhelming. Experience had showed them how strong one has to be to overcome the pressure of a society seeking control over every secret place within.

In "Why I Wrote *The Crucible*" (*New Yorker*, October 21, 1996), Miller made this astonishing statement:

> My own marriage of twelve years was teetering and I knew more than I wished to know about where the blame lay. That John Proctor the sinner might overturn his paralyzing personal guilt and become the forthright voice against the madness around him was a reassurance to me, and, I suppose, an inspiration: It demonstrated that a clear moral outcry could still spring even from an ambiguously unblemished soul. Moving crabwise across the profusion of evidence, I sensed that I had at last found something of myself in it, and a play began to accumulate around this man.

Miller elaborates in Gussow's *Conversations*, describing the center of the play as the guilt of John Proctor and the working out of that guilt.

"Indeed, it finally exemplifies the guilt of man in general. I believe in a seamless linking of the internal life of the person with the social situation. You can't have a witch hunt over a period of time in a society that is not riddled with guilt . . . it's the hidden enemy."

Out of the chaos of the human situation, with great roles for actors, as he said, Arthur Miller made his art. It is wrong to think of him as a "preachy" playwright who wrote direct, clear, moralistic plays, easily read, easily fathomed. His body of work is both morally clear and morally ambiguous, as life is. He rubbed our noses in our responsibility to the family of man but also challenged us to find what belonged only to us. He revealed us blind sometimes, driven by feelings we couldn't understand or control or by Fate, and he chastised us to look at the consequences of our actions. He offered deep sympathy for our struggles in an indifferent society but refused to let us delude ourselves about who we were. He challenged us to throw off the great weight of guilt and write our own true names on the world, even as he showed the awful price of freedom. How hard it was to be free and fully human.

I know it's an honor for this young company to be living tonight inside what we hope is the true word of *The Crucible*.

First rehearsal remarks, NYU Graduate Acting Program, April 2005.

ONE HAND AWAY:
AWAKE AND SING!
BY CLIFFORD ODETS

(2005)

I'm looking at this old photo of my mother, probably five years old and "fresh off the boat." As closely as we can figure, it was taken in 1905. Arrived from shtetl life in Lithuania, then part of Russia, she comes with her parents, joined in loveless marriage by arrangement and lacking the practical skills to make their way. One younger brother comes with her, perhaps; in the next few years, three more brothers and a sister will appear. The family will begin the struggle, with overtones of despair, to stake out its portion of the American dream. It was for this they had packed their few belongings and crossed the ocean in a crowded ship. I wear with pride and love this shawl that my grandmother prized sufficiently to take with her on the journey, along with several large copper cooking pots, unfortunately lost to Arena's prop department in the mid-fifties.

I imagine that my mother Ida is wearing her one good dress, freshly washed and starched to look her best for the photographer. She is a touching little girl—my heart goes out to her—but in the solemn, private expression in her eyes I think I see intimations of the anxiety, tension, and even hopelessness that will underscore her life. Only five, she had already experienced oppression, and this experience will be the counterpoint to her life's jokes and joys.

My sister only recently uncovered the original photograph, of which mine is a copy. Gazing on it has been part of my research for directing *Awake and Sing!*, helping me recall early memories of my own life in the Depression years of the thirties, the period of the play we are about to explore, deepening my awareness of how people who were, to me, Daddy and Mommy, Bubbe and Zayde, aunt, uncle, neighbor, classmate, teacher, and friend, were also figures in the third wave of Jewish immigrants to the United States, the greatest mass immigration in history—figures who became integral to every part of American culture.

The sudden, catastrophic failure of American business in 1929 struck the Berger family of Odets's play with more force than it did my own, though we felt the change. My father had come from "the old country" in his mother's arms, worked his way through MIT by sewing on a pedal machine and assisting the customers in his father's tailor shop in Quincy, Mass. At a young age he became a leading physicist and inventor, Head of Research and Development in the National Bureau of Standards. He provided us with a careful, even-keeled life. Harry loved Ida ("Ida, sweet as apple cider," he would croak), and Ida loved Harry ("I'm just wild about Harry and Harry's just wild about me"). But nothing could lay to rest the litany of fears she shared with her Jewish middle-class friends. Was there enough for a new pair of shoes? Prices were high—two dollars for a child's dress—and we were saving for a house, so five-cent popsicles had to go. Would her children thrive? Were they eating enough? (Eating enough? Eating enough? An obsession!) If they went to summer camp, would they drown in the lake? What if her daughters fell in love with someone who didn't "make a good living"? Or—God forbid—with someone who wasn't Jewish? "What will the neighbors say?" (A refrain.)

Over Bessie Berger, too, hung a host of dangers. Just being alive was dangerous. It will ask deep empathy from the actors to understand the daily unease of strangers in a foreign land, the estrangement and isolation. In Yiddish, strangers are *die anderen—the others*—to be guarded against and feared. No wonder there were self-constructed ghettos in New York City, clusters of one's own people.

It was humiliating for the Bergers to be poor, living tightly on a pooled yearly income of under thirty thousand dollars in today's dollars, not able to be who they wanted and deserved to be, standing close to the American dream, seeing it and not able to grab the brass ring. In the play's one-year span, things get worse instead of better. Poverty corrodes the human spirit. Its weight falls most heavily on the wife/mother of the house. Bessie's weapons against poverty are her mop and dust rags—her house stays "neat as a pin"—a line of credit with the butcher, a boarder, financial help she finagles from her rich brother and, especially, her children, whom she manipulates, so their lives will conform to her standards. "Life shouldn't be printed on dollar bills," moralizes Jacob, the Marxist grandfather. Yes, but what if it is, "shouldn't" or not?

Where was comfort, safety, comradery, good food, a good fight with someone who wasn't going to walk out, respite from being the *Other* to someone else? My mother's magic word was *heym*: home. When the world provoked too much anxiety there was always home to retreat to, home as sanctuary. Home might be contentious for Bessie, Myron, and their family, a place of cross-purposes, criticism and, mostly stifled, explosive disappointment, but it's also safe haven, holding the possibility of laughter and warmth. Love means putting up with and standing up for each other. There are three meals in the four scenes of *Awake and Sing!*, and while this *heym* sizzles with conflict, it also bursts with the laughter of life.

In a recent issue of the *New Yorker*, John Lahr, its senior drama critic, reminded us that Clifford Odets's centennial was approaching and called for new productions of his plays. Naming him "the big, brave, brokenhearted, voice of the thirties," he noted Odets's link to Mamet and Williams, his fine craft, crackling authenticity and stylized fast talk. "Come on, artistic directors, reawaken Odets and let him sing!" exhorts Lahr. As if on cue, here we are, scheduled for an anniversary production of the play that catapulted Odets to renown: Fifteen curtain calls—the balcony especially went wild—when *Awake and Sing!* opened on Broadway on February 19, 1935. Before long it had been translated into too many languages to count. The world turns, and something in the air brings a play center again. What struck a chord then strikes a harmonic chord now. New light is thrown upon a forgotten classic. I've seen that happen many times—how lucky that we now have theaters ready to receive them.

I want to acknowledge Margaret Brenman-Gibson's exhaustive biography of Odets,[1] the product of ten years' work, which has provided me with much of the information and many of the quotations that follow.

Clifford Odets was born on July 18, 1906, in America, the son of Eastern European immigrants who married here. He died nearly broke in Hollywood in 1963, a rapid death over two weeks from stomach cancer. "This mountain blown to dust," his son named the death. Marlon Brando said, "To me he *was* the thirties" and dubbed him "a wild man and a noble man." He quoted Odets that "life was a one hand any way"—a term from weight lifting where you get yourself off the ground however you can. This was Odets was in a nutshell! How to get himself off the ground?

Upon his death, the public verdict of his career ran from "casually contemptuous" to "faintly accusatory," according to Brenman-Gibson. *TIME* Magazine, for instance, which had in 1938 celebrated him on its cover, dismissed him: "The artistic potential everyone expected to materialize was somehow never quite fulfilled." Odets would have agreed. Two years before his death he had rendered his own judgment: "I may well be not only the foremost playwright manqué of our time, but of all time. I do not believe a dozen playwrights in history had my natural endowment . . ." And yet the playwright so many felt had sold out his talent in Hollywood had once wanted to save the world with his art: "When I started to write *Awake and Sing!* I didn't have a mission in life . . . When I came to rewriting it, I was going to change the world, or help it."

The early version of *Awake and Sing!* was titled *I Got the Blues.* The one extant copy lives in the Library of Congress on tissue-thin paper, where an Arena staff member was allowed, wearing gloves, to copy by hand differences in the script from the published Broadway version. How fascinating! The earlier script is more Jewish—more Yiddish—than the later one. The Yiddish phrases, a number of which come back to me from my grandparents' house and from our own dinner table, had been deleted as the script approached production.

1. Margaret Brenman-Gibson, *Clifford Odets American Playwright: The Years from 1906–1940* (New York: Atheneum, 1981). Reprinted by Applause Theatre & Cinema Books, 2002.

The text was made more general, less Jewish. For example, in the Broadway version, Ralphie's girlfriend is unacceptable to Bessie not because she is Gentile—a *shiksa*—but because she is an orphan. The family name is now Berger, rather than Greenbaum. Odets had told Harold Clurman, his director, that he wanted to appeal to an audience broader than the Jewish one (that balcony audience who "went wild" at the opening), whom he expected to recognize and identify with the characters. In subsequent plays, like *Rocket to the Moon*, *Golden Boy*, *The Country Girl*, Odets also attempted to get away from the Jewishness of the characters he drew, and to create "universal" characters.

In this production we've restored the Yiddishness of the original, imagining that if Odets were alive today, with Yiddish having entered and affected the English language, he would agree and find it in tone with the lyrical lift of blunt Jewish speech, boiling over and explosive, that characterizes his writing. *I Got the Blues* ends upside down from the final version. Broadway's optimistic ending, full of hope, however youthfully naive, was evidently worked out in rehearsal between Clurman and Odets. I'm glad it was. In the original text, no one awoke, and no one sang. Poor Moe got carted off to jail.

Was Odets a Communist? What did he know of Marxist doctrine when he wrote the play? This is an interesting question. For a few months Odets was a member of the Communist Party, until he was thrown in jail in Cuba later in 1935 as part of a visiting labor delegation and resigned. He was called before the House Un-American Activities Committee in 1952. I have read this extensive interchange and can see why the talented actor Zero Mostel believed that Odets's compliant testimony stopped up, for the rest of the writer's life, access to his creative self.

The largest truth of it, as told by Brenman-Gibson, is that Odets, on close terms with Whitman, Thoreau, and Emerson, knew little of Karl Marx beyond a romantic awareness of the *Communist Manifesto* and *Das Kapital*. He shared, however, with many of his generation an inchoate hunger to make sense of human society, a hunger that sharpened as religious meaning and hope ebbed. In *Awake and Sing!*, Marxist doctrine, as held by Jacob, forwards the central love story— between Jacob and Ralphie, grandfather and grandson—and its generational legacy: to stop just talking and complaining, and, instead, to join with others to make a better world, a utopian socialist solution.

Unlike many socially committed playwrights of his time, Odets wrote the play not as a conscious political tract but as an expression of his own personal "blues," experienced at a particular time in history. The final impact of *Awake and Sing!* comes less from its protest against the horrors of poverty than from the potent spirit of its people, as they "struggle for life amid petty conditions." By daring to put the lives of these recognizable people onstage, Odets created the first deeply felt and theatrically achieved realism in the American theater.

First rehearsal remarks at Arena Stage, December 19, 2005.

THE LONG REVOLUTION

THE FUTURE OF THE RESIDENT PROFESSIONAL THEATER IN AMERICA

(1967)

The regional theater movement is such a big thing they ought to make a musical out of it.

Some people don't like to call it a "movement"—they object to the over-structuring implied in that term. But if you ask me, it's a movement. I mean, no formal directorate or coordinator; no manifesto; a network held together by no more than shared attitudes or a few passwords, like:

> "Got any good grants lately?"
>
> "What's really on Mac Lowry's mind?"
>
> "How's the subscription drive going? Three hundred percent over last year!"
>
> "Attendance eighty-nine percent! Deficit for the year? $100,000 over last year! Well, not so good! Trouble with the board? That's bad!"
>
> "Company X took three of your actors this year? Listen, that guy you hired away from me has gone to *him* now. They doubled his salary, what are you going to do?"
>
> "Know any good TD's? Voice teachers? Business managers? Actors who will play supporting roles for $175 a week?"

"Hear *The Balcony* was too much for Boston. Funny, it did well in Baltimore and Hartford. What do you think about it for Poughkeepsie?"

"Liked your brochure. Looked just like ours. And his. And theirs and theirs and theirs."

And so on. A movement. A commonality. Not overt or systematic. More like the Catholic New Left. Exerting influence, making some waves, not toppling anything, informally connected in its manifestations. Organized only unofficially.

Whatever we call it, it's a big thing. Just in terms of numbers alone. Since 1950, when there was the Alley and the Cleveland Play House, when we began, and the Actor's Workshop was about to happen, over thirty companies have come into being. And every time you turn around there's more there. "A slow sort of country!" said Alice's Queen. "Now, *here*, you see, it takes all the running *you* can do, to keep in the same place. If you want to get somewhere else, you must run at least twice as fast as that!" And the regional theater *is* running at least twice as fast—running and trying to catch its breath, proliferating and running, running and scrambling and multiplying itself and panting to "get someplace else." (It is also falling apart, but that's another story.)

This bigness really is part of the scene. Take the recent news release sent out by one of the leading companies, headlined "All National Records Shattered." "Company Y offered 296 performances of 16 productions in rotating repertory at 2 theaters. No other theater company anywhere in the country equals the size of this repertory or number of performances within a comparable period of time." The release reports the number of paid admissions and compares it with another company operating in New York. New York company comes in second. Box office receipts get compared: New York comes in second. Capacity percentages are compared: New York runs second.

And then there's this American phenomenon, the Cultural Boom-Boom, within which the regional theater blare takes its place and shape. Of course, the resonance has been pretty much taken out of that one by the William Baumol and William Bowen book *Performing Arts: The Economic Dilemma*, which cautions in a tone of dry reserve and some sadness:

More regional theaters and local symphonies, longer dance tours and a few new opera companies are signs of a cultural boom, but the extent of the cultural boom has been exaggerated. While an increase in consumer expenditures for admissions to performances would seem to indicate a substantial cultural upsurge, this increase mainly represents growth in population, prices, and real incomes, rather than a substantial rise of interest in the arts.[1]

This is hard to swallow past the lump of one's national pride, one's human feelings and one's personal ego. One so wants to be soothed by the social goodwill of say, the March 1965 report by the Rockefeller Brothers Fund entitled *The Performing Arts: Problems and Prospects* which, while it surely does not minimize the troubles that the performing arts are in, still soberly envisages a nation teeming with drama devotees, concertgoers, and ballet-lovers, and gives us cultural hope by the now-familiar exhortation that the place of the arts "is not on the periphery of society but at its center . . . They are not just a form of recreation but are of cultural importance to our well-being and happiness."

One inclines toward the human grace of Marya Mannes expressed in a November 19, 1966, article in the *New York Times*, "Topics: the Select Many." This intense and articulate lady declares that: "Intelligence crosses the boundaries of education and condition. So does the yearning for the unattainable, not in goods so much as in good. The great majority of humans, whether they are aware of it or not, would like to be better than they are, know more than they know, feel more than they have felt."

And one is surely seduced by the statesmanship and optimism of Arthur Schlesinger, Jr., peripatetic theoretician in Kennedy's Lyceum, writing in the *Progressive* that Americans have most of the things they need for the good life. What they want now is quality control. The new "qualitative" issues replace the old "quantitative" ones. For example, instead of "a job, a suit of clothing, three meals a day, a roof over one's head, and a measure of security for one's old age," people are now concerned with the state of the arts and the beauty of the environment, and so on.

1. Published by MIT Press, 1968.

How is it *really*? What *really* gives? And what's going to happen?

My topic is the Future of that "Big Deal," the resident professional theater-movement or not-movement.

A year ago I got a letter from Richard Schechner of the *Tulane Drama Review* saying he had liked *Oh! What a Lovely War* (though he didn't like all of our productions) and that he felt our repertory—"the selection of plays, the kind of work you do, is the most exciting in the country. Yours is the only theater that directly challenges its audiences, that looks for material that is new and probing." I thought his compliment generous and overstated. At any rate, he asked me to do an article about how we go about selecting the plays and about the entire notion of running a theater "that is not only artistically successful but often socially upsetting."

I wasn't in the mood to write the article, so I didn't. I was too depressed. It was the end of the subscription campaign and, after 16 years and the production of about 150 plays, we had lost half of our subscribers—that is some 8,000 of them. (Twice as many as usual.) The loss was accompanied by many letters, calls, and conversations. The gist: Our work had become too "special," too "in-group." Not as much "fun" as it used to be.

Complaints were centered not only on the season just past but on the one before it as well—the year when I had finally decided the theater had an audience and could begin to close in on the kind of repertory that really interested it. There had already been the long, patient years—hopefully un-patronizing—of spice and variety in between pieces of meat: the Program for the Education, Pacification and Diversification of the Audience. And it seemed time for something beyond eclecticism. Brecht's *Galileo* (before it did the resident theater circuit); Anouilh's *The Rehearsal* (the first production outside of New York); *Billy Budd*; *Heartbreak House*; Andreyev's *He Who Gets Slapped* (in a surrealist production that emphasized the alienation of the artist from society); O'Neill's *Long Day's Journey into Night*; and *Hard Travelin'* from Millard Lampell, a musical satire on the Depression period to go with *The Lonesome Train*, Lampell's eulogy of Abraham Lincoln.

Schechner saw that last bill and liked it and wrote about it in the Fall 1965 issue of *TDR*. He said that it and other of our "excellent productions" were spoiled by an audience that was not diversified enough. Where were "the poor" to bring counterpoint and sharp vision to the otherwise homogeneous audience, whose values the play attacked? Since then, Schechner's language has become more pungent: "The Marshmallow Theater" is what he called the "movement" this summer, attacking most of our next season.

I'm really not debating Schechner. I'm debating his innocence and the innocence-by-association of many people who think his way. For what we did—to survive!—what we *had to do* was to acknowledge that the audience was our Master. What we did was to plan a season that would please our Masters—no trick, actually, after so many years of experience. *Macbeth, The Magistrate, The Crucible, The Inspector General, Look Back in Anger, The Andersonville Trial* (replacing a new script not yet ready). No terrible compromises. Just ones of "quiet desperation." The result? Subscriptions up, audience happy, seats filled, no strain, another day, another dollar. They *could* make a musical of it!

Where were the poor? Mr. Schechner, you ask. Where were the well-to-do? I ask you. The well-to-do who have the money and the habit by now and the education and supposedly are in the midst of replacing "quantitative" issues with "qualitative" ones? Where are they?

So here we are: fat, happy, big as life. Bigger than life, because we're Art, and Art is bigger than life. And getting bigger. Hallelujah! So we make our compromises here and there. After all: If Politics is the Art of the Possible, why shouldn't Art be the Politics of the Possible?

Only, our deficits are showing. More and more. And it's not one of those self-terminating problems, like intestinal flu. It's more like pregnancy—a progressive thing. Will it end in birth? Is our sickness like a pregnancy that will end in birth? Who will help us to know?

I have here a Ford Foundation press release dated May 19, 1967, which quotes W. McNeil Lowry, its vice president and our leading artist of benefaction; a bona fide friend. He says:

> On the financial side, it is clear that in a period when tax support has not reached a scale on which these nonprofit institutions can depend, the most urgent priority is the development in a theater's community of a tradition of the annual maintenance drive long associated with other kinds of performing arts organizations . . . With or without the support of national foundations, resident companies often fill their

houses to capacity. But, as welcome as this development has been, it will not by itself give permanence to these groups.

Being faintly paranoid, the first flag that goes up for me is the word "permanent." Arena Stage is seventeen years old this month, the Alley Theatre is three years older, the Cleveland Play House older still. Many of the theaters are new, but we are old, old, old. How old do you have to be to be "permanent"? How far up is "up"? Where are you when you are finally "there"? When do they finally give us a key to the front door? A credit card? One night out a week? Permanent?????

When I get up in the morning I feel about twenty-eight days younger than the Comédie-Française. When will the proof be acknowledged to be actually in the pudding? How long must we scramble, pushing that damn stone up that damn mountain only to have to push it up again? How long, O Lord, how long? Arena Stage for one (and there are others) *is already permanent.* If it should die for lack of funds it will be a permanent—I prefer the word viable— organism that dies.

Mr. Lowry sees as urgent "the development in a theater's community of an annual maintenance drive"—as is traditional for symphony orchestras. The Detroit Symphony initiated such a plan in 1951. Of the $600,000 raised each year about one-third comes from individuals and the rest from the business community, with representatives from local companies each giving $10,000 or more a year. One does not question the plan: It is lucid, imaginative, public-spirited, effective. It has a lot to teach us, if only in a mechanical way. It stands also as a warning.

Howard Harrington, the newly appointed manager of the Detroit Symphony, praised their newly appointed conductor: "He has never become too aroused about modern music. Detroiters are the same. This city has not heard so much music that it goes searching for new sounds. Beethoven, Brahms, the flashing French pieces, a little Wagner, these are what the city wanted and needed."

Is this really what we must have around the country—to live with and grow on—subsidy by the townsfolk who know little about modern art but know without searching what they want and need? Hell hath no fury like a patron scorned. The hand that rocks the cradle may well end up picking the repertory.

If the danger is there in the world of music, how much more dangerous is the world of the word? Nobody uses four-letter words in playing Beethoven's 7th! (Aloud, at any rate.) The word can destroy old shibboleths and create new hopes. It is the mascot of both conscience and controversy. The playwright's power to inflame has a great tradition: Remember the exile of Max Reinhardt, the blacklist of American writers, the social scorn afforded Ibsen, the sheriff at the opening of Strindberg's *Miss Julie*, the bloodshed that attended the Brecht-Weill opera *Mahagonny*.

What will happen if neither the foundations nor the government will give to us on a continuing basis or if they will not give to us in time? In reply I ask—with Bernard Shaw—"What price salvation now?"

"Art needs comfort, even abundance," Leon Trotsky remarked more than forty years ago. And I agree. But we must not equate abundance with the capacity to reveal. Large, busy theaters can be very bleak ones—gay places with light everywhere except in the minds of men. We are in danger of this. An electric mixer makes a pint of cream seem larger by whipping in nothing but air.

The gift of the artist is the gift of sight. Sometimes he achieves great beauty and wisdom with slim means. Jerzy Grotowski's Polish Lab Theatre, one of the most impressive and inspiring experimental theaters in the world, produces only one play at a time. He employs six actors and six students; his theater accommodates forty spectators. His artistic ambitions and penetration are immense.

We need money, but as much as we need money we need—individually—to find, heighten, and explore the *informing idea* of our theaters. We need to find our own faces. Not by looking at each other but by looking within ourselves. We already look too much alike. It has become a bore. And when we know what we are about, that is when we will have real acting companies instead of merely collections of actors.

An interviewer asks Igor Stravinsky: "Have you any late-hour prescriptions for a young composer, Mr. Stravinsky?" The maestro replies:

> If he can turn an honest million outside music he might seriously consider neglecting his talents for a time and turn it. Otherwise . . . he should go directly underground and do nothing but compose; that is, not strive for foundation awards, academic prizes, college presidencies, foreign fel-

lowships; not attend culture congresses . . . not give interviews . . . and not, either insidiously or directly, push, promote, maneuver, advertise, finagle, operate.

"Push, promote, maneuver, advertise, finagle, operate." The story of our lives. "Getting and spending we lay waste our powers," as Wordsworth wrote.

Mac Lowry has noted "the steady deterioration of personal vitality" on the part of theater directors and the high risk of their being overwhelmed. He does not overstate the case. We will not be overwhelmed only if we refuse to give ourselves up, only if we can experience ourselves as autonomous. For me, this means leaving the wheeling and dealing to others and going back to where I came from, to the theater as an art. We may be overwhelmed anyway. But, then, let them take us while we are doing our own work and not at a fundraising dinner.

Real power resides within the art we make and not in the techniques of manipulation, marketing, and promotion. If we seek the Negro audience, we should integrate our acting companies and find plays that speak to Negro concerns. If we want younger audiences, we must compete with films in the vividness and size of our work, its tempo and color, immediacy of themes. If we wish to attract what philosopher Herbert Marcuse calls "the new working class"—engineers, technicians, researchers, and teachers, who are not economically depressed but sensorially dead—then we must attract them with our work's directness, its abrasion, and physical energy, its life.

And, finally, we must achieve in our repertory a dynamic tension between past and present, between old and new. And insist that a strong function of taste be to keep the new from being *merely* new. A true theater is not a museum or library. The first consideration for a play is its relevance to the audience for which it is to be performed. More new works, born of our own time and place, more playhouses devoted chiefly to new works—these are what we desperately need.

History solves only those problems that are capable of solution. One can, therefore, only try. And hope that by defining the problems and engaging them with deep, personal passion, we will strengthen the side of the angels.

From remarks on a panel at American Educational Theatre Association, 1967.

THEATERS OR INSTITUTIONS?

(1970)

I have been asked to write about the future of what is called the regional or resident theater movement in this country, and this is my third attempt. I am wishing they had given the assignment to someone else, for, you see, I have been with this "movement" for twenty years, was part of its beginning, and will be part of its future, if it has a future and my psychic energy remains equal to the task. I know too much about it really to know anything. Someone doing one of those personality stories on me (a painful business) called our son at home the other week and asked him what I was like, how he would describe me. I heard him say: "It's an impossible question, I refuse to answer, how can you know anyone you've lived with for eighteen years?!?" Intimacy is so much easier between strangers.

They should have gotten Julius Novick, who did the resident theater circuit a couple of times, and came out with a book filled with such perception and insight that I am quite smitten with envy. Or Martin Gottfried who manages to describe us unequivocably, prescribe for us without need of consultation, and tinker with our morality, our aesthetics, our public visage, and private heart with the authority of a high priest. And there are others I could list who might have been called upon, all so highly qualified, with diagnoses and opinions positively oozing from their pens and tongues. But if I follow out this train of thought, I will never get to my own, and that is what I am trying to do. Besides, I would end up in a battle fought on someone else's terrain with weapons that they have chosen. And something in me rebels at the thought.

Karl Marx reminded us that you can't tell from the taste of the bread how the miller lived. So I suppose the reason that I am writing rather than someone else is that I am the miller, or one of the millers, and not one of the masticators. I can, therefore, possibly, describe some of the felt meanings and not only the surface contours. I am writing because I find the writings of Herr Critics and Travelers largely one-dimensional, like picture postcards of well-known buildings. And because, perhaps, not knowing, I know better than anyone else who knows.

The signs are not right. If one looks around with even a slight degree of open-mindedness, one can come quite quickly to the conclusion that the signs are not right and, indeed, the portents are dark for the survival of this wee beastie wearing the hat bizarrely labeled (from what attic did it come?) the Regional-Resident-Repertory-Theater of America. The signs are not right, and I am not a good reader of signs, so maybe I can be of some help.

I learned to read by the see-say method, not phonetically. The flash cards flicked and we tried rapidly and intuitively to latch onto a meaning. Pick, pack, pluck, poke, park, puke. At the beginning it was a random process indeed. It got better with the help of context: Obviously Daddy *packed* his bags; he didn't *pluck* them. But areas of fuzziness always remained. I remember once when I was five or six going with my father to his laboratory at the Bureau of Standards and waiting outside and wanting to pick the dandelions growing on the grass. But the signs said NO PICKING so I didn't pick. Years later, in retrospect, I realized that the sign had probably said NO PARKING not NO PICKING. This was a key experience for me, however trivial on the surface. From it I learned that one's behavior is conditioned far more by what one thinks one sees than by what one sees in fact. Reading the signs is, to a degree, a subjective matter. Reality is very private.

Out of all the "signs" to be read in the world, one chooses those that "signify" according to personal vision and need. We carry a camera and choose our shots, enlarging precisely those we choose, excluding areas of reality outside our lens range and selecting sight. The sign that said NO PARKING had no meaning at all for me, even if I had read it right, since I had no car to park. The sign that I read as NO PICKING had enormous meaning for me as it signified that I must leave my dandelions in the earth and wait impatiently for my father without them.

I want to say what signs I now see. Negative signs, most of them. And how I think we might angle them so that they may read better in the long run. Some remarks, too, that will catch up the history of this movement (Genesis before Exodus?) and then place it within a framework, or pincer, which I think of as "Theaters or Institutions?" "A subject for a short story," a character of Chekhov says ironically. There is a sadness in the words and a sense that the subject would not fit even into a very, very large book, that it would need a lifetime of experience to plumb.

The Regional-Resident-Repertory-Theater Movement was, to corn a phrase [sic], an idea whose time had come. Its impulse was highly American, in that it represented a better way of doing things. This doesn't mean to imply that the revolution was not also aesthetic; but first of all it was, in my opinion, in its first birth cry, organizational. I do not mean to depreciate the artistic work that is done (nor, on the other hand, do I mean to over-praise it), or to underrate the hazards o'erleaped, or to minimize the courage, talent, and initiative of any of us, because I think we moved mountains. Or maybe even made them and then moved them. And surely organization is creation. But I think we should all get it clear for ourselves that we started differently and therefore *are* different from the European models to which we so frequently turn for standards and precedents in the absence of any others. A lack of clarity about this has the tendency to get us off course, to keep us from seeing fresh paths, and to make us chastise ourselves for not being what we are not and cannot be.

This organizational revolution began around 1950 (a few years earlier for Margo Jones and Nina Vance, and still earlier for K. Elmo Lowe and Bob Porterfield) and took a great leap of second-generation energy in the sixties, which increased the number of theaters from about a half dozen to three dozen or more. It began when some of us looked about and saw that something was amiss. What was essentially a collective and cumulative art form was represented in the

United States by the hit-or-miss, make-a-pudding, smash-a-pudding system of Broadway production. What required by its nature continuity and groupness, not to mention a certain quietude of spirit and the fifth freedom—the freedom to fail—was taking place in an atmosphere of hysteria, crisis, fragmentation, one-shotness, and mammonmindedness within the ten blocks of Broadway. The most that could be said for Broadway was that there was singular excellence, even though the excellence was always singular. On the other hand, the literature of the stage was being lost. Classics and revivals of still-living older plays simply had no market. New plays were done, yes, but it was the case of good deeds for dubious motives. And important plays like *The Crucible* never did find their audience in New York. Audiences themselves had ceased to exist. Even in New York high ticket prices kept away all but the well-to-do.

We had to prove, even, that there *was* someplace outside of New York. We had to convince theater workers themselves that people lived and breathed out here. One actress in 1955 wanted strong assurances that she could get fresh tomatoes as far from New York as Washington, DC. Outside of New York there simply *was* no audience for any kind of theater except for touring companies with stars. So we looked around and saw a mess, saw that the art of the theater was dying, and thought of a way to keep it alive.

I say "we." There was a "we" though we didn't know each other. It was I, and him, and her out there someplace until around 1957 when Mac Lowry, the Ford Foundation Mac Lowry, found us all and stuck some adrenaline into us by the very act of finding and seeing us and taking notice, not to mention the grants to save our skins that came later. He introduced us to each other, saying, "Look, did you know there was someone else besides you working on this thing?" I met Jules Irving for the first time, and Joe Papp, and John Reich, and Herbert Blau, and a lot of my other coworkers through W. McNeil Lowry.

Separately and then together, we forged these theaters, these instrumentalities, these constellations of activities, these collective outposts, these—God forgive me!—institutions in order to preserve and re-create, in new forms, the art of theater then fusting in us unused. We found a better way of doing things. Found? We forged a better way, we scratched it out, hacked it, ripped it, tore it, yanked it, clawed it out of the resisting, unyielding nose-thumbing environment. We taught ourselves how to direct, produce, administer, raise money, entice an audience, work with acting companies, work without acting companies, make grant applications, raise budgets, raise standards, build buildings, teach and involve a community, change the taste of a community, fail and rise again like the phoenix or, in some cases, fail and not rise again, play a season of plays, then another season and another, search out new playwrights, learn about the crafts of the theater almost without teachers. We taught ourselves how to survive. That we found a better way is our essential *Apologia pro Vita Sua.*

We must not forget that while this is so, the opposite is also true. Among us there has been no Antoine rushing into his makeshift theater with his mother's dining room furniture and real meat from the butcher down the street, discovering the breathtaking reality of an actor daring to turn his back on the audience. No Stanislavsky and Danchenko putting together out of an amateur theater and some acting classes—and out of the work of a genius playwright whose plays demanded a different vision—an entirely new system of behavioral acting based on the physiology of the human body and connected to biological and psychological research of the day. And where is our Molière? Inventing plays to act in for himself and his troupe, elevating and freezing into art his own interior experiences, building a dramatic tradition on the shoulders of the improvisational *commedia* form, mocking himself, mocking his age, mocking his fellow man, and still catering to and pleasing both? Yeats and Lady Gregory and O'Casey and the Abbey, making a theater of protest after their own style, making a literature to help make a nation: We have not yet made one of those. Bertolt Brecht, where are you? To teach the masses so that they might remake the world. The masses stayed away and the intellectuals sat in their seats, but in Brecht's institution the aesthetic was the cause, and the cause was the aesthetic. Who is our Bertolt Brecht, theoretician, transformer of form, social architect, director-dramaturg-dramatist–institutional head all in one mind and body?

We are not even like the European models we most resemble. We are not like the provincial (if only the word vibrated with ideas of nature, or geography, and not with a kind of squarish isolation, a distance from the pulse!) repertory companies throughout England and Germany, companies that also find their life in the preservation and dissemination of theatrical expression. We are not like them. We are usually better. We have longer rehearsal periods, rely less on imported "names." Our contributing arts of scenery, costume, and lighting are more advanced; our actors are far better paid—American company actors earn more on the average than Broadway actors—and are often of the highest level in the land. An English director will say of an actor he doesn't like, "Oh, he's so rep-py," meaning that he's a stock actor, where American directors use the term repertory actor to connote an actor of versatility and range, staying power and commitment, a gifted artist-citizen.

There is no real way of likening us to other culture carriers such as the British National or the Royal Shakespeare Company or the present Moscow Art Theatre, since we are all of us broke and have small companies instead of very big ones. We spend half of our life at fundraising dinners and defending play choices to citizen boards of directors, since with the impulse that we should have theaters in our land came also the impulse that the community should be part of them, should put up some of the money, should even have a voice in them, and—now hear this!—should even commission theaters into being and hire artistic directors to run them. These artistic directors soon leave, out of enormous fatigue bordering on the Sisyphean, or out of wrath at non-professionals meddling in decisions that are hard enough to make all alone, or out of a general feeling of: "Who needs it? What I really want to do is direct, not run an inefficient branch of IBM."

The impulse, then, was to remedy a grievous fault and reverse a direful trend—the contraction and imminent death of the art of the theater. This goal has been, to a large degree, accomplished. Not secured, but accomplished. And in the process of the accomplishment, which has taken place roughly over the past twenty years— in itself a mammoth undertaking—we have also managed, if not entirely to shift then surely at least to cause to lean, the fulcrum of aesthetic excellence away from New York and toward these whad-dya-call-'em theaters. Outside of the musicals, in which New York is unbeatable, and outside of specific and singular Broadway and Off-Broadway productions, these whaddya-call-'em theaters (and some of them *are* in New York since New York *is* a "region," and New York *does* have residents—you won't get any reverse snobbism from me!)

have achieved the highest consistent (repeat, *consistent*) standards in the contributing arts of the theater—architecture, stage lighting, scenic design, playwriting, acting, and directing. And insofar as playwrights and actors and directors are concerned, they have done more to provide a laboratory and proving ground for their skills than any other theatrical mode, or modus, in our history. The American theater has begun to have a tradition: a past, a present, a future, a somewhat coherent way to look at itself and to proceed.

Theaters or institutions? In my mind now these two words exist in a state of uneasy tension, a kind of dialectic opposition, where once they seemed to me to be one and the same word. It seemed to me until quite recently that when a theater finally stopped being on the way to what it was to become and actually became it, then it would be an institution. Resonances that were very seductive to me hovered around the word: an end to the scramble, time for inwardness, time for creative rest and re-creation, a way of work evolved through continuity of association and a common vocabulary, the possibility of sharing power or even passing it on, an administrative environment for creative work that would release it, let it go outward without the random stuttering and bucking brought on by disorder. Tension where it belongs, within the process itself, but purring in the machine. All good things. But it hasn't turned out this way, a seduction is what it really was, a leading-from-the-self. I wonder why?

Perhaps I do precisely what I warn that we must not do. I cling to European institutional models—the subsidized, well-staffed, anything-that-money-can-buy theater. I strain to give flesh to runaway dreams. Between the idea and the reality falls the shadow, and I look at the shadow I cast, and it has a surprising shape. I do not recognize it. It isn't what I had in mind. When you and I talk, six people are having a conversation: the person I am, the person you think I am, and the person I think I am. And then there are the three of you. You say that we are institutional theaters, but I want to know what that means to you? To me? What *is* an institutional theater precisely? What is it when you look at it? What is it when I dream about it?

My thoughts continue apace. I travel around a bit and am on various committees and panels, and I find work that is good—spirited, personal, inventive, vivacious, specific—and a lot of work that is simply there: repetitive, unoriginal, stylistically barren, coming from no particular individual vision, institutionalized. And I find myself too often restless, bored, and boring in the presence of my opposite numbers, the conversation turning and then turning back with a dreary passion upon the life-and-death within subscription statistics, the cloak and dagger relationships with boards or heads of edifice complexes, the Name-of-the-Game-Is-Grants, the gold rush for new scripts that bring prestige—as important as money to irritated egos— and the general problem of how to get from this day to the next, this week to the next, this month to the next without dying, the general problem of how to endure, how to function as part sitting duck, part magician, and still invent.

What is that look I see on the faces of my friends? It is a look that varies, of course, with the day and mood and personality, but it is a certain look that bears dissection. Secrecy? Hidden thoughts, like those of dress designers before late-summer showings (what is it to be this year, two inches above the knee or two below?). Confusion? Where do I turn next? What are my priorities? Loneliness? Nobody knows the trouble I've seen; nobody knows my sorrow. And I'd better not tell, because to tell would be to admit self-doubt and weakness and all the secrets of one's heart, and to reveal these is to be nakedly vulnerable in the presence of one's successful, smiling peers.

What price salvation now? What price institutions now? If this be living theater give us death. Joe Papp: Does anyone ever think how much time and spark-plug energy Joe Papp gives to the endless job of fundraising? To the point where his bones ache with Joe's fatigue, and his temper snaps with Joe's frustration, and his stomach grows sad with Joe's own sadness. And for what? For money. "What's Hecuba to him or he to Hecuba that he should weep for her?" What would you do if you had the motive and the cue for passion that he has? On how many levels can a man be creative at one and the same time and still hang on to his humanity?

I was very rude to a close, close friend recently. He called me to say that the chairman of his board would be in Washington the next day and could she come to talk with us about the festivities one arranges to prop up the opening of a new theater building. I was deep in conference with a playwright, trying to wrest the logic from inside the script. I was on the battlefront, I thought, and I didn't want to be bothered with peeling potatoes in the rear. But ten years earlier I, too, had opened a theater, I had been preoccupied with the same peelings, and I should not have been rude. Yet, I was justified.

"Style is world outlook," wrote a leading Russian director, Yury Zavadsky. And here we are at the heart of the artichoke. Style is world outlook. What is on our stages is who we are and the way we look at ourselves, at each other, and at our world. The psychic engine (it is a biologic law not a metaphor) requires inputs, returns, in order to generate new impulses. The artist must hear his own voice, at best a highly intricate process. Next to impossible within the cacophony of these institutions of ours. So the directors, the conductors of the collective creativity, supposedly the fount for the energy and spirit of the Thing, by getting and spending lay waste their powers. Dust fills their brains and mouths, and when it doesn't they use up half their gut to keep it from pouring in.

So what road are we on, and where's the next toll bridge? Over there: the Swedish National Theatre, the Théâtre National Populaire, the Royal Shakespeare Company, the Berliner Ensemble. Or if you want to take the other route, there are the loose, or looser, creative units such as Joe Chaikin's Open Theater, which plays only briefly in New York, trying to stay clear of the settling down; or Judith Malina and Julian Beck's Living Theatre, hounded to Europe, split into three units, each trying to find its own way, the Becks coming back, trying to hang institution-free, trying to hammer out an aesthetic, a personal style-as-world-outlook artwork with which to penetrate the social barbwire, trying to do it with only as much institutional baggage as is necessary to get from one discovery to another. And Ellen Stewart. Café La MaMa. The seedbed of tumbling, heterogeneous creative projects. Until recently Ellen Stewart kept her dress designing job to keep up her theater. Ringing her bell, passing the hat, juggling projects, she presided over the birth of new playwrights, new actors, new thoughts. Now she has a building and the responsibility of that (the power of that, and the responsibility) and of a continuum of productions.

What happens when the money comes in a little? When you get enough from the Ford Foundation or the National Endowment to move ten squares and buy the Atlantic City Boardwalk? Is it migraine headache time? What time is it when you are suddenly endowed with all the blessings of institutionalization? (Mind you, the blessings aren't something that are forced on you. They're something you ask for without quite knowing what you're getting.) Time for the Table of Organization? Time for specialization of labor? Time to begin to consider the internal distribution of wealth now that you've got some? The promotion, marketing, and distribution of the product? Ways to increase efficiency, ways to rationalize use of time and manpower, ways to diversify so as to appeal to a broader base, ways to close the gap between income and spending? It's headache time and surprise! time. One has become a private enterprise in a capitalistic society. The "not for profit" in your papers really says No Parking. Shades of Adam Smith and the Ford Motor Company of America, and Pan, where hast thou fled?

Next question: Can a group hang with it without a formal structure? Can an individual remain pure in a corrupt world? ask the parable plays of Bertolt Brecht. It's easy to be angry, Mother Courage puts it to the hotheaded Young Soldier. What's important is how long it can last, this anger, before you capitulate to things-as-they-are. How long can a theater stay poor? Long enough to carry out its aesthetic intention? Anything short of that is not long enough. How long is long enough? It took Joe Chaikin several years to evolve his two ritual dramas, *The Serpent* and *Terminal*, and they were "worth" every minute of the time. Does he have enough poor-time left (poor—not in the sense that Grotowski meant poor, which is really rich, rich in the quintessential meaning of the art, poor only in the trappings—but poor in the sense of hungry, insufficient, lacking in stuff with which to make the artifact: time, cloth, concentration)? Does Chaikin have enough poor-time left in him to follow his work to the end of where it is leading him? Must institutionalization eventually follow, follow inevitably—must it then "follow as the night the day"?

Last question: If money corrupts, does absolute money corrupt absolutely? I think not. We have all grown up in this pure society and know that the love of money is the root of all evil. And we have been taught by our well-bred mothers not to talk in public about how much things cost (I suppose for fear the gods will get angry and jealous and take all the stuff away). But I, for one, do not fear the corrupting power of money, and I do not feel alone in my courage. I agree with Trotsky that art needs comfort, even abundance, and I know that the devils of the artist are within him and have their own well-stocked armory and need no help from the outside. On the contrary, I believe in the sublime benevolence of absolute money. Not unlimited money. Absolute money. No more is needed than the amount which will absolutely bring into existence the vision that is being born. It would, of course, be silly and would not meet the test of reason to give Jerzy Grotowski—evolving his work with six actors, able to accommodate only a maximum of one hundred hungry souls a performance, grounding his aesthetic in a poverty of physical means—the absolutely same amount of money as one would give to the National Theatre of Great Britain.

Stark Young wrote: "Behind every work of art is a living idea . . . a content that will achieve a form that will be inseparable from it. A perfect example in any art arrives not through standards but when the essential or informing idea has been completely expressed in terms of this art, and comes into existence entirely through the medium of it. This is perfection, though we may speak of a perfection large or small." All we absolutely need is enough money to conduct the search for the form of our idea, each in his own way, and in the hope that there's a fighting chance of achieving it. If that is not somehow done for us, then we must stop being teased with the concept of institutions, taunted with it, for it is a dance macabre and can end only in despair and death.

There is so much indifference. The Association of Producing Artists folded, and nothing skipped a beat. A short column in the *New York Times*, one in *Variety*, the APA had folded and Ellis Rabb, who created it in the late fifties and steered it into being one of our leading theater companies, was moving into the acting company of the American Conservatory Theater in San Francisco (which is retrenching and giving up its second smaller theater). Whatever the reasons for the disbanding of the APA—the money just gave out, or a bad season topped a series of other problems and down it went, or internal conflicts ripped open the structure—whatever it was, it all slid away so softly, so silently, we hardly knew it had left.

There are troubled sounds from Theatre of Living Arts in Philadelphia, and the resident theater in Atlanta is going or gone. The Loretto-Hilton theater in St. Louis is now no more, and the Seattle Repertory Theatre has been shook up. Joe Papp had to shorten his summer season in the Park, and there are tremors reported through-out the land.

We all need more money than we are getting, and we must get it in a different way. Arena Stage has just received a terminal grant from the Ford Foundation which, partially matched by a grant from the National Endowment for the Arts, will just about cover our deficit for last season, this one, and next. We have in the past received other grants from these and from other foundations, among them a three-year grant for the training at minimal salaries of young craftsmen under a production intern scheme, a three-year grant to increase the salaries of a ten-person nucleus of an acting company. This was very early on, around 1958 or 1959—to entice actors from the magnetic field of New York. And finally, we received a year-by-year grant which keeps at a minimum level of life our Living Stage, an improvisational troupe that performs action skits on the suggestion and with the par-ticipation of young people throughout Washington's inner city.

I mention these in particular to make the point that, while it may be better to have loved and lost than never to have loved at all, these grants had a seminal meaning for our organization. When they were withdrawn, or, more accurately not renewed, the trauma was so intense that one wondered whether it would have been better not to have had them than to have had and lost them.

Not knowing from one year to the next whether there will be a spring, or only summer, winter, and fall, one simply does not know how to organize one's closet. I suggest an end to this tithing tease. I suggest a recognition that either subsidy is here to stay, or we cannot possibly. Further, I suggest an extension of the arc of thought on the part of the policy-makers from three to, say, seven (a lucky number that, with all kinds of mystic overtones) years, so that there may still be part of the grant left by the time we have learned to use it wisely, and so that the benefits can endure for at least as long as it takes our skins completely to replace themselves. The seven fat years of the regional theater. Yes, seven seems a goodly number.

I am not very strong on community giving, except perhaps when it represents only a small percentage of the total. I think we could well do without the hand that rocks the cradle, for the hand that rocks the cradle will also want to raise it in a vote and mix into the pie with it. While a theater is a public art and belongs to its public, it is an art before it is public, and so it belongs first to itself and its first service must be self-service. A theater is part of its society. But it is a part which must remain apart since it is also chastiser, rebel, lightning rod, redeemer, irritant, codifier, and horse-laugher. Separateness is the first law of relationship. Nowhere is the paradox more profound, and nowhere must it be more urgently insisted upon. The first law of the theater is success; without success there can be no theater. At one and the same time, success can be arrived at only obliquely, as a by-product of a personal point of view strongly expressed. Success in the theater cannot be voted on or voted in. The proof of the pudding will be in the eating.

There has been a kind of folksiness in the RRRT Movement, engendered chiefly by the principle of matching money: so much from the foundation, so much from the community. Historically, the motivation was sound—if these cities wanted their theaters, let's see tangible evidence of the desire and wherewithal. But the hope on the part of the foundations that the communities would continue to run with the ball, after they had left the seedbed and withdrawn, turns out to have been a false one. We have lived long enough to see how the grass grew. What we are seeing now is that, as the deficits get larger and larger, the folks get tireder and tireder, for they discovered that the need for money has no bottom. As the folks get tireder and tireder, they also get fuller and fuller of opinions about what is going wrong and why. In the world at large, two wrongs don't make a right. In the theater two rights don't even make a right! It has to be *one* right, for the tougher the artistic decision, the fewer the number of heads who can make it. So, then, let the money be given at a distance, once removed, and let it be awarded by a jury of one's peers. Let the audience be only the judge.

Money from a mixed bag of donors, yes I think we would like that. And we must learn to protect for ourselves a share of commercial earnings from works which we have evolved. If we are of use to Broadway and the film industry, if our better way is now producing fruit, let us reap some of the benefits in a direct financial way. Let us have a share of earnings in the marketplace to feed back into our work. This seems an overstatement of the obvious. But our critic Martin Gottfried trembles over the loss of innocence that may result in a liaison with the sources of money (winding up a recent article with what must be the statement of the month: "There's no sense in being naive about purity . . . But there's no sense in being cynical about purity either."). It took Howard Sackler, author of *The Great White Hope*, to tell me how it really is, or ought to be. It was this play, nursed at Arena Stage, that became the big baby boy that won the Pulitzer Prize, a sale to the movies for something like a million dollars, and wrenched the axis of dominance for the production of important new works toward the regional theater. When we asked Mr. Sackler for a small financial pat on the back, he consulted his morality for a while and decided that since we had posed to him as a high priestess of the arts, and were now reversing roles, we had disqualified ourselves from his responsibility. Let it be known that I am no high priestess of the arts. I am dedicated, fanatic even, and, after a good night's sleep and with a production on the boards that I like, I may even exude a certain charisma. But I am of the world, not above it. I require, and now have learned to demand, a worldly portion of what we help to bring about. I speak for my brothers and sisters in this matter I am sure.

There are other signs that money will not right, but which cannot be righted without money since money is the exchange commodity of our life.

We have not found out how to evolve acting companies for our theaters. No, we have found out how to evolve them but not how to hold them together. Arena Stage has had three acting companies over its twenty-year history: one—and its best—in the first phase from 1950–1955, which broke up when we closed our tiny 247-seat playhouse to seek one large enough to pay the bills (we were still self-supporting in those days); one in the Old Vat, our second phase, which drifted off one actor at a time to Broadway or television or to other new companies coming into being around 1960–1965; and one which was split up by the transfer of *The Great White Hope* to Broadway in 1968. We have not abandoned the notion of company, although some of our fellow theaters have. But we have had to broaden our definition of what constitutes a company and enlarge our vision of how to create one.

Again, we have had to teach ourselves to be independent of European models. American companies, operating at a distance from the film and television centers where most of the money can be made,

and not able to afford companies on a yearly payroll, must be conceived more fluidly. Company membership must be defined more by
artistic point of view and shared experiences, and less by uninter-
rupted geographical residency—although, of course, there is no reason why a company nucleus cannot be held together in one place over
a considerable period of time. Further, companies are not companies
simply because the actors share the same working hours and dressing
rooms. This is a parochial concept. It explains why our critics complain, and justifiably, that many of our theaters have yet to evolve an
identifiable style and remain hard to distinguish one from the other.

A company is brought into being chiefly through the force and
power of an artistic leader. A company develops as the aesthetic ideas
of the leader are given body and substance by the individual talents
collected around him. Brecht's actors were not Stanislavsky's actors
were not Meyerhold's actors were not Grotowski's actors. Actors are
not interchangeable ciphers, and companies are not stamp collections. Companies also require leading actors in order to emerge and
present themselves as individualistic units, although in this country, with its egalitarian ethic, we seem to feel ashamed to say so. The
Moscow Art needed Olga Knipper and Ivan Moskvin; the Berliner
needs Ekkehard Schall; the Group Theatre needed Luther Adler, Lee
J. Cobb, and Morris Carnovsky; the National Theatre of Great Britain,
Maggie Smith and Robert Stephens. Not "stars," but leading actors to
carry the weight, fill up the space, connect the audience to the play
with their special strings, and give the timbre of uniqueness to the
goings-on. Plays are written about exceptional people within exceptional circumstances, and even ordinary people in ordinary circumstances are given incandescence by the magnifying and transforming
art of the stage. We need large voices, both vocal and human, to head
our companies.

When the artistic leaders of our theaters can be freed for the task
of artistic leadership, and when the theaters come to be seen by actors
as a first choice for a way to live their lives, then we shall see if we can
produce leading companies or not.

Along with ways to free artistic leadership to do its job, means
must be found to train people to head up theatrical institutions. This
is one lesson that we can afford to learn from Europe: the know-how,
if not the temperament and talent, for artistic leadership can indeed

be taught and learned. Some sort of planned discipleship had better happen soon in this country. Until we experience a successful transfer of one of our more personally created theaters from one pair of hands to another, the term "institution" is not only tedious but euphemistic. The closest we have come is with the recent assignment of Michael Langham to the post of artistic head of the Tyrone Guthrie Theater in Minneapolis, Peter Zeisler—the last one of the triumvirate who began it in the early sixties—having decided to leave. But this represents an idiosyncratic solution and not one that we can count on repeating. Michael Langham and his association with the Tyrone Guthrie tradition of theater began long before Minneapolis. Furthermore, not all of our theaters will want to perpetuate an English or Canadian style; they will want to develop in more personal and individual ways.

A transfusion of funds and a reassurance that artistic leadership can follow his or her shining star and need not be tub-thumpers and board-pleasers would serve to attract director-producers rather than administrator–business managers to the helm. This latter course has turned out badly in a number of instances. I most strongly recommend the joint participation of a funding agency and some of our artistic directors in planning love-match apprenticeships to their positions. The way things stand now, our theaters are destined to become the mules of theatrical history, incapable of reproduction.

Was it Napoleon who said that it is easier to conquer a city than to occupy it? It is also easier to fall in love with a city than to stay there, easier to launch a revolution than to batten it down. For artistic directors the syndrome is a malaise of doubt: in the audience, in oneself to create and lead a meaningful artistic entity, in the "relevance" of our repertory, in the validity of theater itself within a technocratic society. For some of us it has felt (or feels) that a whole artistic life had been misdirected and that, somehow, we were part of a great betrayal, with no one to blame but ourselves.

The younger people are going to the movies—at least seventy percent of movie revenue now comes from those between sixteen and twenty-nine. "See me, feel me, touch me, heal me," sings Tommy in the rock-media opera at Fillmore East. And the lyrics of Paul Kantner from *Easy Rider* exclaim that "We Can Be Together." To a lot of young people of Woodstock, the Vietnam Moratorium and the Marches on Washington these nervy "now" sentiments seem to have more to say than we do. Had we outlined our day even before we had served up lunch?

There is an article in *Theatre 1* by Harlan Kleiman (he was the manager of the Long Wharf Theatre in New Haven and has since left it) which says: "As we move into a more cybernated, electronically oriented era, the spoken word as a dynamic means of advancing theme or plot in the entertainment media diminishes in importance . . . it is not a matter of economics; theater as we know it is too static and nonsensual. It belongs to their [the young's] parents' generation." And the brilliant young critic, John Lahr, in an article in *Evergreen Review* a year or so ago, writes that Shakespeare is passé, coming from an age whose manners and morals find no equivalent in today's society, his images and syntax are archaic, and that the best that remain are his large metaphors of power, fear, conjuration, psychic dislocation. This was by way of reviewing Richard Schechner's rendering of *Makbeth,* which he liked very much—the audience as members of the feast where Banquo's ghost appears, the witches hanging by their knees, downward, from branches of trees.

Tyrone Guthrie's prediction, dating from the same edgy period of mid-sixties onward, is also dire. Writing in *A New Theatre* of his own experience with the Minneapolis theater that bears his name, he observes that after the honeymoon period ends—the initial years of operation—the audience diminishes, as do the box office receipts, and consequently the very core of the theater, its repertory, is affected. He writes,

> *Three Men on a Horse* is immediately substituted for *Oedipus Rex* in an effort to broaden the appeal. Still the audience continues to dwindle to the point where the resident theater, which five years ago was hailed as the great salvation of the American theater, is now viewed as an additional fiscal burden on communities already overloaded with "worthy causes."

One cynic even goes so far as to say, when asked to explain the regional theater: "If a play was produced on Broadway ten years ago and made an extraordinary profit, was then done in summer stock all over the country nine years ago and was again a box office success, it will now be done in the nonprofit theaters at a sizable loss." And I noted in an August 1967 speech that, while "the regional movement is such a big thing they ought to make a musical out of it," much of its size could be attributed to too much air whipped into the cream, that its overt communality was only the underside of a covert conformity. The whole Movement's shadowboxing relationship with its audience, I added, its fickle and fleeing audience, an audience, whom we both love and hate, can best be expressed by Hughes Mearns's jingle:

> Yesterday, upon the stair
> I met a man who wasn't there
> He wasn't there again today
> I wish, I wish he'd go away.

Something sidetracked us from having to deal head-on with the signs represented by these criticisms and self-castigations of the mid-to-late sixties. That was the quite accidental success of *The Great White Hope* (for success is always an accident; only failure can be counted upon) and the subsequent *succès d'estime* of *Indians*, both of which originated at Arena, both of which had roots deep within contemporary life. And the attention given to the Mark Taper Forum production of *In the Matter of J. Robert Oppenheimer*, in Los Angeles and in its New York incarnation, and to *Murderous Angels* and other plays from other theaters, which subsequently moved or tried to move in one form or another from their homes to Mecca. My good and respected friend Gordon Davidson has been so reassured that the new play's the thing that his conscience is entirely caught. He's now devoting an entire season to new works, and perhaps the future of his theater, though I don't know this latter for a fact.

It is not hard to fathom that new orientation. What more important move is there than to open our arms, to open our theaters to new voices now being raised, to say new things in new forms to new people who are living in a world that has never been lived in before. The search for and the production of new works have their origin in Good Deeds.

But is that the voice of the Tempter I hear? I am not sure. It is nothing if not funny that the write-up of *The Great White Hope* in *Newsweek* Magazine, after singing the praises of James Earl Jones and

Howard Sackler, then nodded in our direction. With this production we had achieved a national reputation, Arena and I, overnight (a night of biblical proportions, having lasted some twenty summers and twenty winters!). We had demonstrated beyond contradiction our right to be. Who can say for sure that it is not the Tempter's voice we hear? The competition to do the premiere production of a new play has become part of inter-theater politics since *The Great White Hope*. One theater director was totally exercised over not having presented the American premiere of a new script that he loved, but, after it was premiered in another theater, he would not do it in his, even though it still would have been new for his particular audience. What kind of love is that, that "bends with the remover to remove"? Is it not, indeed, a love subject to temptation?

This does not mean that good deeds cannot be done out of questionable or mixed motives. But it does raise in my mind a most interesting formulation, a hypothesis as it were, with which to wind up this reading-of-the-signs. (One can beg a question, but one cannot steal it away. The question remains.) Broadway was onto it a long time before we suffered our first little inkling: A new play with a good press and a good word of mouth (in our particular situation we can even do without the good press) means lines at the box office and a feather in our caps, as *Variety* put it for us with *Indians* (a bad pun?). But what about the rest of it? Should we nag ourselves to death with self-doubts on the subject of relevancy? Are we out of sync with the rhythms and sounds of our time? Are our audiences really gone? Is *Macbeth* done for? Without *The Great White Hope* what kind of a hope are we? Are we worth the money it will take to keep us alive? What do the signs tell us?

I don't know in an empirical way the answers to any of these questions. I am in the position of most people who have to make decisions and follow a course of action. We don't know enough to satisfy our intellect; we have to use whatever facts we can get hold of and piece them out with our emotions, our inclinations, our prejudices. I feel more optimistic than I did three Augusts ago. I am glad that I heeded Emerson who exhorted one to work on without despair, but if we despair, then to work on anyway.

Frantz Fanon was onto something when he wrote that language was "the god gone astray in the flesh." There are two meanings here. One, that language is the highest evolutionary achievement of the human animal, a gift toward the gods. And second, that language is a function of the body, of the flesh, not, in the medieval sense, of the "soul" or "spirit world." Man is the animal who expresses himself with his body, this expression sometimes emerging as speech. No gifted actor or director will find anything new in Julius Fast's *Body Language* book that is now the talking-piece of dinner parties.

Ask any good actor. The theater is a place of physical actions and physical adjustments that when they reach their height, their straining point, their necessity, burst into speech. Just as song is speech unable to contain itself. Or it is a place of physical actions and adjustments which are themselves a form of speech, a language of the body, either denying or demonstrating what is being "said." I don't know what kind of theater Harlan Kleiman was referring to as "static and non-sensual" except to theater that is dull and without style. When theater is alive, the words are an extension of gesture, both psychic and physical. Or the gesture *is* the word. Or the gesture and the word, together, are life made concrete. The experience is as mobile and sensual as life itself. That the theater's movement and sensuality are different from the film's is, of course, true, but that is not what Kleiman or others who agree with him are saying. It may even be true that the medium of the film is more readily accessible to the psychology and habits of today's young people, challenging as it does the one-at-a-time-ness of events in the theater, freed by the camera as it is from the dimensions of time and space, exploding as it can the synapse between thought and the body, the connection for logic that theater requires.

On the other hand, at the cinema one is not immediately witness to the event. One is not present in the flesh or, more accurately, the flesh of the event is not present. So the sensual experience is once removed, is it not? And why can't we have both, the theater *and* the film. Our thirteen-year-old son saw *Alice's Restaurant* and a dress rehearsal of *The Cherry Orchard* last season, one right after the other on the same evening. I asked him for his feelings. "The movie is bigger and moves faster," he said. "But I wasn't there in the same room with the people when it was happening. I liked them both. Why can't we have both?"

There are more good films than good theater productions. There is too much theater; especially, there is too much bad theater, theater with no roots in human soil. It is very easy for theater to be bad and very hard for it to be good. I believe that bad theater has done much to send kids to the movies, where at least the images and the transitions between images are outsized and rapid and exciting—and you can eat your popcorn and go to the bathroom and get a drink of water when you want to. Bad theater and, of course, habit. Young people are not in the habit of going to the theater, because it is "good for them." But you have to go to the theater for the same reason you read a book or fall in love.

And this goes not only for the young people but for the young people's parents, who also find bad theater boring and lifeless and not worth leaving their television sets for. Imagination is the nose of the public: By this, at any time, they may be quietly led. I think it was Edgar Allan Poe who said this. But it is I who second it. It is I who, out of my experience with bad seasons and good seasons, changes in administrations, deep affronts from disappearing subscribers, horrendous problems with matters of urban decay, the increasing crime rate in the central city, the high cost of money, fury at critics who don't know bad work when they see it, much less good, the endless invention and reinvention required to keep the people coming and to replace the ones who leave, it is I—faced now with more per capita competition than any other city in the United States—the emotion rising up in me to counter the doubts and question marks—I who agree with him, who second him. Right on, Mr. Poe! Imagination is the nose of the public: By this, at any time, it may be quietly led.

Poe aside, I disagree with everyone else. I disagree with John Lahr, with Dr. Guthrie, and with the other critic who said we do the plays at a loss that Broadway and stock did at a profit. First of all, I think there is a place for *Three Men on a Horse* alongside *Oedipus Rex* in the repertory of an American theater for reasons of its theatrical exuberance, the deliciousness of its design, and its sly, askew glance at the American way of killing the goose that lays the golden egg by not knowing when enough's enough. In its funny and unpretentious fashion, that play deals with the precarious nature of the creative process itself. I may even produce it again some time. For a repertory is a place for finding things, and *Three Men on a Horse* should be found, discovered, come upon by succeeding generations who have never before found it and to whom, therefore, it is new and— here's that word—relevant.

I once asked our older son what the word "relevant" meant to him. He answered me simply. A subject or, in this instance, an artwork was relevant if it tied in to what was currently of concern or importance to him. Or it was relevant if it was simply beautiful in its own right. Or it could be relevant on both counts. Of course, there is a beauty that is large or small, and we would be on sounder ground with *Oedipus*. But I feel on sound ground with *Three Men on a Horse*, and it is good ground from which to make my point.

I think one must guard against uppishness. Plays like *Room Service*, *You Can't Take It with You*, and *Three Men on a Horse* are not "trashy comedies," as our same Gottfried article calls them, nor do we produce them in an attempt "to alchemize dated commercial theater into American folk art." Nor is there any feeling of "scorning the audience" or "concealing the camp" when they are produced. The fact that the plays were once commercial successes does not automatically cancel them out as "folk art." Reasoning in reverse, one could argue that, because these comedies were popular successes, they were "folk art" ahead of their time. I hold to neither view very strongly, but I prefer the second to the first. I do not have the same aversion to commercialism as do many of my friends. My aversion is to art that has everything but creative energy, everything but life.

At any rate, I produced *Three Men on a Horse* and *You Can't Take It with You* (and over a hundred other plays from the past including Molière, Giraudoux, Shaw, Shakespeare, Pirandello, Brecht, and O'Neill, to an average of ninety percent of capacity over the years) *for the life that is in them*. And, particularly, for the life that, like a tuning fork, sets off and responds to vibrations that are in the air today. I produce them for the continuum of life that they provide and for the sight they permit into the astounding ebb and flow of experience, its repetition and circularity, though each time with a difference. It's to laugh at and to cry over, to puzzle out, to give up on, to take sides with, to be put off by, to delight with recognition at. It's a face in the present looking at a face in the past and seeing something of itself. Doing old plays provides a bridge between past and present.

A work of art is always relevant. A work of personal genius has perpetual life. Human nature does not change so rapidly. Thornton Wilder, in that wise and gentle voice, wrote in his novel *The Eighth Day*: "Human nature is like the ocean, unchanging, unchangeable.

Today's calm, tomorrow's tempest—but it is the same ocean. Man is as he is, as he was, as he always will be."

Why does John Lahr have troubles with *Macbeth* without the "k"? Could it be because he has seen productions without specific human reality or without an interpretation of the environment of the play that would make it come to life? Douglas Turner Ward and Robert Hooks of the Negro Ensemble Company once told me that they felt the "classics" held nothing for young Black kids, and really nothing for the Black population at large. But I wish John Lahr, Doug Ward, and Bobby Hooks had been at Arena Stage to watch inner-city Black high-school kids watch Macbeth, propelled by the hunger of ambition, thrown out of control by it to the seducing of dark forces, to the blood of murder and the hallucination of deeds-gone-awry and, finally, to his own destruction. And they knew faster than anyone in the play could that Lady Macbeth was up to no good, what burned in her heart, and why she went mad. And then there was the bonus of all that language that *Mission Impossible* just never gave them. The language was not so hard for them as we might pre-judge, since the words rested on emotions, and the emotions rode out high on physical action. Tomorrow and tomorrow and tomorrow. And life's a walking shadow. And life's a brief candle. And we're too far steeped in blood ever to turn back. And we're just poor players who strut and fret our little hour upon the stage and then are heard no more. All well within their lives to understand. And within ours. Within our life and times as social beings. And within us, deep within us, as human beings with such a brief and bloody history.

So, let us not impale ourselves on doubt. Plays by new writers, of course. But the theatrical past will die—the past itself will die—will fall into shadow, unless we prevent it. There must be a tension between the old and the new. And the answer to the question: "Without *The Great White Hope* what kind of hope are we?" has got to be: "The only hope we've got." And the answer to the question: "Are we worth the money it will take to keep us alive?" is, "Yes, I think, on balance, we are. But from whence cometh our help?"

Originally published as part of "The American Theatre 1969–1970" in *Theatre*, a publication of the International Theatre Institute of the United States (New York: Charles Scribner's Sons, 1970).

ARENA AT TWENTY-FIVE
(1975)

Either the cup is missing or the wine. There's an old Russian proverb to the same effect: "Never the time, the man, and the occasion all together." Life is built this way. We all know how hard it is to get things together. Either the stomach is ready and the purse is poor, or else the larder is full and the cholesterol count too high. Either the cup is missing or the wine.

Arena Stage is in its twenty-fifth season. If making a production is making a world—with its own special psychology, look, rhythm, architecture, sounds, reverberations (and we have made over two hundred of these worlds) then twenty-five years is a very long time indeed! Time to accumulate a lot of wine or spill it, time for the potter to come up with a good solid cup or to reduce one to smithereens.

The wine at Arena, the wine *of* Arena, has aged and mellowed into a pretty good bouquet. This year, following the Russian tour which finally identified us as a creative collective and gave recognition to and permission for our deep and serious theatrical aims (neither of which had ever been given fully in our own city or country, alas), we made a jump into artistic maturity. A critic intuited the achievement of our production of *Death of a Salesman*: "This is the rarest of happenings," he wrote, "the meeting of a masterpiece and a company in full possession of its artistic means."

It was perceptive of the critic to see this, because during the rehearsal process—though no one said a word about it—this sense of being in full possession of our artistic means was somehow there, infecting every moment of the work, making it ride out on a wave of ease, of serious yet joyous investigation, of camaraderie, of collective discovery, of a kind of sureness and concentration that made it clear that, at least for this period of our life, we had become what we had gropingly sought to be. Something in the air felt different.

Our wine will not stay so sweet. Individual productions will fail, and some years will show better than others. But having found a way of being together as a group, and knowing that this communicates to an audience, we no longer doubt that we can touch the source of the wine. It took twenty-five years to reach that sense of identity, that maturity, so we can, I think, be forgiven if we have some quiet pride.

That is the wine. Now what about the cup? I'm talking about "the cup" of Arena Stage. "What's the trouble here?" one always asks of a script to find out the drift, the thrust, of the life within it.

You see, feeling good, I'm also feeling bad. People have such faith that Arena Stage will continue. As it was in the beginning, so it will always be. But there is really no guarantee. Where is it written that American society is capable of identifying Arena's contribution (*function* is maybe a better word) on its own terms? Or, even if it should identify it, where is it written that the theater will get the tangible support it needs to enlarge upon its achievements in some kind of peace and surety.

My mother used to say, "Where is it written that . . . ?" (My grandmother said it, too, in Yiddish.) Meaning: Who says so? What authority insists? On what stone tablet is it engraved, by what holy law made manifest, that such-and-such has to happen in such-and-such a way? The saying represented the embodiment of folk wisdom. In tone and body language, "Where is it written?" implied that *it isn't really written anywhere*.

Arena Stage's future now hangs in the balance, and nowhere is it written on which side the forces of history will come down. I have never before in our twenty-five year history felt or said that, so it would be unjust to accuse me of crying "wolf"!

Of course Arena's problems are economic, as are the problems of every arts institution in America, many families in America, and of America as whole. Still, to get hooked on the idea that Arena's problems are only, or fundamentally, economic would be very foolish indeed. That would lead us to take actions that could only solve the very short, short-run, and end up making us increasingly impotent, as we discover that the actions that might be okay in December don't work at all in May, when the going gets tougher.

Of course, our problems are economic. The cost of everything we use keeps going up, especially the cost of labor power, since theater is an art made by people (particular people who are not interchangeable parts). With the cost of tickets fixed within a very small range, if we wish to keep the audience we have built, and for whom our work is designed, our deficit will grow larger each season.

The Ford Foundation has us on a terminal grant, which ends the year after next. It is rumored that Ford's Arts and Humanities Division, which peaked at spending about $25,000,000, will be stabilized at $5,000,000 for the foreseeable future. The business community of Washington gives practically nothing to Arena Stage. In a building fund drive in 1960 to complete the present Arena, of $300,000 raised in the community, only $9,000 came from Washington businesses. Obviously we could not matter less to them. Were it not for our individual patrons and our 17,000 subscribers, the Washington community as a social force would score a minus-ten in the area of economic contribution to our survival.

Local foundations have been critical to our life, but the two major local foundations are finding increasing pulls on their attention from other worthy projects, and there is no guarantee about their continued level of support. With no state government to give us help, no municipal government, and with a big blank in the area of local government giving, only the National Endowment for the Arts stands there as a fairly dependable source for what is needed most—support for our general program. And even here, one wonders what the future will bring. We can only hope for the best and try to keep a stiff upper lip.

There is but one way to read a system of values at work, whether in a family, a theater or other institution, or in a government. That is, to see how much of the wealth is assigned to any particular item/

idea. The pattern of spending (giving, assigning, differentiating)—where the weights and measures fall—tells what a society-in-little or society-at-large values.

Where will the weights fall at this moment in history, and how will the measures be made, and by whom? We have our doubts, but they are no longer, as they have been in the past, about whether we could make this institution viable. The doubts—no, the single doubt—the point that pierces the skin—is this: Does our city and our country care about an institution whose central and sole aim is to create images by theatrical means in order to demonstrate, crystallize, intensify life? Does it care enough to come down strongly on our side at this critical time?

When I ask if society-at-large, through the assignment of its wealth, will make clear that it values creativity as creativity—and not as creativity-cum-ambassadorial or creativity-cum-ceremonial or creativity-cum-social or creativity-cum-political activity—I ask a question that goes right to the basement of the whole building. Works of art and arts institutions appear and are sustained not as isolated benefactions from Heaven, but as peaks emerging from a continuing living process. Shakespeare could not have happened without the turbulent complexities of the Elizabethan age. The great violin makers evolved their expertise over centuries of song and string playing. Gothic churches came from the yearning of entire populations to reach toward God. Nothing comes from nothing. And nothing subsists on nothing.

The living process that gives rise to artworks depends on a culture's willingness to support tangibly, in whatever historical mode, the effort of its artists. That willingness comes from the value assigned to what is being made. One does not yet know the degree of mere stylishness involved in America's "cultural renaissance." Arena Stage is neither alone in seeking reassurance nor in its susceptibility to being reassured. We are brooding but alert. We watch anxiously.

We would be grateful if foundations responded to our real needs for general institutional support. Our hearts would beat stronger if Washington business firms came to see giving to the community's arts on a par with giving to the community's charities—something unconscionable *not* to do. If local foundations recognized their pivotal responsibility in keeping alive our city's cultural treasures, our anxiety would be much allayed. And what about a line item in the city budget for the deficits of worthy institutions? Or an endowment fund set up by rich national corporations to umbrella our nation's theater companies, as if they were sister institutions of universities and not outcast cousins?

Each of these suggestions is entirely within reason; none is outlandish. All are needed. There is a natural tendency for human endeavors to fall apart (either the cup is missing or the wine). We need a strong and passionate taking of sides in all of these areas, if Arena Stage and its companion institutions in the city we hold dear are not suddenly to spill away.

These remarks, prepared for Arena's silver anniversary celebration, struck many of the same themes as Zelda's Ralph L. Collins Memorial Lecture at Indiana University in the 1974–1975 season. [T.L.]

THE LONG REVOLUTION

(1978)

I have a snatch of wisdom, a nugget, a pearl even, stumbled-upon and shining: We must hang on to our despair. Without despair, everything is hopeless.

In the past twenty years—longer for me and a few others—we have made a revolution. And while revolutions can pulse with the joy of change and ride on the back of optimism and imagined good, the energy for them comes from despair. Despair creates anger, and anger creates energy, and energy turns things around.

The dictionary offers up a number of definitions of "revolution." I focus on two: "a sudden, radical, or complete change (as in revolution in thought)," and "a basic reorientation and reorganization (as in revolution in technology)." We engaged in both: a revolution in thought and a revolution, not in technology, but in methodology—near enough. It was despair that transformed one into the other.

Of course, everything started with thought. If the very fabric of our thought had not changed, we would not have been able to change reality. The new perception of theater that came to us had many facets and implications, and each of us emphasized something different. But the basic synapse in our thinking was simple: that theater should stop serving the function of making money, for which it has never been and never will be suited, and start serving the process of living, its revelation and shaping, for which theater is uniquely suited, for which it, indeed, exists. The new thought was that theater should be *restored to itself as a form of art.*

There's a lot of confusion about what this radical though simple thought really means. In his new book, *The Subsidized Muse: Public Support for the Arts in the United States*, Dick Netzer talks about "art qua art" but never really defines it, except to say, "the arts are generally viewed as 'merit goods,'" are "good for us," and that "their production and consumption should be encouraged by subsidy because they are meritorious." Nor is Congress or even the National Endowment for the Arts yet comfortable with the thought. They struggle to define professionalism; they use geographic and other extraneous criteria as guidelines; they blur aesthetic considerations with considerations of "availability," "enhancing the quality of life," or "increasing the multiplicity of services." They broaden definitions to include funding for activities that may be worthy but are not art.

Because of this confusion, public policy about the arts is confused. Even artists are confused.

What is an art form? When I say we wanted our theater to be about art, what exactly do I mean?

First of all, I mean that art is *something of its own and not something of something else.* It is not education; it is not social betterment. It is not about civic pride or better international relations or group therapy. It is not "merit goods." It is not *goods* of any kind. It may serve many worthy ends and, indeed, it does—all of the above and more. But it serves these ends tangentially, as spillover from itself. Art is not created for these ends and does not exist for them. It is self-serving and lonely. Self-standing and fragile. Self-defined and searching. It is what it is.

Art objectifies a private reaction to some portion of the universe. As a result, it is always personal. It originates—as do our dreams, neuroses, ideas, beliefs, as does thought itself—from within, and from within a single sensibility. It is a way of looking at reality and rendering up that vision in one medium or another. Even though theater emerges in a collective way, and sometimes as the aesthetic will of a collective, still its core is a singular vision.

The social aspects of art come from the human need to share, from our nature as gregarious and empathizing human beings. Having audiences to fill up our houses has its economic necessity, but it has a deeper psychological one. We want and need to share what we make and do as deeply as we want and need to love: "Look, Ma, no hands!" "Take a look at this, will ya! Ain't it something?" This need is at least as old as the ancient tellers of tales: "Gather around, and let me tell you how it happened."

Art is a way of knowing reality. And we want to know; it gives us pleasure and power. Art not only records civilization; it *is* civilization. It is the process of the mind knowing itself and sharing what it knows. Art exists outside of time. It is not faddy. Images may differ in different periods, but they always carry an echo, always follow a thread. Art is as persistent as human nature, because it is rooted there. Possibly, the need for truth has some physiological basis, like the need for oxygen—a necessary way of knowing.

Art mediates primary experiences through form. It, therefore, requires technique, study, training, mastery of the "rules of the game." Each art form is a special discipline, as complex and serious—with a high playfulness—as law or medicine or banking.

We have to make people understand these things. But first we have to get clear ourselves, to sustain our energy and keep ourselves on track. Then we have to explain it all to others. If we don't, the sources of national support for our revolution will drain away, channeled into things that look like, but are not, art.

A revolution in thought has a certain motion. It starts with the question: "What do I want that I haven't got?" It then moves to the next one: "What is standing in my way?" Finally: "What is to be done?" Once you answer this third question you begin the long, long labor required for that other kind of revolution, the basic reorganization and reorientation of method. In other words, you begin pulling the damn wagon back and forth across a hostile landscape.

We said we wanted theater as an art form. When the despair set in, all we had was Broadway, an industry built upon one-shot-ness, Mammon-mindedness, crisis and hysteria, lest all be lost on a single throw of the dice. We needed quietude of spirit and continuity, the freedom to fail and still go on working. We had actors stuck in long-run hits and stagnating, or not working at all. Directors and designers with limited outlets. Architectural monotony: That is, the proscenium arch and nothing else.

Our stage classics were lost to us because they couldn't support a commercial run. We had new works from established playwrights, but new playwrights couldn't get a foot in the door. There was some excitement Off-Broadway, but almost none in the rest of the country. In Washington we had no theater at all, not even road shows. The American theater was a contracting knot of insularity and predictability and the turning of a buck. With its high ticket prices, it shut itself off from the lives of all but the most well-to-do Americans and the New York City expense-account audience. We were sad and mad. We looked around for another way to organize things, and we found it.

And that is how we came to be, with our differences in style, world outlook, taste, and personality, but with unity in setup, in our needs and deepest concerns.

To sustain a revolution you have to deal, constantly and well, with lots of counter-revolutions. Alas, things evolve not in a straight line but in a spiral, or, as Lenin put it about the big one in Russia: two steps forward, one step back. Every revolution partakes of the incompleteness of all human endeavor.

Our instrument as a revolutionary alternative to the commercial theater was the nonprofit corporation, previously associated with education, science, and charity, but not art or culture. Without the nonprofit income tax code, our American theater would not exist. Being nonprofit, however, does not define us—our goals, our aims, our aesthetic, our achievements. What defines us, measures us, is our capacity to produce art. That capacity, it so happens, has come inevitably to produce deficits as well. We remain part of commerce and have to deal with all aspects of it in our working lives, because we exist in a culture that still values us too little.

As it is, our "nonprofit-commercial" theater still has to tango with that other commercial theater from which we broke, out of despair and anger, because it offers some opportunity to make ends meet. For example, The Public Theater covers sixteen percent of its expenses at its box office, nine percent from other earned income, twenty-five percent from grants and contributions, and the remaining half from *A Chorus Line* and *for colored girls* . . . Without these two Broadway productions it would not be surviving. If that represents a blurring of the purpose and function of our theaters through increasing participation in the commercial sector, then we have had this "greatness" thrust upon us.

Still, I don't produce in New York. I experience dread when "producers" come down to Washington to discover "properties" ripe for the picking and offer grudging percentages in exchange for risk, development, labor, and love, and then more often than not, turn what they saw and liked into something altogether else under the terrible pressures of Broadway production.

It behooves the arts to get their act together and talk hard with American business, the government, and the public at large about this matter of art as art, how important it is and how much commerce it takes to produce and sustain it. Perhaps when the government understands deeply that a theater is an art form and therefore dependent on a single personal vision, money for our long revolution will be made available.

However impractical, production by permanent acting company remains the method organic to theater as an art form. It remains the ideal. But it gets more difficult to hold actors together long enough to evolve the unity of style, camaraderie, and identification with common goals we so passionately want. Arena Stage has had roughly four companies in our long history, each of which eventually drifted away in response to the power and glory of commercial transfer. I grieve when we lose actors to Broadway (or TV or film), which still holds some vestigial attraction for them. Is it futile for us to want to keep them with us? Is it impossible to achieve? Should we abandon the idea? Are we at fault by not enlarging our loyalties to company actors, offering better roles, plays chosen for them, continued training? What is to be done about this troubling counter-revolution?

And while we are on the subject of actors, what is to be done about the director/producers who lead them? How are they to be developed to replace those of us now at work, when it comes time? Artistic leaders may be born, but not full-blown out of the head of Zeus. We are rich in the resources to train the talented people capable of top leadership, but we aren't doing it and, so, are wasting what can never be retrieved: human experience. We are not preparing successors to inherit the traditions of any given theater, however they may be altered in the succession. Again, art is personal, and new artistic leadership has to be continually identified and supported wherever it can be found. We must all fight for that.

We set out to create a form for theater that would enable us to insert meaning and beauty into our culture so that people could reach out and touch it simply and directly. Despite hazards and harassments, we have in our various ways done just that. Our greatest achievement has been to decentralize or make "popular"—that is, part of the lives of people all over the country—the art of the theater. It is a miracle of sorts. For not only did we have to construct the method to carry our idea, but we had to train an audience to know that they wanted to have what we wanted to give them. And that was not an easy struggle. It still goes on.

Liviu Ciulei, my director-friend from Romania's Bulandra Theatre who directed our *Hamlet* this past season, sends me what he calls "data about the typical subsidized repertory theater" in his native country. For example, his theater's personnel list: four directors, two assistant directors, three set designers, two assistant set designers, two literary managers, one librarian, seventy actors, four stage managers, two technical stage managers, two master sound technicians, two sound associates, two masters for makeup and wigs, two assistants for makeup, one hairstylist, six gentlemen tailors, six ladies' dressmakers, one shirtmaker, one hatmaker, one embroiderer, three warehouse keepers, one laundry person, thirty administrative jobs, and so on. This is just an introduction; the total company and staff number 232. The Bulandra operates two theaters, mounts eight–ten new productions a year and keeps eighteen productions in repertory. National subsidy covers all salaries and represents about two-thirds of the total budget. The rest of the budget is covered by the box office, which needs to sell eighty-seven percent of the seats to about six hundred performances per season in Bucharest (three hundred for each house) and thirty–forty performances on tour.

We do not ask for that much. Yet Liviu's letter should be required reading for those who write about the "subsidized muse" in the U.S. It should be read into the *Congressional record*. It helps me understand our fatigue, why it's so hard here to sandwich in a personal life or trip to the movies.

The dictionary labels another meaning of "revolution" obsolete: "A winding or curving form or course: twist, bend." It may be obsolete, but it rings a bell. Our "course" will continue to be a winding one. A great suppleness—as in "twist, bend"—will be demanded of us for years to come.

Sweet are the uses of despair.

Without despair, everything is hopeless. And there is still so much to be done.

From a keynote speech to Theatre Communications Group's National Conference in 1976.

BEYOND BLACK AND WHITE

For much of her career and from the vantage point of Washington, DC, a city with segregated theater spaces when Arena Stage was established in 1950, Zelda cast the civil rights struggle in Black and white terms. What now might be discussed as "equitable representation," "inclusion," or "anti-racism," she then saw as the work of "integration." In the following confidential proposal to the Arena Stage board, later edited and published in Washington's the Sunday Star, *Zelda uses terminology of that day—a year after the founding of the seminal Negro Ensemble Company—to talk about the deeper, more vital artistry she envisioned from a fully integrated company. Her later writings, including all those that follow, replace the word "Negro" with "Black" or "African-American." "Integration" would, by 1991, become "cultural diversity." Of course, in 1968 many people had already adopted this different language, but for whatever reasons, Zelda had not yet done so. When two decades after she quotes this earlier essay, she rewrites herself, using the term "Black." After much thought and conversation, I've kept her original language here, not only for historical accuracy, but as an unvarnished guide to Zelda's own evolution within the profession she pioneered and the era and predominantly white culture of which she was a product. She would want nothing less than the truth. That said, I apologize to any readers who are troubled by this now rejected nomenclature. [T.L.]*

TOWARD A DEEPENING AESTHETIC
(1968)

A VIEW ABOUT VITALITY

In some sense all channels for large purposes are woefully unworthy of their task. A theater institution is not exempt from this humbling truth. However, since progress is only in the process, there is nothing better to do than to stay as alive as possible to the forces at work and get on with the job.

This "staying as alive as possible" seems to me the key to survival and growth. In an art institution it is surely the key to unique, personal expression and the avoidance of copycat formulae and hardening of the arteries. It may also help us avoid the trap of eclecticism, which is the death of all art, especially art made by institutions.

Harold Rosenberg deals brilliantly with these problems in "Parable of American Painting," an essay in *The Tradition of the New*. Though the essay is about modern painting, it is also a parable of theaters and men and institutions in general.

I recall in my grammar-school history book a linecut illustration which shows the Redcoats marching abreast through the woods, while from behind trees and rocks naked Indians and coonskinned trappers pick them off with musket balls . . . The Redcoats march in file through the New World wilderness, with its disorder of rocks, underbrush and sharpshooters, as if they were on a parade ground or on the meadows of a classical European battlefield and one by one they fall and die.

I was never satisfied that the Redcoats were simply stupid or stubborn, wooden copies of King George III. In my opinion what defeated them was their skill. They were such extreme European professionals, even the Colonials among them, they did not see the American trees. Their too highly perfected technique forbade them to acknowledge such chance topographical phenomena. According to the assumptions of their military art, by which their senses were controlled, a battlefield had to have a certain appearance and structure, that is to say, a style. Failing to qualify, these American trees and rocks from which come such deadly but meaningless stings are overlooked. The Redcoats fall, expecting at any moment to enter upon the true battlefield, the soft rolling greenswards prescribed by the canons of their craft and presupposed by every principle that makes warfare intelligible to the soldier of the eighteenth century.

The difficulty of the Redcoats was that they were in the wrong place . . .

Institutions and movements atrophy. Theaters wither away or become stale, when contact with reality is weakened and when imitation or repetition substitutes for direct experience and constant improvisation. Theaters in America face that danger at this very moment. They are like the Redcoats in Rosenberg's description. They are marching according to the "canons of their craft" and do not see what is behind the trees.

WHERE DOES ONE LOOK?

One looks back and forth between the art itself and outer reality. A theater must have one foot inside the building and one foot outside.

It must suffer this awkwardness in the knowledge that the posture is a necessary one for genuine creativity. A theater must penetrate the mysteries of its own art and perceive the hovering phenomena of its own particular time and place. It must take the largest possible view of its destiny, not the smallest, or it will soon become, as many young theaters already have, an administrative machine for the output of "plays."

One must stay as alive as possible, yes. One must stay "tuned in" and unafraid of solutions that have only one, *singular* application. Arena Stage is almost twenty years old and has faced the dilemma of fresh perception more than once.

For a thing to become what it is capable of being, power must be present. Indeed, the Greek words for power (bia) and life (bios) reflect their essential relationship: Power is basic to life. Without power, life cannot become what it must be.

A theater, to serve its highest artistic function, must be a power-producing agency. It must be an enabler, a facilitator of human growth. And it must release power by means of what it is: its own nature, its own self-definition. In short, a theater uses: (1) the artist; (2) molded experience—that is, the play shaped into event; and (3) the audience. If it fails to develop these forces to their fullest potential and to create the most powerful interplay among them, it has not yet become what it can be. (We have no voltmeter, no Geiger counter, but we know what we mean.)

Everything becomes relevant: the environment that allows artists self-direction, initiative and personal growth; training programs undertaken for self-perfection; a repertory whose continuing themes relate to what people, both inside and outside the theater, really think and feel; a system of production (such as rotating repertory) that keeps aliveness and interchange at its peak; a rehearsal process that maximizes personal expressiveness within the necessary discipline and emphasizes direct rather than repeated experience; the highest development of all the components—playwriting, design, the management of production; the arrangement of architecture and space as a way of defining the relationship between audience and event; and, finally, the arch under which all takes place, the conscious channeling of all this energy, choice, and process outward, so that the theater's ultimate power—to change the environment and man himself—can be realized.

The more a thing knows its own mind, the more alive it becomes. The total release of the power contained within a theater occurs only when the three elements—the artist, the event, the audience—know what is in them to be known and can share it.

AESTHETIC POWER AND THE MOMENT

Where are we at Arena Stage? When we look around, inside and out, what do we see?

Arena's record has been, all in all, a good one. A way of work has evolved over the years that, without being rigid or over-codified, seems to release the life locked behind the words of the script. A theater structure of architectural distinction, designed to meet the needs of an existing company and make a strong statement to make about the collective nature of theater, has been put up and paid for. We have, little by little, gathered around us an audience with a real, rather than opportunistic, relationship to the theater. Our personnel tend to want to stay, because they tend to expand rather than shrivel in this environment. A company and "company style" have emerged. "Artistic standards," sometimes excellent, never fall below a certain level and, considering the lack of subsidy, are phenomenal. Our repertory is satisfactory-to-challenging—a constant, often significant examination of the human condition via plays that speak to our own age and audience. After eighteen years, three homes, and a hundred-and-fifty productions, Arena looks and feels young. And healthy, with houses over ninety-percent filled and a deficit no bigger than it should be.

When I look around, however, beyond our too-perfected technique and what Rosenberg calls the "canons of our craft," a deep, visceral intuition tells me that the power of our art is being blunted, deadened, and caged. We are, like the Redcoats, in the wrong place.

Washington, DC, the nation's capital city, is the first city in the country to become predominantly (sixty-three-percent) Negro. Its school system is over ninety-percent Negro. Yet we have no Negro actors in our permanent company, and attendance by Negro members of the community—except for plays like *The Great White Hope*, *Blood Knot* and *Othello*, which have Negro actors onstage—is practically nil. The Kerner Commission on Civil Disorders' recent report concluded that "our nation is moving toward two societies, one Black, one white—separate and unequal." It warned against the development, in our major cities, of an urban "apartheid." This is the single most pressing social phenomenon of our day and, with isolated exceptions, absent from our stage. One would think it did not exist.

The Negro's struggle for power—economic power, business power, political, intellectual, psychological, *human* power—foundationally affects his relationships with other Negroes, with whites, and with himself. This struggle reverberates through contemporary American life. Each of us feels its vibrations every day. And yet we come into our theater at night as if into an unreal world: A white audience sits around a stage upon which a white company tells "sad tales of the death of Kings." Surely, we are in the wrong place! And it is not a geographical dislocation; it is a profound *aesthetic dislocation.* The style of our art is cut off from its source.

In *Tell It Like It Is*, provocative Negro columnist Chuck Stone remembers:

> My minister in Hartford always told the story of a little boy who used to race the old trolley cars pulled by horses. The boy would run along for a while with the trolley car, sprint ahead, and then drop back to taunt the motorman. "What say, Mr. Motorman, can't you go any faster?" "Yes, son, I can," replied the motorman, "but I've got to stay with the car."

We are all—all the theaters—simply staying with the car. By doing so, we deny to our work a dimension of tension, abrasion, contemporaneity, connection, immediacy, aliveness—a dimension of power.

Arena Stage proposes to leave the car and try running it alone. It proposes to enlarge its present company to include a substantial number of Negro actors. And it proposes, for a minimum of three years—or as long as the self-definition and self-determination of Black people and the relationship between Black and white people is the most pervasive circumstance of our lives—to select a repertory that makes organic—aesthetic—sense for an interracial company. In this way we can best discover and release the power within our art. In this way we can deal, spontaneously and directly, with what is behind the trees.

THE PLAN

First of all, there is no sociological motive behind it; the motivation is not to employ Negro actors for their own good or out of white guilt or social responsibility. These are worthwhile reasons, but they don't enter here. Nor do we have in mind enticing the middle-class Negro dollar into the box office till. Conversely, there is no polemic involved. The social environment is a character in all significant plays, and the examination of human values is at the core of dramatic experience. But the notion here is not to reroute Arena Stage onto the road marked "Protest Drama." We may protest, we may affirm, or we may simply investigate. All modes of dramatic expression remain open to us.

We are also not interested in warping the thematic of any play by forced interracial casting. In *The Iceman Cometh*, which we are now rehearsing, Joe Mott is a Negro and his "pipe dream," as opposed to the pipe dreams of his bar mates, is tied to that fact. If the play were cast interracially, one would rip O'Neill's tapestry apart, for Joe's inner life is uniquely defined by illusions of acceptance into the white man's world. We are not on the moon, and we must not cast as though we are. We are in the here and now. The fabric of realistic human relationships must be handled with great sensitivity or belief will be shattered. The Black-white relationship is too central to our life to pretend that it is not.

The plan is not conceived of as eternal. It is rooted in the terrain and will need constant tuning as the terrain shifts. It seems likely, though, that some extended form of it will emerge as permanent. Our national life is finding its identity within the interrelationships of Black and white people, and a living theatrical art can hardly do other than follow the example of the life it seeks to illuminate.

THE ACTOR

We approached the plan by exclusion and negation—what it is not. Now we should examine it from the opposite angle and see how it adds to, deepens, and enriches the art of the theater by means of the artist, the audience, the stage event.

The art of the theater concerns us first. Any single Negro actor is an individual and, therefore, not like anyone else, a state he has in common with any white actor. He is also an artist with the desire to use his talent in the appropriate way: to share his human insights by demonstrating human actions on the stage. This, too, he has in common with any white actor.

But every human being is what he[1] has been born and what he has experienced. We are each a constellation of traits of personality, mind, body, and behavior, some there in the cradle, some picked up along the way, and we are what happens to us. When two people meet, two pasts meet; we encounter one another encumbered. Surely the Negro actor, coming into power at this moment of history, knowing exclusion from the dominant white culture and therefore having a special view of it, has the capacity for a unique and particular expressiveness on the stage.

The movement of the Negro adult now taking place within American life is cataclysmic. It offers the artist, who comes to grips with our moment, catalytic opportunities for emotional confrontation and human change. If Negro playwrights can find their audience. If Negro actors have the talent and opportunity for sufficient training and experience. All the stuff of art and life is presently at hand and ready to be shared: loneliness, anger, guilt, love, paranoia, hate, derision, need, role-playing, duplicity, hope, failure, treachery, injustice, randomness, emergence, frustration, despair—the whole kit and caboodle of being alive.

The fact of Blackness is something white people simply cannot feel or know. It is like no other exclusion. "Wherever he goes, the Negro remains a Negro," says Frantz Fanon in *Black Skin, White Masks*, written from his experience as a Negro and psychiatrist in the Antilles. Fanon dissects the psycho-existential created in the Negro by virtue of his Blackness; by analyzing it, he seeks to destroy it. Fanon's book describes the odyssey of a human soul from the deep-

1. As with the language of race, I have let stand Zelda's distinctly mid-twentieth-century use of pronouns, specifically what might be called the "universal" he. While Zelda often referred to directors and artistic directors as "she," as late as the sixties, she still defaulted to the masculine for actors, playwrights, and others. In her final years I found her increasingly curious about the range of pronouns and nonbinary gender designations entering common usage. [T.L.]

est darkness into the light, the widest arc of human experience. It is an Everyman story of neurotic personality recovering into health, a journey most of us have not taken and from which we have everything to learn.

When we exclude the Negro actor from our stages and company, we not only deprive him as an artist of the opportunity to use his talents and to grow, we deprive our work of a mine of human experience that could only enrich it and shake it up. We deprive our work of tonalities and reverberations and attitudes toward white society that may be benevolent or not, that may be abrasive or not, but that are bound to be particular, deeply felt, and urgent. We deprive our work of a degree of motion, confrontation, personal exposure, contact, friction, union—of a continuously alive dialectic of change through experience—that a company of both white and Black actors could achieve, but that one of only white actors is less likely to. We deprive our work of complexity, immediacy, verticality, and learning. We deprive it of power.

THE AUDIENCE

Without the audience as terminus, the art of the actor—the art of the theater itself—does not exist. I have my own version of the old scientific riddle about whether, if no one is there to hear it, a tree that falls in the forest produces a sound: That is, when the tree falls, what is the listener (assuming he is there) called upon to do?

When a play happens, the listener, the audience, becomes a primary doer. He has an urgent and inexorable task to perform: He must answer back—not always out loud, but as good as. He has to catch the ball of action and return it to the players in a shape changed by his own reaction. Based on the rules of the game we call theater, the audience must keep up this *play* of reciprocal connection for the whole evening. Because change can come about only through direct experience and not through passive watching, it is this very rule that causes change in him.

Audiences don't just come to see our work, they are a part of it. The nature and composition of the audience has a great deal to do with the "success"—that is, the degree of aliveness, expressiveness, tension, depth, and energy—of a performance. Which is to say, the audience has a great deal to do with whether or not a performance achieves its power as an art. Actors know this by instinct and experience. "What kind of house is it?" they ask. Not the stage event alone nor the audience alone, then, but the two together in the moment-to-moment life they invent and share: a spiraling excitement of discovery and gift.

Homogeneous audiences, who connect with a play in a predictably uniform way, with one pervading attitude, are anathema to the pulse of a living art. It isn't coincidental that, in all its years of history, Arena seemed most alive while we were playing *The Great White Hope* and *Blood Knot* this year, both with interracial casts, both drawing an audience more diverse than usual with regard to race, income level, age, education, occupation, human experience, preoccupations and interests, patterns of entertainment, and expectations about theater and life in general.

Certainly, the sight of an all-white audience in a theater that professes engagement with life outside its walls—in an urban city with a majority Negro population—evokes Disneyland. It goes beyond the preposterous to the gut of art itself. Said Henry James: "Art lives upon discussion, upon experiment, upon curiosity, upon variety of attempt, upon exchange of views and the comparison of standpoints." He did not have in mind, of course, the "conversation" between audience and performance, but he might have. The human dialogue. It is the silent but essential process for the making of a pulsating theatrical art. One can almost "hear" it going on—not only between play and audience, but also among the audience themselves. It is the real movement taking place—the movement between men's minds.

Nothing could serve the theatrical art more profoundly than the presence of a heterogeneous, diversified, interracial audience. Our American theaters have already suffered hugely, deep within the core of their work, for the lack of it.

THE PLAYS

If a theater seeks Negro audiences for the enlivening of its work, it should integrate its acting company. The key to the Negro community is the Negro performer. The Negro community will find out very quickly that the theater knows it is there, knows what it, as a community, is doing and thinking about, and that its interest and participation are welcome.

Plays that "speak to Negro concerns" come second. These concerns may be specific goals: greater representation in the political structure of America; more control of economic capital; accessibility to education and training; job advancement without discrimination; the creation of Black community institutions; desegregated housing economically within reach; the achievement of excellence in a given area through racial unity, etc. Still, the overriding, all-embracing concern, which contains and compels all others, is the emergence of the Negro into full humanity, into the entire possibility of every man, woman, or child's human power. For all its special frustration and historic particularity, this is a universal striving, dramatized in world stage literature from the Greeks until this present day.

It would be a parochial mistake to think that the Negro people in Washington would only come to the theater if we did *A Raisin in the Sun* or *The Blacks* (although we might do them, as well as new works by Negro playwrights). Furthermore, the "Negro community" is not monolithic. *The Slave* and *The Toilet* by LeRoi Jones might find as many Negro detractors as white, even though Mr. Jones is a Black playwright.

One must guard against glib assumptions. Bertolt Brecht wrote and directed his own plays and even evolved a unique acting style, all designed to draw into his theater the German working class in the hope they would be incited to remake the world they lived in. But the working class stayed away. Brecht's audience was, instead, made up of artists, intellectuals, and the educated bourgeoisie. We must keep reminding ourselves that the power is within the art itself. We must use that art with full vigor and with full faith. We must not undercut its power by picturing other people in our own image, rather than as they really are. We must not predict too much about too many things.

Still, certain plays suggest themselves for an integrated audience and creative casting from an interracial company. Classic or modern, they will tend to be plays of size and scope, rather than small, realistic works centered around family life. More often than not, they will veer away from the naturalistic, their gaze turned outward. They will be plays of major repercussion: classics whose modern implications are inescapable (*The Bacchae, Orestes, Troilus and Cressida, Coriolanus, Major Barbara*); contemporary plays whose psychology and circumstance illuminate the human condition at large, rather than special sectors of it (not *The Tenth Man* or *Juno and the Paycock* so much as *The Caucasian Chalk Circle, Of Mice and Men,* and *A Memory of Two Mondays*). Multiracial casting won't work as well with plays too tightly welded to their own period (*A Doll's House, The Importance of Being Earnest*), but will suit plays that constitute "models" for reality (*The Good Woman of Setzuan, The Visit, Camino Real, Waiting for Godot, The Trial, The Balcony*).

The creative casting of Negro and white actors in the right repertory should help us to explode the theater event and, in this one place at least, connect the work onstage with the reality outside. New images should pop out at us, new understandings, new connections—all from new combinations. Relationships will gain dimension, revealing complexities that might have passed us by. A motivation deepens or contradicts itself, shifts its ground. A conflict becomes more ambiguous, or less so. Tensions already in the play erupt with yet another force. We are given new eyes with which to see old plays, and meanings from the past zoom straight into the present day. Perspective deepens, widens, curves back upon itself. The stage holds all the world.

Excerpted from "Confidential Plan," March 1968, later published in revised form in *Sunday Star*, Washington, DC, June 30, 1968. Both versions were drawn upon here.

CASTING FOR A DIFFERENT TRUTH
(1988)

Theater belongs to the world of the imagination. It is no one place; it is every place and any place—an empty space to be filled in any way we wish. We have always had it. It is as old as our curiosities, our fears, our hungers, our need to understand and control our lives. It is a game we organize quite deliberately and play out with a proper sense of seriousness and ceremony to discover what our dreams are telling us, why we have done what we have done, where our feelings could take us, and how we can overcome our enemies from within and without.

It is a universal game: Everybody believes in it in one form or another, and grown-ups believe in it the same way children do ("You be daddy, I'll be mommy, we have dinner, then you get mad, and I . . ."), that is, we believe in it even though we know it's all make-believe. We believe in it because we want to, because we need to. At the very center of the theater event is the will to imagine—both for the actor and the audience. "Think, when we talk of horses, that you see them," Shakespeare's Prologue to *Henry V* tells us. "Suppose within the girdles of these walls . . ." SUPPOSE!

Suppose that there were a fine acting company made up of white actors and Black actors and Hispanic actors and Asian-American actors; women and men; young actors, older, and old; deaf actors and the hearing; actors with other special characteristics. And suppose that one assigned roles freely, without prediction from history or from one's old habits of thought. What if one took nontraditional casting as far as one could? Suppose the premise of this theater company, its founding principle, was that the human spirit could be embodied in unpredictable and newly imagined ways, astonishing the spectator and revealing meanings never before anticipated, sloughing off old ways of looking at things and opening them up to their very heart.

Suppose, in some universal space, the actors could strip private identities to the core, lose the accidental shells of personality, date of birth, gender, and national origin, and become purely human— thought answering thought, feeling responding to feeling, action following directly upon intention.

Anthropologists tell us that we sense our belonging first to our species, second to our gender, and last to our race. And that we would give up these attributes, if we were forced to, in reverse order. We are all more simply human than otherwise, and isn't it that which speaks out, in the end, in the theater? In every culture, there is a resemblance between the face of anguish and the face of ecstasy. In the theater we recognize—re-learn, re-remember, re-know—our common past and joined fate.

I can imagine such a company, and it excites me. I can imagine it, though I wouldn't yet know how to make it real. Surely it is not an abstract possibility. A thrilling aspect of Peter Brook's *The Mahabharata* is that actors come from eighteen countries and speak English in their various individual accents. Here is a beginning model for the kind of company one could envision as an ultimate form of nontraditional theatrical expression.

Every play is an archaeological dig that tells or suggests how people lived their lives, what their mode of thought was, what gods they believed in, how they made their money, what books they read, what they ate, sat on, and wore. Plays are temporal and age-rooted, and for that reason go in and out of focus for the culture that looks back upon them. They are now "dated," now "relevant," showing themselves this way and that, like phases of the moon.

Casting a role is giving a specific living and breathing persona to the imagined figure who exists in a specific social, political, and philosophic imagined world. The tapestry of events and relationships is created out of the actors/characters of this world. Once you have cast this play, you have more or less predicted the outcome of the event, for you have bestowed life upon the characters.

Besides choosing the play itself, the single most important creative act of the producer and director is to "fill the roles." For once those two have removed themselves, the actor and the audience will be left to share the implications of each other's presence within the tale enacted between them. The actor and the audience, then, share a highly political act of communication and empathy: They speak to each other, through and under the lines of the play, of their daily lives and of what they want to come of them, for themselves and for their children. Nontraditional casting in the end becomes a matter not of employment, but of politics and of art.

John Kani is appearing now as Othello at Johannesburg's Market Theatre, South Africa's first professional production of *Othello* with a Black actor in the title role—an example of nontraditional casting with a twist! He plays to an almost all-white audience of 520 a night, and it comes as no surprise that in a country that prohibited interracial marriage until two years ago, Othello and Desdemona's first passionate stage embrace briefly but palpably startles theatergoers.

Not very long ago the spectacle of Kani kissing blond and fair-skinned actress Joanna Weinberg full on the mouth would have triggered a national debate and probably violent demonstrations by white supremacist groups. Indeed, Kani recalled, when he appeared in Strindberg's *Miss Julie* at the Market just two years ago, half the audience walked out as he put his hand on the thigh of the white actress playing the leading role. The next night, Kani needed the protection of security officers to leave the theater safely and, subsequently, the government curtailed the run of the play. While one can doubt that two years have changed fundamental attitudes so radically, production photos of *Othello*'s racial intimacy now appear on the review pages of South African newspapers without a murmur of indignation.

Howard Sackler's master play *The Great White Hope* caused a similar—though much milder—kind of ripple when it opened at Arena Stage twenty years ago. Basing the play on the career of Jack Johnson, who in 1908 became the world's first Black heavyweight champion, and on the subsequent search for a "white hope" to topple him and redeem the Caucasian race, Sackler tossed upon the stage a microcosm of American attitudes on race. With James Earl Jones as Jack Jefferson, the character based on Johnson, a figure both heroic and personal, and Jane Alexander as his white love Ellie, a woman of heartbreak strength, the play rocked audiences in Washington and later, in a shorter and more melodramatic version, in New York. Jefferson is picked up on a Mann Act violation in the midst of one of the most romantic, most tender love scenes I have ever watched onstage. The audience audibly reacted when the lights came up on Jefferson and Ellie in bed, and several of the actors felt the need to have their phone numbers unlisted to eliminate harassing calls.

The social climate changes. Every reaction is special to its time and place. There is an identifiable "feel" and even sound for what passes between the actor and audience as the world that lives in the play meets the world that the audience brings in from the outside. The issue of nontraditional casting derives its electricity and, yes, its complexity, from the contemporaneity of the act of theater. The ideas behind it, rightly, are being examined and discussed, for theater casting policies have not kept up with American life, much less led the way.

Twenty years ago, I wrote in a grant application that "the creative casting of Black[1] and white actors in the right repertory should help us to explode the theater event and, in this one place at least, connect the work onstage with the reality outside. New images should pop out at us, new understandings, new connections—all from new combinations . . . We are given new eyes with which to see old plays, and meanings from the past zoom straight into the present day."

One wonders what Arena's experiment in the late sixties with a totally integrated acting company would yield today. For a variety of reasons, this experiment was not successful, despite goodwill on all sides and a number of productions that were, as I remember them, both theatrically vivid and revealing human. I recall with pride and warmth Frank Silvera's Lear and Mary Alice's vulnerable Cordelia with Ned Beatty as the Fool; and Olivia Cole's tempestuous Stepdaughter in *Six Characters in Search of an Author* (the "second family" was a cast with Black actors) opposite Richard Venture as the Father, alternating as the Leading Man in a rotating repertory schedule with Robert Prosky. The accompanying third production,

1. Zelda uses the word "Negro" in the earlier grant proposal she mentions but has rewritten it as "Black" here, twenty years later. [T.L.]

Brecht and Weill's *Threepenny Opera*, missed somehow, but the idea of an integrated society for this work has always seemed just right to me. The idea for the company began to pale with *Marat/Sade* and *Indians*—actors and audience drifted away; the center would not hold.

Was the idea ahead of its time? What variants would make it work today? Should the aesthetic have been based on "blind" casting (casting without regard to color) rather than on the casting of Black and white actors in a conscious manner meant to be creative? Were Black actors then more concerned than they are now with new Black plays and burgeoning Black theater companies? Is a Black audience any more interested in a traditional Western repertoire (even with an integrated cast) than it was twenty years ago? Would mature Black actors prefer to pursue, as the majority of white actors do, opportunities in film and TV, revisiting the live theater only when a role is particularly compelling? Do young, Black, would-be actors see enough future for themselves in the American theater to warrant spending the time and money to train for it?

Looking back, is our earlier concept of repertoire for an integrated company out of date? At the time of that company, around 1968, James Earl Jones said in an interview, "If I walk onstage in a part where race is not supposed to be an issue, and the play is not broad enough in scope to support me, it doesn't work. I did Lenny in *Of Mice and Men* . . . and it worked perfectly. He is a classic loner. Only plays that are large in scope can be appropriately integrated now." Is this still true? Today, would we "believe" James Earl Jones as Willy Loman or Big Daddy? Have times changed?

In the same interview, Jones suggested that white actors should at some time play Black roles so that they can find out what it feels like to be Black. What kind of personal transformation might occur for a white actress if she were to play Lena Younger, the mother in Lorraine Hansberry's *A Raisin in the Sun*? Or would this casting be creative only for the individual actress and blur the racial issues central to the theme?

What about women in men's roles when women occupy such "roles" in society? A female Willy Loman? One has seen the exquisite performances of men as women in the Japanese Noh dramas, roles that are inherited from their fathers and studied for years in every minute gesture and nuance. Shakespeare wrote his plays to be performed all by men. Several women have played Hamlet, Dame Judith Anderson and Sarah Bernhardt, among them.

But nontraditional casting poses a different question. Can Willy Loman become Wilhelmina or Wanda Loman without destroying the fabric of the play? How large are our imaginations? *Death of a Salesman* is a family play and contains profound information about primal relationships (mother and son, father and son, mother and father, sibling rivalry) as do all family plays—*Oedipus* or *King Lear* or *A Raisin in the Sun*. It centers on a family in a particular culture and the roles that different members of the family play. *Salesman* speaks about the American value system—about selling and about selling one's self, about America as a nation of consumers who are losing touch with the land, and about lying. Its point of view and primary images are male, for its roots are in American business created by American men.

If I could accept Wanda as Willy, perhaps I would have achieved the furthest reaches of my humanity. I would concur that gender is a secondary characteristic of being human. I would have torn myself from my aesthetic viewpoint: that plays contain complex information about the lives that give birth to them. I would be lying if I said I had yet arrived at either of these two points, though they are worth considerable thought.

Another interesting question: "Should actors be cast on the basis of talent only?" I think the answer to that one is "Yes." Quickly adding, not necessarily on the basis of evolved and mature talent, of ripe and visible talent. No latent gift should go untapped. The responsibility of a training program is first to be able to recognize talent in the bud and, then, to organize a curriculum, faculty, and environment that will bring It forth. At the same time, producers and directors—especially of companies—are responsible for the evolution, the development and growth, of artists. They must provide experiences—roles as well as continued training—that require and stimulate growth. This is especially true for young, minority actors who otherwise might never find their place in the American theater.

The growth of our actors ultimately benefits the audience and the art. When the individual goes to the edges of his or her own ability, it spurs forward leaps of creativity in the group as a whole.

Published in *American Theatre*, May 1988.

A PROGRAM FOR CHANGE
(1989)

CONTEXT

In the year 2000, a third of the population will belong to minority groups. Within that century, minorities will become the majority population of our country. Of the next 20 million people to join the job market, only 3.6 million—18%—will likely be native-born white males. While, at the same time, skill shortages rather than job shortages are likely to become the dominant employment problem.

I have kept an informal file over the past year on issues relating to the nonparticipation of minorities in the various endeavors of our national life, a subject that vitally interests me both as human and as theater worker. I've done no special research, just clipped articles from the two newspapers I read, the *New York Times* and the *Washington Post*, and here and there from other popular publications. The file is now four inches thick. And the documentation is overwhelming and heartbreaking.

A study done by the University of California at Los Angeles in 1982 shows that 30% of Hispanic[1] college students and 41% of Black

1. As elsewhere, I have stayed with Zelda's own—history-bound—terminology for race and ethnicity, even as it evolves over the years and in these pages. [T.L.]

students, as opposed to 61% of white students, got degrees. In addition, the number of Black male undergraduates continues a decade-long decline even as enrollments increase for Black women; the number of Black high school graduates going on to college declined from 34% to 26% in 1985. In teacher-education programs, the teachers for elementary school level are 90% white, for secondary schools 92% white; in our foreign service there are only 6 Black ambassadors out of 150 worldwide. The boardrooms and the rosters of CEOs in corporate America; the list of senior partners of law firms; the ranks of PhDs in law, medicine, language, and science; the number of homeowners in nonsegregated residential areas all show a pattern of exclusion and/or of nonparticipation for reasons that can be discerned: racism, poverty, the "curse of low expectations," the breakdown of the family, the cycle of drugs and crime.

When Jesse Jackson proposed that Blacks henceforth be officially called "African-Americans," Black columnist William Raspberry found it evident of "despair" and a "renewed sense of our outsideness." He sensed "a new line of racism popping up," as evidenced in the Howard Beach incident,[2] outbreaks of racial hostility on college campuses, and the continued failure of whites and members of minority groups to have much to do with each other outside work.

Everywhere, but everywhere, there is a deep awareness of this one, single, fundamental, overriding fact of our future: the ever-increasing growth rate of minority populations as against their disproportionate underrepresentation in our institutional life and, especially, in the echelons of influence and power. What interests me, beyond the pervasive recognition of this fact, is how our institutions attempt to do something about it—if not out of conscience, compassion, and good citizenship, then for reasons of economic survival and the perpetuation of these institutions.

For example, a growing number of schools are trying to attract more Hispanic-Americans, recruiting tools ranging from rock videos featuring prominent Hispanic-Americans to dormitory floors set aside for Hispanic students. Miguel A. Nevarez, president of Pan-

2. In the early morning of December 20, 1986, two Black men whose car had broken down in the Howard Beach section of Queens, New York, were beaten by a group of white men. One of the beaten men, Michael Griffith, was killed by a car as he tried to flee.

American University in Edinburg, Texas, said, "It doesn't take too much imagination to realize that this is the future workforce. Someone will have to keep the Social Security checks alive." Last March, two thousand educators gathered in Washington, DC, for the National Conference on Race and Ethnicity in American Higher Education. The major theme: the plight of Blacks on all-white campuses. The major worry: the coming shortage of minority professionals to do the nation's work. At the private Walden Club on the top floor of a downtown office building in Chattanooga, Tennessee, May 2, 1988, several of the city's financial movers and shakers huddled over drinks. The topic: third-grade geography. American business has reached out and adopted individual schools, has provided scholarship incentives for good marks and graduation, and, indeed, has now begun to reach in and shape the very curriculum itself—these are just a few creative instances of comingling the impulse for good with the need to create a pool of workers who can propel tomorrow's technology and, of course, its profits.

It isn't yet clear that the responses will be sufficient to answer the flood of need, displacement, fear, and anger that minorities are experiencing. It is encouraging that selected university, community, and political leaders, as well as psychiatrists, church leaders, authors, journalists, and futurists, seem to share an understanding that, if public policy is to change, it must change by deep and real revision in the institutions through which we lead our lives: the place of learning, of child-rearing, of work, of worship, and—dare I say it?—the institutions where we examine and celebrate our lives in the presence of other members of our community—the art place.

A German radical—whose name I have forgotten—wrote of "the long march through the institutions" as inevitable for deep and lasting social change. I agree. There isn't any other way for the peaceful in-gathering of the human tribe in all its gorgeous variety but the way of the institution. For a member of the now-white majority, the only response to minority exclusion and disengagement is a multicultural one. At the same time, of course, we institutional leaders of the majority must acknowledge, support, and even sponsor parallel movements for the creation of minority institutions that are separate from ours and carved out from within or away from our own examples.

My whole life led me to these thoughts and this need to cause change at Arena Stage, of course, but the immediate impetus was my five years as chair of the Graduate Acting Program at New York University. I found that I could cause major change there by affecting a few individuals. By encouraging and finding subsidy for a small number of talented minority students—four or five a year—I could influence the whole field and the flow of other young actors into the program. This success inspired me to look for a way, using the greater resources and reach of Arena, to revamp our institutional life and bring it into line with the needs and realities of today. The plan is very specific, geared to providing opportunity and training that can help transform individuals and, therefore, segments of the society; I believe it is simple, doable, and imperative.

THE PROGRAM[3]

Arena Stage wishes to embark on a four-year, five-part program to address one of the nation's most urgent concerns in the area of theater. Located in the nation's capital, with a population of 70.3% Black, 2.8% Hispanic, and 1.05% Asian (1980 figures), Arena has become increasingly aware of its failure and, indeed, the general failure of American nonprofit theaters in urban centers to have sufficient multicultural representation on its stages, in its audience, among its personnel. For us, this cultural apartheid has come to feel artificial and false, to isolate us from our community, and to deprive the creative process itself of reality. We are sure it must be so for other theaters in other cities as well, and that a change in one of them will have reverberant meaning for the others.

We also feel deeply the necessity to attract into the theater young members of minority groups to whom it might never occur to search for a career there. There is today a severe shortage of trained minority arts administrators, for example, and hardly any trained minority

3. While the voice of these remarks is distinctly Zelda's, the proposal-like form and language of the next sections, I suspect, were written in collaboration with other staff members—specifically development/fundraising staffers—at Arena. Though I have edited all of it liberally, I felt it important to preserve at least the outline, if not the finances, of the plan for Arena. [T.L.]

technicians—not to mention directors, designers, literary managers, producers, or actors who are trained to perform in the classical repertory. Talented minority professionals don't emerge because they see no place for themselves; there is no place for them because they haven't emerged. It's necessary to break into this cycle by hiring qualified minority group members whenever possible, but also to create for the young real incentives to enter the field and real training opportunities.

We believe that the following program for increased participation of ethnic minorities in the theater can have perceivable effect on the field in a fairly short period of time. Our intentions are:

1. **To launch a Fellows Program.** Each year approximately ten talented young people from minority groups would be identified and assigned to an appropriate area of the theater—acting, directing, design, dramaturgy, producing, stage management, technical theater, public relations and marketing, business management, box office, and house management. Identified through local and national community and educational institutions, they would train and work under the personal supervision of Arena's top creative and management staff and could spend time in adjacent areas of interest. They could stay for two years if warranted. Fellowships would be awarded in the amount of $10,000.

2. **To produce large scale Black or other minority work and to undertake further nontraditional casting of classical and contemporary Western drama.** Next year, we plan to produce one of the Federal Theatre Project plays—*Big White Fog* by Theodore Ward or *Stevedore* by George Sklar. *Big White Fog* has to be cast specifically by color, as the issues revolve around the racial discrimination practiced by Black people among themselves. Each of these plays is very large, and the budgetary implications of these choices are clear to us.

3. **To evolve through training and rehearsal techniques a unity of style and a common artistic vocabulary among a company of eighteen to twenty members from various backgrounds.** After an intensive preseason training

period, trainers would remain on a part-time basis for the rest of the season.

4. To add to our staff a director from a minority group to serve as Artistic Associate and participate on the highest level of artistic planning for the selection of repertory, the formation of the acting company, and the assembling of artistic personnel. The Artistic Associate would direct one or several of the productions each year and nurture young minority playwrights.

5. To hire a Program Coordinator from a minority group to administer the Fellows Program, both in the recruitment phase and, once underway, within the institution, including helping to place people at the end of their training.

BACKGROUND

As it approaches its fortieth birthday in 1990, Arena Stage feels qualified to undertake the complex, elusive, and challenging program outlined here. We have already begun. Over the past two years, Arena has made strong moves to turn things around, to reflect more nearly the concerns of the population among whom it lives. By its choice of repertory, the engagement of artistic talent and of several Black members of the community in available staff positions, and the formation of a Community Outreach Advisory Committee, as well as extended marketing and promotional efforts, Arena has been able, in a surprisingly short time, to initiate change in community perception and participation—to engage with people who thought that Arena Stage held nothing for them.

Last season, we presented the Yale Repertory Theatre's production of August Wilson's *Joe Turner's Come and Gone*, Lloyd Richards directing; Lorraine Hansberry's *Les Blancs*, Hal Scott directing; and in our new Stage Four series for new American plays and playwrights, Ron Milner's *Checkmates*, Woodie King, Jr., directing. These productions plus the gospel musical *Abyssinia* last summer and *Playboy of the West Indies* by Mustapha Matura, which just closed, both directed by a young, Black director, Tazewell Thompson, have brought in primarily Black audiences, several of these productions playing to 95%

capacity. All were artistically and, with the exception of a negative review of *Les Blancs* from our one major critic, critically successful. Over 28% of all roles were filled by minority actors, principally Black. While multicultural attendance at plays from the Western repertory has not significantly increased, even though we have moved strongly into nontraditional casting, we expect that pattern will improve over time.

Otherwise, the rewards of this turnaround have been high and heady. The spirit within the theater is enlivened. The bonds with our community seem tightened. We feel we are on the right road and have a strong chance for success.

Arena has originated and presented many Black works over its thirty-eight-year production history and employed a large number of Black actors and a few Black directors and designers. For two seasons in the late sixties, we had an acting company, supported by the Ford Foundation, that was twice the size of our current company, in which Black participation was 50%. That phase of our evolution did not succeed, but it was a valuable experience, as we revisit the idea. One of the reasons for failure was that, while the acting company represented our community well, our staff was all white. Also, there was no representation on the level of artistic leadership. Nor did our public relations and marketing efforts engage the community beyond drawing audiences for the productions.

Arena is more confident about how to go about this today. The climate is much more favorable, as we again take up this important theme that is woven into our history.

These remarks were presented at the Ford Foundation on February 8, 1989. Later that season, the National Endowment for the Arts awarded Arena a one-million-dollar challenge grant to make this plan a reality.

OUR TOWN IN OUR TIMES
(1991)

Cultural Diversity: I have to keep asking myself what it is and how to express it as it lives, breathes, transforms under the pressures and experiences of the world and the theater.

Cultural diversity is about responding to that world and bringing it into the theater. It's about making the theater contemporaneous with life, but more than that, about making the theater a leader of perception and not a follower. Not in the rear guard of our times but in the forefront. There was a controversy in the *Washington Post* this past year about the nontraditional casting of *Our Town* at Arena Stage: Out of twenty-six members of the cast, seven were Black and one was Hispanic.

There were two pairs of interracial siblings and Dr. Gibbs was performed by a Hispanic actor. It was a controversy I had been waiting for, hoping for, and welcomed, since it aired issues that needed to be addressed. It was the contention of the journalist that the casting policy made the production bear no relationship to reality, either Thornton Wilder's or New Hampshire's. He pointed out that as recently as 1980 that state had a Black population of less than .05 percent, and a Hispanic population of .005 percent: "New Hampshire comes about as close to being lily-white as any of the American states, so to represent it otherwise may be noble but it is also preposterous." He made other arguments—for example, that the casts of certain plays have distinct racial and ethnic compositions, as do certain families and communities in the world itself, and to represent them otherwise is to *mis*represent them.

Supporters of Arena's policy responded to this article by defending theater as an imaginative art, with educative power and a capacity to stretch the minds of its audiences to new possibilities for human life. Others pointed to the need for a larger rather than a smaller artistic sensibility, and the danger of using the question of "historical accuracy" or "the relationship to reality" as a hiding place for old habits.

But for me, the keenest response had to do with the contemporaneity of the theater-going act. What does it really matter in the larger scheme of things about the demographic statistics of New Hampshire? Is that really Wilder's central point? And, if it is, is it one worth making in today's world, in Washington, DC, with its particular struggles and needs? Theater is an art of the Now. Everything we say in it we say in that moment the actors share with the audience—this very moment, this Now. The past must be seen through the eyes of the present. If our present eyes see nothing in that particular excavation of the past, then it shouldn't make its way to the stage. It serves us nothing to retrieve it.

The audience who came to see *Our Town* came from a world where racial hostility on American campuses is increasing. Black students often face stereotyping as cruel as any faced by their grandparents. In response, some universities are reconstituting dormitories along culturally specific lines. (The Hispanic house at Stanford, for example, felt that its forty-three percent representation made for a good protective balance.) Our audiences also live in a world where heated arguments over politically correct behavior abound. In a recent televised debate, for example, the president of Yale said that he felt that any limitation of speech was against the principles upon which universities were formed. His opponent said that a racial epithet was a spit in the face, and what did that have to do with free speech? Finally, our audiences know a world where harassment in all forms is increasing, as civil rights achievements of the sixties are dismantled, gay-bashing is a daily hazard on the streets, episodes of virulent anti-Semitism escalate in America and are officially tolerated (or sponsored) in the Soviet Union and the countries of Eastern Europe.

Today a young, Black male has more chance of going to prison than to college, and Pittsburgh is talking about separatist high schools organized on the special needs of Black male youth. In the eighties the Hispanic population of Washington, DC, increased by 130%, the highest increase of the nation's 30 largest metropolitan areas. For the past 17 years, children have been the poorest age group in our society—nearly twice as likely as adults to live in poverty. Yet federal funding for children's programs grew at only one quarter the rate of overall federal spending increases for the eighties. In the District of Columbia, where a decade ago nearly 40% of children lived in married-couple households, only a third do now. More than 19% of Washington's girls aged 15 to 19 became pregnant in 1989, and there were more than 2,000 births, a 14.5% increase from the year before. A report titled "One Nation, Many Peoples: A Declaration of Cultural Interdependence" was recently delivered to New York's education commissioner and ignited fierce debate about the recognition in our educational system of the history and achievements of American non-white cultures. I could go on and on with these examples, but I think you see what I mean.

How could one present *Our Town* today, with our eyes closed to the world in which it is being presented? Of what importance in this year, in this time, is the hypothetical statistical accuracy of the racial composition of this mythological Grover's Corners at the turn of the century? Within Wilder's imaginative construct of man's daily life and the events that, with all their cultural variants, define us all, how discordant is it really that a contemporary production took certain liberties with rigid historical accuracy?

With every play that we do—new play or classic—we ask ourselves: How do we bring this play into our world? How do we make it alive for our audience here and now without destroying it or distorting the imagination that birthed it? How do we speak to our spectators, as they walk from their own worlds into this one, the theater? How do we make use of a model of experience—the theater event—that is not something ungrounded and unreal and inconsequential and hypothetical, but that takes place truthfully in the audience's midst and is of them and their daily life? We continue to ask these questions and to answer them as best we can, constantly and in good conscience attempting to serve what was in the play when it came into being, and what is in it now in the time of its new life. We think cultural diversity in a theater is about that questioning and answering.

In the sixties, Arena Stage attempted in a very serious way a program about cultural diversity. And, in terms of the life on the stage, we succeeded rather well. We had an acting company of thirty-two members that was totally integrated and mounted a number of distinguished productions. However, our attempt and our success was incomplete; it didn't take hold and fell away after a few years. We had not yet come to understand that the entire institution had to become multicultural, intercultural, cross-cultural—that the whole spirit of the institution had to change, not only on the stage, but also upstairs, downstairs, on every floor, and in every department, in every mind and soul. We must have designers, directors, dramaturgs, playwrights, fundraisers, business managers, subscription managers, costumers, scene painters, as well as actors from all cultures. We must especially have them from the second wave of immigration that is changing America in a way and to a point from which there is no return. It isn't enough to just talk and write about multiculturalism. The reality must be concrete. And if that is true for us, so is it true for all four hundred theaters across the land, which, taken as a whole, constitute the American theater. When Arena speaks with its own voice, we hope it can speak as an example for many other institutions.

We like to think that this thrust is not *affirmative* action—a term which in the current climate carries all the controversial semantic baggage of quotas, segregation, restitution for past injustices, and the meaning of "qualified"—but *affirming* action—an attitude which regards each individual as special and discoverable and openable and not to be wasted. Affirming action regards the brain itself as subject to organic transformation, depending on what it sees, hears, touches, and experiences.

America cannot be a melting pot anymore. That's an image from a phase of our life that belongs to the history books, a time when, by dissolving one culture into another, we thought to create the signature of our land: *e pluribus unum*—out of the many, one. Now, in its second wave of immigration, America must learn to be a land of conglomeration, recognizing through its institutions that various cultures add richness, complexity, variety, individuality, juice. Yes—add diversity. The highest attribute of nature is its diversity. It has taken billions of years to evolve its manifoldness. One day the highest accomplishment of man-made civilization, following nature, will be precisely that—its diversity. And our present challenge is to learn how to organize and manage that diversity.

Published in *American Theatre*, October 1991.

CREATIVITY AND
THE PUBLIC MIND

ON CREATIVITY
(1993)

In the famous interview scene in Oscar Wilde's *The Importance of Being Earnest*, Lady Bracknell interrogates Jack Worthing as a potential suitor for the hand of her daughter, Gwendolyn. "I think a man should know either everything, or nothing. Which do you know?" The flustered Mr. Worthing replies: "I'm afraid I know nothing, Lady Bracknell."

I can only say that on the elusive subject of creativity, I stand with Mr. Worthing. However, he goes on with the scene anyway, and so will I.

Some ruminations:

On the front page of the *New York Times*, there is a photo of the dark shadow of flying birds against a white, cloudy sky, and the caption: "Along the Platte River on the Nebraska prairie the arrival of thousands of sandhill cranes is a good sign. Nebraskans know spring has arrived when the horizon turns gray with the birds' swooping, six-foot wings."

As with the cranes, creativity is in us as a force of nature, arriving in season with our birth, part of the natural plan. And if it isn't killed by too-early socialization, or by the stifling norms of an educational system designed to elicit conformity from within, or by a world that threatens physical and spiritual health—survival itself—it can have, in some of us, a wingspread of six feet and even more!

Someone has said that every child is creative, at least for five minutes, and I agree with that perception. It seems that creativity—that power to make new things, to come upon, assemble, and bring into being new objects, new thoughts, new ways of doing things, of using natural forces even to transcend them—the flying machine which overcomes the force of the Earth's gravity, for example—it seems that creativity is part of the survival equipment of mankind. Our repertory of behavior (limitless beside that of the bee) and the range of possibility and choice contained in our imaginings—these are the wellspring from which we build our civilizations, create our artworks, and love our beloved. Man is the animal who adapts. Man is the animal who creates.

I am at this moment working on Anton Chekhov's *Three Sisters* with my students at NYU—one of the great impressionistic plays of all dramatic literature. Once again, I am awed by its apparent unmanipulated flow of life, its seeming lack of organization that conceals an artistic method as strong and tensile and mysterious as a cobweb.

One night, between rehearsals, I had dinner alone at a nearby restaurant and spent the meal watching and listening to the conversation between a mother and her four- or five-year-old daughter. So intimate: The mother's eyes gazing in love at her child, knotting up the child's prattle and giving back to her, in some changed form, responses the child's flitting talk seemed to ask for.

I toy with the idea that Chekhov engaged his play in the same way that the mother engaged her child: finding out what *it* wanted to do next, talking with it, now entering into it, becoming it, now stepping back and listening, attending, then moving in again to shape and perfect the living moment. I think, too: Maybe the primary model for creating a formal work of art exists in our earliest relationships with the objects around us, the first of these being, of course, the relationship with the mother. How she gazed at us, shadowed us, ushered us into an understanding of the premises of our world. How she served, attentively or even critically, to make us into ourselves. Or, perhaps, how that all happened not beneficently, but badly. Creativity, unfortunately, is not always a benign affair.

The imagination of man applies itself willy-nilly. It is the immeasurable power and range of this imagination that enables us to outdo any other animal on Earth in conscious cruelty. No animal but man could have imagined the concentration camp or the social construct of the Holocaust.

Dr. Alice Miller, the German psychoanalyst, in her four extraordinary books, explores the psychological mechanism by which the child's sadism is elicited and schooled in the forms of cruelty already practiced by the adults. Her chapter on Adolf Hitler and the deformed shape of his creativity provided me a source of understanding for our production of Ari Roth's *Born Guilty*, based on interviews of the children of Nazi perpetrators that we commissioned and produced at Arena Stage several years ago.

From the conscious to the unconscious and back to the conscious; from what is known to what is unknown and back to what is, now, more nearly known. This is the creative method. An endless interaction between logic and technique with the hidden forces beneath, often dark and not directly subject to our will—dreams, memories, the vestigial structures of our evolutionary past. A rich reservoir to be tapped for our creative enterprises, an underworld Freud dubbed as "as deep and mysterious as the Zyuder Zee." In comparison, the powers of rationality sit atop it as thin as surface tension in a glass of water. But we need these cooler powers. They are our tools, our levers, to reach the deep and fertile images out of reach, and then to organize them consciously into completed products of the mind.

We treasure the early sketches of a visual artist or architect, the improvisations of an actor, the first drafts of a poem or novel. In them we find the original, visceral impulses of the artist; we touch him or her most deeply, intimately, before the work has become an organized whole, a balanced system of thought and feeling, before the rough-and-tumble of creative process closes to us.

"The brush mark is the man," a Chinese calligrapher says. The creator and the created are bound to each other. We are not interchangeable in our creativity. There is no Hamlet, only clues to action—or inaction—on the printed page. The Hamlet that lives, is an embodied persona: *his* Hamlet or *his* or *his*, with that particular way of moving, speaking, thinking, that particular rhythm of being and that particular set of memories. We say to the student playing Hamlet, "Half of Hamlet is *you*, so you better be good and not shortchange him."

Why one person acts, another paints or sculpts or makes a dance, while another makes a cabinet and another a garden—we do not precisely know. We know that multiple intelligences exist. We know that dancing and painting and playing the piano are all forms of thinking and perceiving, perhaps different forms of thinking and perceiving. We observe that a particular form of creativity may run in a family: Michael, Lynn, Vanessa, and Natasha Redgrave, for instance—a combination of genes and exposure, perhaps. Molière's father was an upholsterer, and Meryl Streep's father a pharmaceutical executive. Was there a great-aunt somewhere we don't know about? We don't know if creativity runs in the families or runs away from them.

As Nobel Prize–winning chemist Max Perutz reminds us in his preface to *Is Science Necessary?*:

> Renoir painted every day of his life, and when old age had made his fingers too arthritic to hold a brush, he got someone to tie the brush to his hand. Haydn rose early each morning to compose; if ideas failed him, he clasped his rosary and prayed until Heaven sent him fresh inspiration . . . When Newton was asked how he had arrived at his insights, he answered, "By keeping the problem constantly before my mind."

There is an obsessive quality to deep creativity that makes of it a dangerous rival for worldly concerns—wealth, family, even romantic love. Creativity is a form of romantic love, perhaps.

The artist creates in what the psychologists call a "flow" state, an altered awareness found in people performing at their peak. First identified through studies in which people from rock climbers to chess masters described moments of sublime achievement, flow characterizes the thrill that motivates artists to keep at it year after year. That elastic sense of time—vanishing into a kind of hyper-speed or crystallizing into stop-frame slow motion—is a mark of this flow state, where a person's skills live in exquisite balance with challenges facing them, where the measure of time, which is the very measure of life, bends in a new way, and, even death, one feels, can be defied.

In addition to their auditions and interviews, applicants to the Acting Program at NYU are asked to write an essay. One essay quotes Tom Spanbauer's novel, *The Man Who Fell in Love with the Moon*, in which a philosophical cowboy tells his Indian friend:

> There's really only a very short time that we get hair and teeth and put on red cloth and have bones and skin and look out eyes. Not for long. Some folks longer than others. If you're lucky, you'll get to be the one who tells the story: how the eyes have seen, how the hair has blown, the caress the skin has felt, how the bones have ached.

Each of us longs to be the one who tells the story. In one way or the other, to share with someone else the experience of being human, to create new bonds. Lucky are we who get to do it.

Speech to the Cosmos Club, a private social club for women and men distinguished in science, literature, the arts, or public service, located in Washington, DC, March 27, 1993.

CREATIVITY AND THE PUBLIC MIND
(2002)

I'm honored to speak in the annual lecture series in memory of Nancy Hanks and her achievements as chairperson of the National Endowment for the Arts from 1969 to 1977, roughly thirty years ago. I've titled my remarks "Creativity and the Public Mind." I'd like to speak first about the second part of the title, following Nancy Hanks and the NEA into our own times, before pondering the role art plays in human society and how the Endowment has affected the creative process itself.

Nancy Hanks. As a frequent NEA panel member and grant recipient as producing director of Arena Stage, I had the pleasure to know her somewhat. That complex, private-yet-loving, tender-but-tough, indefatigable woman followed Roger Stevens to become the second chairperson of the Endowment. Tutored by Nelson Rockefeller in the ways of politics and gaining valuable experience as vice president of the Rockefeller Brothers Fund, Nancy had no real artistic background and never tried to conceal that fact. Somehow, she knew what artists needed. She knew about making institutions grow, and she had the courage and creativity to see that things were done the way she thought they should be. Under her stewardship the Endowment experienced a burst of energy and optimism that, for a time, promised democratic culture in America at the highest level. Helen Hayes, at her last meeting as a member of the National Council on the Arts, said, "I have stood on many mountain peaks, but this was my Everest."

All of us artworkers in the field had those same feelings. The NEA beckoned us to our Everest. By her ability to defuse conflict and her knowledge of how to work a system to her will, Nancy was able to achieve bipartisan support in Congress, an astounding 1,400% increase in appropriations, from $8 million to $140 million and, by hook and crook, to keep censorial politics at bay. She became "a mother to a million artists," as one fan said. She brought equal weight to bear on arts institutions, leading the arts for the very first time into national consciousness.

Nancy's years were turbulent ones in American history: the women's liberation movement, the revolt against our involvement in Vietnam, the civil rights revolution that brought both upheaval and the exhilarating possibility of change. The arts were an important means of expressing deep-seated bitterness, rage, and alienation; of rejecting traditional values and habits of behavior; of experiencing excitement, empowerment, and a newfound sense of freedom. First through the enlightened support of W. McNeil Lowry of the Ford Foundation, beginning in the mid-fifties, and then with the new structure of public funding growing stronger and stronger, we dared to see the future, and it worked.

We handled setbacks with a quiet heart, perhaps too preoccupied with our new toys. When in response to a $750 grant for a one-word, seven-letter poem—"lighght"—the *Los Angeles Times* weighed in with two poems of its own—"ugh" and "blech"—we laughed at the absurdity. A magazine called the *Brown Bag*, connected to a literary anthology grant, was condemned by Congress as "a subversive organization, at least as subversive as Black Power . . . There you have a Bolshevik bomb, black, round, substantial, with a subversive fuse, to . . . disrupt poetic literary salons." Our response was something like, "There they go again!" As if Congress was a bunch of naughty boys, bound to grow up soon.

In 1972, Erica Jong was one of 60 writers out of over 1,500 to receive $5,000 grants, which yielded up her best-selling novel *Fear of Flying*. This event precipitated a flamboyant brouhaha. "Public Paid for 'Horny' Novel" was the title of a nationally syndicated column. "If some dizzy dame or guy wants to write about her or his most intimate sexual feelings, why should you or I be stuck with the tab for these ravings from a restroom wall?" The reporter's solution was to abolish both Endowments. Jesse Helms called the book a "reportedly filthy, obscene book" and suggested that the $5,000 be refunded.

But Nancy pulled the fat out of the fire yet again. Artistic judgments were not her responsibility, she stated; they were the province of advisory panels, made up of professionals in the specific fields. It was up to the National Council to endorse the panels' recommendations. Nancy put everything on the line, up to the very structure of the Endowment itself. It was Democrat Sidney Yates, chair of the House Subcommittee on Appropriations, who supported Nancy when she appeared before the committee. Prompting her, he suggested, "Perhaps time has a habit of changing values, customs, and attitudes." Nancy, of course, enthusiastically agreed. "One of the dangers art requires is that somebody may say that his creation is trash," he suggested. "You are indeed right, Mr. Chairman," she concurred.

The Endowments were not abolished. Nancy wrote in a letter to Jesse Helms that "nurturing the broad range of the nation's creativity is far more important than a few tempests that arise . . . I say that because of my conviction that the cornerstone of any culture is the nurtured talent of its creative artists." We hunkered down to our work.

Of course, political pressure is a given for any government agency, and we were alert—though not sufficiently alert—to the tensions between the Endowment and Congress. The balances were always tenuous and easily disturbed. The issues prefigured during Nancy's tenure were to run away with themselves, and the threats to abolish the agencies, though at first quite unbelievable, soon gained a sense of possibility, and we came to feel threatened in a new way.

The issue of censorship erupted like a Vesuvius in 1989 and 1990, more than a decade after Nancy. New York Senator Alfonse D'Amato tore up a copy of Andres Serrano's photograph "Piss Christ" on the Senate floor, while Jesse Helms claimed in a loud voice that Serrano wasn't even an artist. Both of them called for the elimination of the arts agency. We remember when the "decency clause" became a part of the NEA's reauthorizing statute; to receive funds we were required to take into consideration "general standards of decency and respect for the diverse beliefs and values of the American public," and also to know that "obscenity is without artistic merit, is not protected speech, and shall not be funded."

John Frohnmayer was to live with the havoc this statute wreaked and, finally in 1992, was asked to resign after three tumultuous years as chairman. He had denied grants, over the approval of the panel, to Karen Finley and three other performance artists who became known as the NEA Four. They brought suit against the NEA—their claims were settled out of court—and then expanded the suit to the Supreme Court, challenging the constitutionality of the "standards of decency clause." Congress was embarrassed and angry.

The American Family Association and the Christian Coalition grew in power over the years and brought into Congress a continuing series of new outrages in an effort to eliminate the Endowment. While the American people supported arts funding in a general way, and offered their taxes willingly, there was never any kind of counter-culture groundswell against censorship. The arts community eventually came to the fore and did its best, but it couldn't find effective language defining what it stood for. It lacked good media coverage; its supporters didn't have enough votes to exert any real pressure. Outside of the Hollywood few, artists are poor and, so, had nothing meaningful to offer to campaign chests. As a strong political force that could affect policy at the highest level, we were better as artists.

Jane Alexander was the first artist ever proposed for chairman of the NEA, and of course we were thrilled. *She* would know how to affect policy at the highest level—the president himself. Nancy Hanks had had the ear of President Nixon and of President Ford and, for a short time, of President Carter. When Jane came to Roger Stevens for advice, he immediately said, "Always talk to the president." Jane tells us in her recent book *Command Performance*, that from 1993 when she was sworn in, until the fall of 1997 when she resigned, she could secure only one official appointment with President Clinton—in March 1995 for about twenty minutes. She was seeking his overt support for the NEA against Republican attacks on controversial art, reassuring him that funds were now granted only for projects unlikely to cause problems. The president replied: "That sounds good, they've got to understand the public won't pay for that." —Meaning controversial art. It's interesting that the first President Bush, in deposing Frohnmayer, wrote to him similarly: "The taxpayer will simply not subsidize filth and blasphemous material." I guess you can say that the Arts Endowment has had bipartisan attention.

Jane concluded after her meeting with Clinton that the president regarded the arts as a "soft issue." "Winning was what it was all about," she writes. She had wanted Clinton "to be not only a skilled politician but also a visionary, with lofty ideals and a dedication to the finest creations of human beings." She wanted more than there was to be had and finally came to know that and left.

She notes that when Sid Yates was asked whether he felt politics and art were antithetical, he answered that as support for the arts gained around the country, the cry for accountability of public funds would increase as well; the tension between "high culture" and democracy, he believed, was inevitable. "He may not have liked the erotic photographs of Robert Mapplethorpe," she adds, "but he never doubted the artist's right to make or exhibit them." Yates quoted Ogden Nash: "Smite, Smoot, / Be rugged and rough, / Smut if smitten / Is front-page stuff."

Matters of content have been brought under control. An era of grand possibility on the federal level has slipped away. No more grants to individual artists—they're the ones who cause all the trouble. No more sub-grants on the part of institutions—in case they might bring in the individual artists who cause all the trouble. In fact, no more general support for institutions, which is what they most need. Grants are awarded only for projects in certain designated categories. The NEA continues to serve well and importantly in areas that remain to it, especially on a state and local level, especially in the areas of arts in education, architecture, and access to the arts.

Surely, we must press to keep the Endowment alive and see it better funded. But many of us who were ardent believers in a long and high reach for public funding have come to doubt that the tension between artist and politician will ever be resolved. I was one of those ardent believers and am now one of the doubters. I regarded the content controversies of those ebullient early days too lightly, as ludicrous or transient, rather than as deeply rooted expressions of our political system. We lost our best opportunity to organize our forces, early on, when the conflict was still in motion.

Let's speak for a bit about the nature of creativity itself, so we know precisely what it is we must struggle to protect. In general, our public representatives don't know what the creative process is or perhaps even how to regard its products. It's not that politicians can't at the same time be artists or appreciate art, nor that artists or art appreciators can't at the same time be politicians. We have examples of good men and women who combine these talents. In our country, however, political power more and more equals money times votes, and art is acceptable principally for its spin-off benefits (civic enlightenment, legacy preservation, community health, economic assistance to downtown, and so forth), rather than for its pith.

At Arena Stage I once had the honor of introducing Nobel Prize–winner Isaac Bashevis Singer, who wrote his novels in Yiddish, thus restoring the language to literary stature. In preparing to introduce him, I went back to his works, reacquainting myself with his wonderful characters. Their culture is Jewish, and we encounter them rooted in the religious and social life of the *shtetl*—the village—of Eastern Europe in the late nineteenth century. Singer so powerfully creates fictional people whose realness is beyond dispute that we can know them above their nationality.

Gimpel the Fool, for example, could be one of us. "I am Gimpel the Fool. I spin yarns," he says, introducing himself by name and occupation. Singer lets him speak a truth that is universal for every storyteller:

I wandered over the land, and good people did not neglect me. After many years, I became old and white; I heard a great deal, many lies and falsehoods, but the longer I lived the more I understood that there were really no lies. Whatever doesn't really happen is dreamed at night. It happens to one if it doesn't happen to another, tomorrow if not today, or a century hence if not next year. What difference can it make? Often I heard tales of which I said, "Now, this is a thing that cannot happen!" But before a year had elapsed, I heard that it actually had come to pass somewhere.

In Gimpel's words lurks not only the source of the storyteller's yarn but also something deeper, something about the very biologic nature of man—our life as a species. Something about the wild, anarchic, animal stuff in us that we try to tame, so that we may enjoy the order and delights of civilization. About that flimsy veil between the conscious and unconscious, between waking and dreaming, what we know and what we don't want to know. About our life's struggle to sort out differences between how we perceive the world and how it "really" is.

Of course, we are the same, you and I—leaves from the same tree. But how are we to know each other across our separate experiences, religions, habits of life, wantings, sufferings, pasts? This grotesque misunderstanding, this confusion and enmity, this war between us! "Now, this is a thing that cannot happen! But before a year had elapsed . . . it actually had come to pass . . ." If Gimpel were among us, he could well be pointing to the seventy-foot crater where the Twin Towers so recently stood and where three thousand of us were incinerated on a golden day that started like any other.

We have always had our *griot*, our storyteller, who seeks to unravel these mysteries for us, hoping to find hints, clues, by walking in the shoes of another, gathering up the cultural strands of time and weaving them into a tapestry of meaning, trying "to pierce the opacity of the world," as Camus put it, and of our human nature in particular. Camus added: "If the world were clear, art would not be necessary."

On September 11th, I became a part of the primal rush of students and grown-ups to the agora, the marketplace, which in this instance happened to be Washington Square Park, the destination for a shared ritual of grief. A link fence surrounds the marble Arch, which terminates Fifth Avenue downtown at Waverly Place, the neighborhood of New York University. It is here that public expressions of sorrow coalesced. Within days after the attack, the fence was swathed in immense white canvases and, on its northern side, a giant American flag. All of these—the flag included—served as vast communal parchments. Hardly a square inch of space remained uncrowded by the fury of written gratitude or confusion, pacifism or unbridled rage. English, Russian, German, French, Italian, and languages I couldn't differentiate spelled out thoughts and feelings, hopes and despair, in every color of the magic markers stacked in small mesh bags, hanging every six feet or so for people to grab.

The storyteller was the community itself. The parchment wall around the monument received a thousand authors. The language of grief had been passed along, person to person, block by block. Television cameras swept over the area, and this ritual grief was transmitted from eye to eye, satellite to satellite, and, again, block by block. There were the "Missing" flyers—copied photos of missing loved ones posted on the fence at Washington Square, as well as on fences, trees, buildings, lampposts across the city. The flyers carried personal remarks by family members. A lament: "Missing, my two lovely twins, age 28." A description, as if the details could lure him out from hiding: "He had a tattoo on the base of his back, no facial hair, his right big toe had only half a nail." Amended by hand: "Gennie Gambale had not been on the 102nd floor, but on the 105th." A child's scribble: "We need you, Daddy, please come back." And instead of a proper funeral: "Yesterday. How we long for yesterday."

The scanned photographs affixed to the flyers echo a ritual from ancient Greece in which sculptured images of the deceased appeared on graves. The dead were often pictured in some final activity before traveling to Hades, living a moment of their lives for the last time. Inevitably, the family members who devised the "Missing" flyer—like the Greeks who sculpted graves for their dead—had chosen the happiest images they could find. So, the missing people stood smiling in wedding pictures; they were poised above birthday cakes, with babies and puppies and at graduations. I pass the marble Arch each day on my way to NYU and back home again, and I reflect on the singleness of our human destiny.

It seems that making something useful is not enough. We must embellish it, in some way memorialize it. We elaborate our homes with great attention to their style and materials and decor or spend concentration and energy on how we adorn our bodies. What shall it be: cloth or leather, buttons, buckles, or bows? Wear corsets or breathe free? Paint our faces, put rings on our fingers or through our ears or nose, tattoo favorite symbols on our flesh?

How shall we think of these things that we do and have always done? The walls of the caves of France, great natural chambers covered with paintings of astonishing vividness of form and facility of design, the first record of civilization that we have. The Gothic cathedrals of Europe, built over centuries by whole communities. The pyramids of Egypt?

What *is* this need to make the ordinary extraordinary? Whether it is wood, stone, or clay; movement or sound or speech; story, image, or a conception of space—what drives us to transform that which exists in nature to a more evocative, meaningful existence in art? Here we are, in every society, adorning ourselves, our artifacts, and our surroundings, making music, creating dances, dramatizing stories, painting and sculpting and writing, assembling in the marketplace to express our collective grief. What lies behind these universal practices?

The extraordinary care and attention given to these matters, as well as their ubiquity, are clues that, in some way the biologists have not yet plumbed, they are, indeed, related to survival and not frivolous cultural overlays. It seems that we human creatures—"poor, bare fork'd animal," Shakespeare calls us—are without defenses but for our creativity, subject to huge vicissitudes of fortune in the course of a lifetime. Aware, despite our talent for denial, that those we love may die, that we ourselves will die, and that, in the end, life's a failed enterprise. On top of those insults to our self-importance, we can't run very fast. We lack the tough hide of the elephant, the long neck of the giraffe, the teeth of the shark. We're subject to a range of bodily and emotional illnesses. Isolated in our separate skins—the only creature who is outside of nature—we find out to our surprise and indignation that the world is not made for us at all; we only dwell in it for a time. (Some of us don't learn this and do great harm to the environment.)

The gods or the one God or our internalized consciences exact a heavy price for the pleasures of life that they allow us. We suffer the feeling that we have little real power over anything much. As Shakespeare's Gloucester said, "As flies to wanton boys are we to th' gods, / They kill us for their sport." As far as I know, he has never persuasively been contradicted. Floods, earthquakes, wars, suicide bombers, anthrax and smallpox, draught and starvation, psychic trauma, untrustworthy leaders upon whom we project our dependencies, economic cycles of poverty and plenty—all seem to be beyond our control.

And yet. And yet. There *are* things we can do! And, as Ralph Waldo Emerson said, "That which a man *does*, that he has." We can know beauty and try to create it. We can reach for immortality through what we leave behind. An actor can surrender to possession by an imagined Other; a political activist, to a compelling cause; a mother, to the miracle of birthing and raising a child. We *are*, then, capable of transcendence and of ecstasy. We can, through imagination and empathy, reach across the distance between us and experience intimacy. We can make palpable in the world whatever we imagine (and alas! we can imagine blowing things up as well as taming them). And, by our capacity to play, we can fantasize alternative universes—other ways that things could be—and make artworks that are these new worlds.

In that sense, we have all the power there is. Through art, we can confront the core of uncertainty at the heart of things. On the whole, artists do this far more bravely than engineers or lawyers or politicians. In a culture of specialists, the artist is something else. Because reality is malleable and can accept any construction put upon it, how one sees it is how it is. The personal vision of each individual artist speaks to us of the elasticity of human perception and makes us wiser and better fit for survival. And in making art, we draw in a conscious way on the deep, rich mother lode of the unconscious. What comes to the artist from that hidden place surprises and enlightens her. And she, in turn, by making the familiar strange, the ordinary extraordinary, shows the rest of us what we may never have seen. Quite literally, she illuminates, she throws new light upon reality. In that way she has the power to make and remake the world.

Tikkun Olam. In Hebrew: "To repair the world." We are the only animal who strives to do that. It's our creative mission. And this mission gives us our identity.

For the individual artist, there is also the precious opportunity to know one's self. The artist can see life more clearly through the eyes of his creative self. Can he not, then, see *himself* more clearly through those same eyes? As creator, you see or feel or imagine a thing and begin in a way that is only yours—to bring it to life. The thing yields to you, for it's your creature and wants to be born.

Along the way of its emergence, it will acquire a life of its own. It will rebel, challenge you, and ask of you what *it* wants rather than what *you* want. You may see things in a different way; you may feel ambivalent, resistant, confused, or angry; you may not have presently available within you what it wants. But if your will is strong or you just can't help yourself, you will keep at it. You will listen to the imagined object as attentively as you can and try to bat down anything that stands in the way of achieving it—self-doubt, fatigue, fear, despair, guilt, rage, panic, the drying-up of impulse, whatever. You must always stand your ground against what Schiller and, later, Freud called, "Watcher at the Gate." The *Watcher* is critical and judgmental; he would censor the flow of thoughts and images out of which the artwork will emerge. You must get rid of him and hang on to your singularity. Without you, this special vision would be lost to the world. Albert Einstein, when asked how he would have felt had there been no experimental confirmation of his general theory of relativity is said to have remarked: "Then I would feel sorry for the dear Lord. The theory is correct." Good for him!

Because of your urgent love for this demanding child you have brought forth from inside yourself, and because of your total absorption in it, you will allow yourself to be revealed to yourself. In time you will know what has to be done next and how you must shape yourself in order to do it. The dialogue will continue back and forth. Hopefully, it will consummate in something that pleases you. And, then, pleases someone else.

Here's an untitled poem by William Butler Yeats:

The friends that have it I do wrong
When ever I remake a song
Should know what issue is at stake,
It is myself that I remake.

Each of us is an original. We come into the world at the coast of alternative ovulations, alternative lives. The chances of our becoming our parents' son or daughter is in the vicinity of one in ten million. We are born with identities that may not suit those of our mother and father; we may be born into the wrong house or even into the wrong destiny. But if we have the talent to create a beautiful thing that wouldn't be there but for us, we feel blessed. This act gives us the opportunity, in addition to repairing the world, to repair ourselves, make ourselves whole, a project that can engage us for a lifetime and for which, I believe, we have landed on the Earth.

Censorship of a certain kind is a good and necessary thing, serving a vital function in human life; we couldn't construct a civil society without it. We're born animals, and we need to accommodate to that fate. We teach our children and relearn ourselves how to repress and rechannel our anarchic desires, which are intuitively selfish and antisocial. Children have to share their toys, and their parents mustn't shout "Fire!" in a crowded theater. Self-censorship, repression, the internalization of certain cultural habits and codes, passed along primarily by our parents, is the price we pay for civilization. In his landmark book, *Civilization and Its Discontents*, Freud acknowledged that the rewards of civilization were well worth the price. He even suggested that repression is the very seedbed of art, where metaphor and symbol, the basic grammar of artistic expression, are born.

Being the antennae of their species, artists have picked up on all of this. Their task, however, is different from that of other members of the community. It is to push through the tall, dense barriers of custom and habit that society has put up for its own perpetuation, and to see the world freshly. The artist struggles for *de*-repression, to recover the childlike, anarchic spirit that was once hers, to join that spirit with her adult knowledge of craft and with hard work to make a new thing the world has never before seen. To play within form is the difficult way of the artist. And, with the force of culture being so strong, rediscovering that earlier inner freedom is perhaps harder than to learning how to use one's materials.

The artist is a lonely creature. His only constituency while he's at work is himself. He lives every day out on a limb. Much as he may wish otherwise, the unseen presence of those who will look or listen or read, judge or award or buy hovers around him. The society of his time never leaves him; indeed, it provides him with his themes. But sometimes he needs to be lonely.

"When I was writing *Joe Turner's Come and Gone*," playwright August Wilson says, "I realized that someone was gonna stand up onstage and say the words, whatever the hell they were. That's when I realized I had a responsibility to the words. I couldn't have the character say any old thing. There couldn't be any mistakes." He communes with himself in the crepuscular gloom of the basement of his home and, if he's lucky, taps into what he calls "the blood's memory," that "deepest part of yourself where the ancestors are talking." In his mind's eye, the audience is there, in the basement with him, waiting to see what he's going to show them this time—the audience who, in various guises, passes through his dreams and keeps him on the edge as he moves through his working days.

Institutional leaders are lonely too. The hardest part of my years at Arena was staying tuned to the life of my community—its preoccupations, its mood, its artistic tastes—and yet not being bound by these. I would try to intuit what needs, what hopes and fears, might be beneath the surface of their individual lives, what feelings that they might not even be aware of. I would try to speak to those. To do that, I had to stay in contact with my own inner life, below the surface of my daily busyness, to know what I was thinking and feeling in this ever-changing moment and place. If I could find myself, I thought I would find the audience. I was looking to be innovative, to bring them something new and unexpected, whether of today or of centuries past, to surprise them, to delight and teach them through something I myself had found surprising and illuminating. I would let them be the ones to decide whether we had succeeded or not.

And, of course, sometimes our coming together was successful, and sometimes it wasn't, but that's how we understood it would be. The marketplace of ideas—this is the best of what our democracy has to offer. I know that other people work this way as well, striving to keep their relationship to the work direct and personal.

Because we have less money than we once had, because we need more and more votes at the box office, because we seek to please our audiences in order to stay alive, we have come to adopt the tools of the politician: the opinion poll and the focus group. While useful for demographic or market studies, these are dangerous to the artist and, in the end, diminish her intuition—that ability to access information so rapidly that it seems to bypass the brain and, at the same time, to feel right. Intuition is a potent gift for an artistic leader to have. The artist must know. Unlike the politician, the artist must lead without first collecting other peoples' opinions, unless they are collaborators. People won't know until they receive an artwork, until they experience it directly—hopefully with an open heart and mind—whether it delights them or not, whether it opens a door for them or not. So why ask them ahead of time? Can you imagine Picasso conducting a poll to see whether people were ready for him to leave his Blue Period and move on to something else—something, say, more abstract? Or for Ibsen to have gathered some of his audience in 1879 and asked how they would react to a play about a woman who leaves her husband and children in order to become a complete human being? Nora's door-slam was heard around the world, her exit so controversial that social invitations of the day requested that *A Doll House* not be discussed at dinner. The homogenization of art pulls its claws, plays to the surface of the public's taste.

There are other forms of censorship that press on needy arts institutions. The issues of donor intent, donor control versus institutional integrity, are as old as the practice of philanthropy. The tension between giver and recipient is often healthy and can make for some innovative and surprising gifts. But the passions, values, and strategic objectives of the donor need to match the vision, mission, and goals of the organization. Leaders of arts institutions understand that how the money is raised dramatically affects their ability to carry out the mission.

Another issue at a time of external pressures is transparency: how to maintain the openness of a place, its ethos of shared truth. "But I'd shut my eyes in the sentry-box, / So I didn't see nothin' wrong," Rudyard Kipling wrote. If there's bad news, no one wants to be the messenger—that's entirely human. But openness requires that board and staff, artists and staff, artists and board stay in touch with each other's work in progress. Complacent cultures and vacant sentry boxes hamper creativity. There can be a general sense within an institution that a policy or trend or budget is not to the good, but no one wants to tell the boss because the boss won't want to hear it. After a string of box-office flops, Samuel Goldwyn reportedly told his top staff, "I want you to tell me exactly what's wrong with me and MGM—even if it means losing your job." No one wants that to happen, but you get the point.

For the artist, poverty is also a form of censorship. So where are we now with the NEA and funding? We reached the peak in 1992, with an appropriation of $176 million. After the huge cut in 1996, the figure fell to $99 million; it stayed there until 2001, when it rose by a smidgeon to $105 million. Compare that to Nancy's $140 million 30 years ago! This little $105 million is a measure of the recognition, acknowledgment, and moral support the federal government bestows upon the arts in America at the millennium. President Bush signed Appropriations Bill H.R. 2217, guaranteeing a $10 million increase in NEA funding for 2002, while Congress considers another $2 million for 2003—token raises for a job well done. No more consternation on the Hill. No hullabaloo in the media. No dirty pictures. All is quiet.

In his departing remarks, recent NEA chairman Bill Ivey said, "I believe we must face the challenge of developing our Big Ask . . . The Big Ask cannot just be about more money for the NEA or for state arts agencies or any entity, although our large vision, our shared vision, will in fact require additional support. We need a bigger, more comprehensive, more real conversation about art and society than has been conducted in the past."

Money will follow imagination; in the arts it always does. We should strive for more NEA support in the valuable areas it has marked out for itself. But for the Big Ask, I suggest we must go outside of the Endowment, to places and people interested in supporting the individual artist or creative institutions, and not frightened by occasional controversy. We need to think outside the federal box. For example, a Boston-based nonprofit agency called Philanthropic Initiative works with individual foundation and corporate donors to identify compatible recipients, a refreshing angle of approach. The Foundation Center tells us that there have been 11,000 new foundations created since the mid-nineties; some of the arts-oriented ones could perhaps be persuaded into fresh patterns of giving, maybe through a regional or even national pool of funds to serve artistic ideas outside the pale of the federal government. The very well-funded National Science Foundation, created after World War II to pay for the training of scientists, might provide a template for training a new generation of artists, from whom we would expect a flurry of new artworks.

The mass media megacompanies shortchange the arts. While they routinely raid nonprofit arts institutions for talent—look at TV and film credits, and you'll see a "Who's Who" of the nonprofit performing world—they don't give back. When Jane pressed them to help fund the Endowment, they evaded, claiming they contributed by paying taxes. We shouldn't stand still for that. Some other entity we set up might persuade them to support the arts as they should and, surely, can afford.

Maybe the government is right after all: Maybe controversial art should be funded by the private sector. I can't believe I'm saying that. These are early thoughts. I dare to speak them in the hope they will provoke conversation and, yes, controversy.

The fifteenth annual Nancy Hanks Lecture, Eisenhower Theater, the John F. Kennedy Center for the Performing Arts, Washington, DC, March 11, 2002.

PROFIT/NONPROFIT

ON RISK AND MONEY
(1986)

A artist can only think about art in terms of risk. Surely that applies not only to a theater artist but also a surgeon/artist or an architect/artist or a lover/artist. Risk is the name of the game. I think of it less as "risk" than as "threat" or "danger"—words that have greater resonance for me. The painter faces the threat of the empty canvas; the writer the threat of the blank sheet of paper. The actor lives with the threat, the danger, or the script in front of her. What do all those squiggles mean, imprints of unknown animals crawling around on the page? How do you create a living, breathing human being out of those peculiar blobs of ink?

Everyone embarks on an artistic enterprise in a state of siege. Alan Schneider used to shiver and shake before he went into rehearsal. In his maturity, after he had directed more than two hundred productions, on the edge of a new production he would visit my office all anxiety, and we'd have a cup of herbal tea. I would reassure him that he was an artistic genius, and he would say, "How do you know that?" I would say, "I just know." He would say, "But I don't know."

The artist hangs in that fascinating, dangerous place between "I can't" and "Oh, yes I can." Between "I'll never make it" and "Oh, yes I will." And absolutely everything is at stake—one's very sense of self, not to mention one's practical means of survival. Inside the artist there takes place the primary snuggle between the *id*, the child that wants to play and make a beautiful object, and the *superego*, the internalized voice of the parents of society or of God that warns, "I don't think that's going to be any good." And that's why the environment of a theater is so important. What comes off the walls, what hovers in the air, what is not tangible and yet is the most tangible thing about a place says to the artist either "Yes you can" or "No you can't." It's so essential that the environment be supportive, permit a "what the hell" attitude, a playful attitude. A place has to come down on the side of the artist's daring and against the dangers that lurk inside and out.

The basis of all art is transformation, the changing of one thing into something else. It is a physiological truth that things are created by one thing becoming another thing. Transformation is a law of nature: It snows, and then the snow melts; it rains, and then the sun shines; you get angry, the anger fades away, and you can love again. The dancer can't organically get to the next gesture until this one extends to the furthest point. The actor can't play another action until what he gets back from the other actor turns his need into a new need. The environment we must create in the theater is one that allows for transformation, change, that moment of ultimate risk where something goes to the end point of itself and, so, becomes another thing. It is a moment of absolute freedom as well as risk.

"The sands take lines unknown." I have that pinned on my bulletin board at the theater. We must support this time of the unknown, in which the artist struggles toward what later will be known. I put a poem by the British poet Christopher Logue on the wall on top of class schedules and announcements at New York University's acting department:

> Come to the edge.
> We might fall.
> Come to the edge.
> It's too high!
> COME TO THE EDGE!
> And they came
> And he pushed
> And they flew.

The students read that every day and understand it, I think.

Now, having said all that about danger and risk and life on the edge, I want to say something else: The first law of the theater is success; without success there can be no theater. I don't think that implies one has to be successful every minute or even every month, but that it would be nice to be successful over a season, and surely over the long haul.

The first law of the theater is success. The theater is a public art; it has to meet its audience. There's a joke: A producer asks his partner, "What should we cover the seats with? Should we cover them with plush or with the tough nylon they use in airplanes?" The partner says, "What difference does it make? Let's cover them with bottoms!" The partner is right.

We think that there were ten thousand seats in the Greek amphitheaters. I recall, though not exactly, the words of Hallie Flanagan Davis, that wonderful woman from Vassar who led the Federal Theatre Project in the thirties: "Once there was a theater with ten thousand seats where people gathered on a hillside and ate their bread and cheese and sat for three days watching their plays. For what they saw there meant more to them than bread and cheese. It was the yeast that made the bread rise."[1] Theater was the experience, she meant, that gave meaning to their lives. That's success!

Theater has to matter to its audience; it has to pay its way in accordance with whatever system prevails at the time. When theater lived within the church, the church paid for it. When the church kicked it out as too secular, the medieval guilds picked up the bill— the bakers' guild, the carpenters' guild, the weavers' guild, etc. The queen paid for Shakespeare, the king for Molière. European socialist governments pay for as much as eighty percent of the budgets of their theaters. (Who pays the piper also pays the tune. My friend Liviu Ciulei lost the Bulandra Theatre in Romania over a production of *The Inspector General* that was deemed insufficiently grateful.) Our particular, peculiar, unique American system—a mix of public money, private philanthropy and box office—is a previously unknown way to support theater, a first in history.

1. The exact source of this quotation is unclear. Zelda is probably paraphrasing from Flanagan's "First Federal Summer Theater: A Report," in *Federal Theatre*, June–July 1937. [T.L.]

Whatever the system or culture, the artistic (producing) director has to produce—that is, lead forth, bring forth. As Liberace put it: "Without the show, there's no business." Brilliant man.

When one thing is true, the opposite may also be true. So, while the first law of the theater is success, the norm of the theater is failure. Success is the exception. You might look at Broadway and think it's all about success, but it's not. It is about failure. Any given year Broadway operates at a loss. A few people get rich; most lose money. Most shows are flops. It is factually a nonprofit enterprise, according to the basic natural law of the theater. If producers, theater owners and unions were sensible, and not so competitive and hungry, Broadway could contribute a lot more creativity to the American theater.

Why is failure in the theater the norm? Because the forces at work are so complex and unpredictable. First, you have to find the right play—whatever that means—and the right playwright (living or dead). Then you have to unlock it properly. Every play is a lock, and every director has her own key to it. So, within the overall artistic vision of the institution, you have to find the right director with the right vision. That director must work accurately and never blunder, because there's no time or money to retrace if things go wrong. At a subsidized theater like the Berliner Ensemble, you can build a set and scrap it if it isn't right, if it won't release the play. Our theaters don't have the resources to start over.

What else makes success so elusive? You have to assemble the right actors. So much to consider: Which actor in the company needs to stretch and grow? Will casting an actor who hasn't yet "stretched" hurt the play? Will he stretch? How do you balance serving the company and serving the play? Which actor needs a large role to sustain his interest and fully use his talent? If you cast an outside actor in a role a company actor covets, what will it do to company spirit? To your credibility? Which designers are compatible with both the play and the director's vision for it? Are they free and interested? The art of collaboration in the theater is subtle, elusive, and mysterious. It doesn't always run by the clock or calendar.

Then there is the question of time. Wise directors brought up in the European system demand it. Lucian Pintilie, who recently directed *The Wild Duck* at Arena, got close to eight weeks of rehearsal. In cohesion, detail, and depth, the production showed it. Sharon Ott got four weeks—three of five-hour days and one of eight-hour days—to work on *Restoration*, because our schedule fell that way. Being a young director, she wasn't in a position to demand more time, and we weren't in a position to change the schedule. Such conditions typically prevail where time equals money.

The interests of the actors, the shop schedule, the appropriateness for the spring benefit or Christmas or school spring vacations, the receptivity of the city (in Washington we are one of some twenty-two theaters), the collective consciousness of the theater and what it attends to at the moment, the needs of a season for balance and variety, and, finally, the nature of a specific audience—all these affect a play's "success." You can see why the norm is failure. You see how complex it is.

Artists know this basic dialectic most piercingly—success is not the norm, but without success there can be no theater. And it is the artist—more than the board or the community, more than the *Washington Post* or the *New York Times*—who want and need their theater. The theater is home to its artists—food, shelter, family, a reason for being.

Art makes money, not the other way around. When the art makes enough money, everything works. We don't then discuss risk because the risk paid off, so there's no need to discuss. It's only when the experiment fails that it's called an experiment. When there's not enough money, when there's a deficit, our tolerance for risk gets reexamined.

Does a deficit mean something or nothing? How much money should theater art be counted on to make? What are the community's expectations? How much does being nonprofit really cost? Does it cost too much for a community to support? Should box office provide fifty percent of the cost? Sixty-six percent? Is seventy-five percent of the cost too high an expectation over the long run? Who provides the balance?

In a deeper sense, what does the word "nonprofit" really mean? How misleading is the term, with its particular reference to the tax code, in our economic world? In *The House of Intellect* (1959) Jacques Barzun wrote: "Many directors of corporate foundations and some university trustees handle money for research and education not as if they were engaged in a nonprofit enterprise, but as if they were engaged in an enterprise that was failing to make a profit. In other words, they do not see where the actual profit lies. It being intellectual and they not, it is to them invisible." Replace some terms, and his statement applies to the arts institution. How do we pay for Barzun's kind of nonprofit?

Arena's board president, speaking out of a great passion and love for this theater and out of dread of its weakening—a feeling we all share—speaks of the deficit as "a very ugly fact." It *is* a very ugly fact. On the other hand, if it leads to a greater understanding, it can be a very beautiful fact. It would be hard to imagine a board thinking of a *surplus* as an ugly fact, whereas it would be quite possible for an artistic director to think of a surplus as an ugly fact, because it suggests that the theater might be doing the wrong things with its money. It might not be creative enough, might not be *risking* enough. *Could* a surplus be looked on as a sick rather than a healthy sign? I think so, though I doubt that a board would. Alas! Artistic directors and boards usually stand on opposite sides of a great divide on this issue. But let's say a deficit *is* an ugly fact because it threatens our security. How do we eliminate it? How do we lick it?

There are points in the life of a theater when it isn't meeting its audience. The obvious way to change that, of course, is to reduce the number of flops and increase the number of hits. There's an old show-biz saying: "There's nothing wrong with the theater that a hit can't cure." I wonder. It's reported that the Guthrie made a million dollars on last season's *Guys and Dolls*. But somehow it blurred its artistic identity in the process and lost its third or fourth artistic director in ten years. It may not be true that there's nothing a hit can't cure.

There's another saying in theater: "You're only as good as your last hit." It's an awful saying. What if we had to live up to that? It's vital that we accept the failures of our artists. America has been cruel about that. We tend to be ungenerous about failure, as if it's a betrayal when artists don't measure up. We were very cruel to Tennessee Williams, for example, and maybe the pain it caused him kept him from rising to his earlier peaks.

One of the first questions a board might ask itself is whether, in a nonprofit arts institution, bottom-line thinking really gets to the bottom of things? If it doesn't, then how could that thinking be revised to coincide more appropriately with the nature of the institution? The feelings of separation and uneasiness between artistic leaders and boards around the country will not be changed until these questions are forthrightly confronted, and answers are sought for and found.

From *American Theatre*, November 1986.

CONGRESSIONAL TESTIMONY: THE CASE FOR THE NEA

(1990)

Chairman and distinguished members of the Subcommittee, I am grateful for this opportunity to present testimony on funding for the National Endowment for the Arts on behalf of Theatre Communications Group; the American Arts Alliance; and Arena Stage; the theater I cofounded and have headed for forty years.

I first wish to thank the Chairman and members of the Subcommittee for their commitment to the Endowment's principles of creativity and freedom of expression during the heated debate in Congress last year, echoes of which have not yet subsided. This interchange posed challenging questions and raised political issues that are by no means clear cut. These were dealt with by this committee with extraordinary patience, fairness, and grace. I would also like to congratulate the Honorable Sidney Yates on his imminent receipt of an honorary degree from The Juilliard School, a recognition to which his championship of the arts in America over decades so clearly entitles him.

Since the late forties and early fifties the American theater has been engaged in a Revolution, a long Revolution filled with stops and starts, periods of renewal and periods of plateau, moods of high energy alternating with despair—a kind of manic-depressive roller coaster whose ups and downs are especially acute at this time.

The Revolution began with a small group of people who were fed up with current ways of making theater and who committed themselves to finding new ones and having them prevail. From a handful of theaters around 1950 (the year of Arena's birth) there are now more than 400 all over the United States, playing to over 19,000,000 people a year, regularly producing new American and foreign plays, interesting revivals, and world classics in contemporary interpretations, uncovering ever-broader audiences through a moderate ticket-pricing policy, taking on the central question of cultural diversity onstage and in the audience, fulfilling their responsibilities in the area of training artists and administrators, and engaging more actors and other theater artists outside of New York than are engaged within New York, the erstwhile capital of the American theater. Indeed, it is to these professional theater companies that Broadway now turns for its primary source of talent and energy—actors, directors, designers and, of course, the new playwrights, from whom all other production arts flow. Only the multimillion-dollar musical remains as the signifying mark of Broadway.

What has been built in roughly the past third of a century is an American national theater—the fastest growth of a new form for the arts in history.

It is a theater admired the world over, especially in Eastern Europe, for its energy, its artistry, its originality, its playwrights, for its amazing survival with a minimum of government support. It is admired and envied for its freedom of dissent, up to now unhampered. We draw closer, the Eastern European theater and ours, as the tyranny of the box office becomes known to them in their shifting economies and the tyranny of censorship, which they have lifted, threatens to become known to us.

The originating thought at the base of our theatrical Revolution was really quite simple. It was that theater should stop serving the function of making money, for which it has never been and never will be suited, and help reveal and shape the process of living, for which it is uniquely suited, for which it, indeed, exists. This new, radical-though-simple thought was that theater should be reclaimed from commerce and restored to itself as a form of art: an ancient and ever-changing artform, where life in all its complexity happens before our eyes. Paradoxically, what was needed to make this artform prevail over the controlling influence of the marketplace was money!

From 1950 to 1959 Arena was on its own, spending only what it could take in at the box office. From 1959 until 1965, the Ford Foundation provided additional support, allowing us to grow beyond the constraints of box office income. By its support, Ford attracted attention to the arts in a way that had never happened in our history. Then, in 1965, with an appropriation of $2.5 million, the National Endowment for the Arts came into the arts world. Since 1965 and until 1990, as Ford and other foundations withdrew from the arts, concentrating on other concerns of society, the National Endowment for the Arts has been our most reliable mainstay—our safety net under the high wire, our sky hook from which to suspend our act, our booster, and our prime enabler in the psychic, muscular straining for artistic excellence.

Surely this was not just about dollars themselves. With an arts budget that represents only one two-hundredth of one percent of the total national budget—less than sixty-four cents per year per taxpayer on everything the Endowment does—we are hardly killing the goose while we enjoy the golden egg!

Federal dollars give us nourishment, warmth, dignity, a place at the table, acknowledgment that we're doing a good job. They fluff up our sagging spirits, strengthen our will, gird our right arm and, most importantly, pry loose resources from private corporations and, by the matching requirements, tap our communities on the shoulder and ask them to look up, please. The $119 million given by the Endowment for grants in 1988 generated over $1.36 billion in private funds. Talk about making your money work for you!

Without this aggregate of funding from the nonprofit area, from which over half our economic resources come, the American theater, a tough but tender animal, is on the way to becoming an endangered species. It cannot survive on box office income alone, and it needs the knighthood that only the federal government can bestow, in order to continue its evolutionary climb.

Does it really matter, in the end? What if it were all to fall apart? What, after all, is the American theater up against the rest of the story: the despair and hopelessness of the poor; the bewilderment of the mentally ill in their barracks/shelters; the scourge of AIDS; the flight from reality into the haze of cocaine; the despoiling of the air and water; the accumulating illiteracy of our young? Do we over-dramatize the case for drama? Are the arts not a flourish, an "extra added attraction" that we can live without? How are we to think of these things?

Before the city, there was the hamlet and the village; before the village, the camp, the cache, and the cairn; even before these, there was the cave. And inside the cave, there were great natural chambers covered with paintings of astonishing vividness of form and facility of design—exquisitely realistic animals or highly formalized and styl-ized men and women, art of enormous aesthetic mastery. One Paleo-lithic drawing on the wall of a cave in France depicts a man dressed in the skin of a stag, wearing antlers on his head, presumably a wiz-ard. Aha! an early actor, trying, even then, over the rim of history, to imitate some other presence, in order to influence nature and imag-ine his fate.

In the rites of the cave, if anywhere, we find the first hints of our civilization. Not alone for the carnal rewards of the hunt or some sure source of water, not for a place for safe mating or protection against the elements or the barbarian, but for a more meaningful and enchanting life, for abundance of spirit. To share with others the day-light fantasy and the nighttime dream, men gathered and made their enclaves.

An old Egyptian scribe tells us that when cities were first built, the mission of the founders was "to put the gods in their shrines." Art. And thought. Giving form to the imagination. Recording the past and the activities of the present, extending in time backward and forward. Attending to the care and culture of men.

I testify on behalf of all our theaters that we must nourish our storytellers, for without them we will have lost our childhood and, with our childhood, who we might become.

On May 15, 1990, Zelda provided this statement in person before the Con-gressional Subcommittee on Interior Appropriation. Her testimony was one response to furious attacks on the National Endowment for the Arts for funding controversial and allegedly "obscene" art.

A HARD TIME FOR THE HIGH ARTS
(1993)

While I was still an undergraduate, lured to a strange new course at Cornell University called Contemporary Soviet Civilization, I had the enormous pleasure of studying Russian History with Sir Bernard Pares, a leading world authority on the subject. I will never forget Sir Bernard, English scholar whose heart was warm, head crammed full, but whose body, at almost eighty, was growing chilly. Against the Ithaca summer he wore long underwear which peeked out randomly and unceremoniously from his outer clothing. One day, he was talking about religion in the Soviet Union. He had the habit of taking long pauses, while his mind wandered to gather the needed supplies. He would look up suddenly and let loose. "Religion in Russia!" he shot out on this day. "Religion in Russia is like a nail in the wall. The harder they hammer at it, the further it goes in." All these years later, history has proven Sir Bernard right.

I think the theater, surely our own American theater, has shared this peculiarly abused yet death-defying destiny. Hammered at, beleaguered, deprived for long years of official encouragement, it has refused to go away. Deeper into the wall every time. The Fabulous Invalid—groaning, coughing, weak with the shakes, still cat-and-mouses its deathbed scene. It has always leapt up at the last moment to announce, in a quavering voice, that its pulse seems to be quickening, that it feels like some tea and toast, and to ask, with a certain pathetic panache: "Where's the stage, and what's the show?"

But is this time different? Or does it merely seem so, merely seem this time that the hammer is not after the nail—is not satisfied with aggression against the nail—but is aiming at the wall itself? A special report by Nello McDaniel and George Thorn put out in 1991 by the Foundation for the Extension and Development of the American Professional Theatre (FEDAPT) described what it calls "The Quiet Crisis in the Arts." Since then, the crisis has grown noisier, not to be ignored.

In the first three years of the nineties, fifteen theaters have closed. Most major dance companies carry debts of six figures and higher, and virtually all dance companies with budgets of three million dollars carry seven-figure debts. Dance Theatre of Harlem laid off their dancers and suspended operations under the weight of an estimated $1.7 million deficit. The Joffrey Ballet's internal artistic and board dispute was punctuated by disclosure that the institution was carrying a debt of two million. Its recent plans to merge with the equally troubled American Ballet Theatre fell apart. Adrian Hall's successor at Trinity Repertory Company resigned in the wake of revelations that the theater was carrying an accumulated debt of $1.2 million.

This crisis is not about incompetent management or bad managers. It is not about lack of accountability or bad boards. It is not about unappreciated productions or bad art. A confluence of factors, financial and otherwise, that have developed over the last ten to fifteen years, have changed the world by happenstance and by design.

About government support of the arts Ronald Reagan was very clear: He didn't believe in it. He expressed, in word and action, his intention to eliminate government support of the arts. After taking office in 1981, Reagan encountered opposition to these plans, though, and had to settle for substantial budget cuts. We didn't welcome the cuts, of course, but it was better than no NEA at all. We adjusted and tried to make up the difference in other ways, accepting, somehow, between 1979 and 1989, an NEA budget that declined approximately forty percent in purchasing power.

But while the arts community was settling in to the situation, the Reagan/Bush ideological and economic policies were penetrating the private and public sector, redistributing wealth and creating a very different order of business, power, and debt. According to political analyst Kevin Phillips: "Under Reagan, federal budget policy, like tax changes, became a factor in the realignment of wealth . . . The first effect lay in who received more government funds. Republican constituencies—military producers and installations, agribusiness, bondholders, and the elderly—clearly benefited, while decreases in social programs hurt Democratic interests and constituencies: the poor, big cities, subsidized housing, education, and the arts."[1] During the eighties an estimated hundred billion dollars was withdrawn from human resources by the government. Daycare centers, nursing homes, museums, symphony orchestras, and theaters felt the pinch.

Non-federal funding sources have been pressed to fill that gap. While federal support of the arts represented a small percentage of contributed income, non-federal funding represented a significant percentage. Having that funding redirected and diffused away from the arts in the face of growing demand in other areas has created stress, tension, the flight of artists from their institutions, and the pointing of fingers within them. Many places have abandoned hope.

From 1980 to 1990, the U.S. went from being the world's largest creditor nation to the world's largest debtor nation, from carrying a four trillion dollar debt to a ten trillion dollar one. A third of all corporate profits in 1990 went toward debt service. Those who assert that the arts need to be more like business and government should take note: The arts have achieved this dubious goal—we are dangerously in debt!

In addition to a shrinking financial capital pool, the past ten years have seen a shrinking human capital pool, both in terms of audience and of workers for the arts. For the first time since the fifties, we are seeing a decline in audience attendance, a startling transformation in our expectations. From the late sixties to the early eighties baby boomers provided an audience tailor-made for the growing arts industry. Bright, young, urban-dwelling adults, with disposable time and income, fueled the rapid emergence and growth of many arts organizations. They also provided for an industry low on financial capital a large, eager pool of young, well-educated, idealistic individuals willing to learn-and-invent-as-you-go at low salaries.

1. Zelda is quoting from Phillips's op-ed essay in the *New York Times*, June 17, 1990. The last three words in the quotation—"and the arts"—are Zelda's own addition. Phillips ends his sentence with "subsidized housing, education." [T.L.]

Now, the boomers are older. They are married with children or heading single-parent households. They have greater job responsibilities. They've moved out of urban areas, which are too expensive and less desirable for raising children. They have less disposable income and, equally important, less disposable time. Many have left the arts for jobs that can better support their families and lifestyles. The same labor shortage afflicting other areas of American commerce also affects the arts. The so-called cultural elite grows less aggressive.

McDaniel and Thorn have proposed pragmatic, creative, and common-sensical, short-term remedies for this "quiet" crisis. Ingeniously, there are three tailor-made approaches offered to suit the institutions that are: (a) "pre-edge" (I presume the edge referred to is the edge of DOOM); (b) "at the edge"; and (c) "over the edge" (i.e., already DOOMED).

Rapidly summarized, we are advised: first, to cease being driven by the equation of Growth=Success that we are used to. The reason: Growth raises expense budgets; income budgets are then created to balance those expenses without regard to whether the goals are achievable. Second, the authors urge us to establish a floor of hard-core income, from which to develop all short-term planning. That is, don't plan to spend more than you are absolutely sure to take in. Eliminate whole major expense sections if necessary. (Echoes of Henry Thoreau: Don't increase your wants; decrease your needs.) When the institution is in balance—if it can be rescued from the edge—then and only then can it be reconceptualized and redesigned; then and only then can it return to its center—the aesthetic which animates it. Always tested, of course, against the question: "Can the artistic needs equal the available human and financial resources?"

The stated assumption underlying all this is that in today's environment, arts organizations cannot be large enough, bountiful enough, to meet the goals many of us thought they would meet, indeed, designed them to meet: hiring more artists for more money for longer periods of time; having an artistic home; staffing well-paid middle-management positions; providing health care, pensions, and sabbaticals, and so forth.

Startlingly, McDaniel and Thorn also point to a redefinition of the term *professional*, suggesting that, perhaps, serious professionals can no longer expect to make their living from an arts institution.

They use the small family farm as an example. A recent study from the Secretary of Agriculture showed that seventy percent of family farm income comes from off-farm labor, only thirty percent from the farm itself. Typically, at least one member of the farm unit works in town to subsidize the farm. How truly disappointing, after all these years of struggle, to think that artists will, likewise, have to learn word processing or marry well.

The process of reconceptualization and redesign must include the possibility of closing the organization—will the Fabulous Invalid stand still for that???—though the authors hold out the possibility for positive outcomes as well. The outside environment may change, freeing more resources. In the meantime, we can develop new ways of thinking, new approaches, new strategies, techniques that reflect "the current environment and conditions." In fact, the report offers, change might be good for us. "Motivated by a new perspective . . . change-transformation refines and integrates. It attempts to heal the dichotomy of either/or, or this-or-that . . . Change no longer seems threatening; instead it absorbs, enlarges, enriches. Each new insight widens the road ahead of us . . ."

Well, yes, but we are left with disquieting questions.

When are we to regard the Fabulous Invalid as having died? How do we pinpoint the moment of *aesthetic* demise? Is it possible for the body of the work to go, for only a faint pulse remain—the Cheshire Cat smile of the work—and the institution still be regarded as alive? Can its intentionality be diminished (rehearsal time compressed, plays selected by cast size, classics too large and therefore gone, staff reduced, acting companies disbanded, pennies pinched, aspirations snuffed) and, by admitting and accepting this diminishment, can the organization nonetheless experience the denouement as "healing, enlarging, enriching?"

Is there a "world in a grain of sand," as the poet William Blake tells us? If, in the Hegelian sense, changes in quantity lead to changes in quality—a thing becomes another thing at a certain point when "more of the thing" has accumulated—does it work backward as well? As one unloads, devolves, reduces oneself, does the reduction become a *reductio ad absurdum*? As we transform backward, will we simply get thinner and thinner as artistic standards bleed from our veins, and end up down the drain? How small can the vision get before it's some other vision or no vision at all? What if the grown-up doesn't want to speak as a child again?

What can be done? I don't know. We are navigating unchartered waters. The poet Antonio Machado quotes a proverb: "Traveler, there is no path. The path is made by walking." How, then, shall we walk?

The melding of cultures occurs throughout everyday life in the United States, a melding that recent events, such as the riots in Crown Heights, Brooklyn; and South Los Angeles, threaten to obliterate. But not yet. We hope not yet. In a brilliant essay entitled, "America the Multinational Society," Ishmael Reed probes this melding and the threat that some feel it poses. He begins by quoting an article from the *New York Times*, June 23, 1983, that I was similarly struck by:

> At the annual Lower East Side Jewish Festival yesterday, a Chinese woman ate a pizza slice in front of Ty Thuan Duc's Vietnamese grocery store. Beside her a Spanish-speaking family patronized a cart with two signs: "Italian Ices" and "Kosher by Rabbi Alper." And after the pastrami ran out, everybody ate knishes.

Ishmael writes:

> On the day before Memorial Day, 1983, a poet called me to describe a city he had just visited. He said that one section included mosques, built by the Islamic people who dwelled there. Attending his reading, he said, were large numbers of Hispanic people, forty thousand of whom lived in the same city. He was not talking about a fabled city located in some mysterious region of the world. The city he'd visited was Detroit.
>
> A few months before, I was leaving Houston, Texas, I heard it announced on the radio that Texas's largest minority was Mexican-American . . . The taped voice used to guide the passengers on the air trams connecting terminals in Dallas Airport is in both Spanish and English.
>
> . . . One of the artists told me that his paintings, which included African and Afro-American mythological sym-

bols and imagery, were hanging in the local McDonald's restaurant. The next day I went to McDonald's and snapped
pictures of smiling youngsters eating hamburgers below
paintings that could grace the walls of any of the country's
leading museums . . .

Such blurring of cultural styles occurs in everyday life in
the United States to a greater extent than anyone can imagine . . . The result is what the Yale professor, Robert Thompson, referred to as a cultural bouillabaisse, yet members
of the nation's present educational and cultural elect still
cling to the notion that the United States belongs to some
vaguely defined entity they refer to as "Western civilization,"
by which they mean, presumably, a civilization created by
the people of Europe, as if Europe can be viewed in monolithic terms. Is Beethoven's *Ninth Symphony*, which includes
Turkish marches, a part of Western civilization, or the late
nineteenth- and twentieth-century French paintings, whose
creators were influenced by Japanese art? And what of the
cubists, through whom the influence of African art changed
modern painting, or the surrealists, who were so impressed
with the art of the Pacific Northwest Indians that, in their
map of North America, Alaska dwarfs the lower forty-eight
in size?

. . . And what of the millions of Europeans who have
Black African and Asian ancestry, Black Africans having
occupied several countries for hundreds of years? Are these
"European" members of Western Civilization—or the Hun-
garians, who originated across the Urals in a place called
Greater Hungary, or the Irish, who come from the Iberian
Peninsula?

. . . Western civilization, then, becomes another confus-
ing category like Third World, or Judea-Christian culture, as
man attempts to impose his small-screen view of political
and cultural reality upon a complex world.

Reed is right about the American elite clinging to this view of civilization, as if it was Western and Western was white. But it is time to
recognize, in James Baldwin's phrase from *Notes of a Native Son*, that

America is white no longer, and it will never be white again. I say that "it is time to recognize." This truth *has* been recognized, in one degree or another, with one degree of success or another, in most of our public institutions. But *least of all* in our arts institutions—ironically, the one place where, while preserving specific cultures and cultural symbols, there might be found as well a common ground of American cultural experience.

Many important steps were made in the eighties to encourage the democratization of American arts institutions. The NEA, state and local arts agencies, and some foundations and corporations are strongly behind the process and even use evidence of its forward movement as criteria for funding. Nonetheless, there remain major discrepancies between the ethnic composition of our cities and that of audiences in our major public institutions, discrepancies that are impossible to ignore.

One public art agency official in North Carolina noted recently that although nearly all public institutions had been integrated in his lifetime—with people from all cultural backgrounds coming together to study, swim, and read in public facilities, the same does not hold true of the arts. He goes on to wonder whether the arts are the last bastion of public segregation in this state.

I think we really *do* know as artists and as institutions which way we must walk on this issue. It is a difficult path for some of us, since our arts institutions are at base the expression of individual artists, whose tastes, interests, and talents incline the way they incline, for reasons that are mysterious and hidden and highly personal. They do not always incline in the way others may want them to. I offer no answers to this but ask for higher levels of questioning.

I believe it necessary that we ourselves—the creators and presenters and managers of art, with our boards and community leaders—seek and support cultural equity in our time. We ourselves, through concrete actions that are both identifiable and doable, must take the initiative for this. Not because it is a duty imposed from the outside, but, first and above all, for the resources and richness that such a policy will provide our art. We must embrace the thought, with curiosity and joy, that various cultures add richness, complexity, variety, individuality, juice. Yes—add diversity. The highest attribute of Nature is its diversity. It has taken billions of years to evolve its manifoldness.

One day the highest accomplishment of man-made civilization, following Nature, will be precisely that—its diversity. Our present challenge—and our pleasure—is to learn how to organize and manage that diversity.

Secondly, we must undertake this course for our very survival. In California, perhaps America's most socially volatile state, a recent Department of Finance report indicates that within thirty years, the population will consist of 16 million Anglos, 14.9 million Latinos, 2 million Blacks, and 5 million Asians and others. It does not take a lot of imagination to visualize the increasing volatility of the situation. If minorities, soon the largest segment of the population, continue to feel the arts are not theirs, the pressure to change the pattern of public support will only grow. The established arts organizations must not fail to see that the light at the end of the tunnel is a train coming our way.

The art we choose to sustain, the artists we put on our stages, the audiences we reach out to and bring into our halls, the power and plans we choose to share with smaller ethnic groups, must attest to equity amid diversity. The need comes at a terrible time, when arts and presenting organizations are struggling to survive, and support structures are stretched to capacity. But we must act individually and, especially, in partnership. We must define what we want to do, get together, lay out means, and do it.

We must not only further democratize our own institutions, but recognize, help to establish, and support, psychologically and emotionally, organizations dedicated to culturally specific work and artists of color.

If we walk this way, perhaps a path for survival and growth will unexpectedly emerge.

In Cincinnati, fall of 1990, eight jurors hearing Cincinnati v. Cincinnati Contemporary Arts Center (also known as the Robert Mapplethorpe obscenity trial) determined the border between art and obscenity. At stake were the First Amendment rights of artists, the survival of the National Endowment for the Arts, the community standards for pornography, and the question of whether the U.S. would become a nation that sustains only an orthodox and official art or a live culture.

I want to focus on the process of that jury's selection and what might be learned from it. The *New York Times*, September 25, 1990, describes the voir dire:

> Eight jurors and one or two alternates are to be selected from among fifty prospective jurors. The questioning so far indicates that few of them know or care much about art, and most are deeply religious and strongly object to pornography and homosexuality . . . Of the eight men and women questioned so far by the prosecution . . . only three had ever been to an art museum. Four others said they had gone to other types of museums, but only on field trips in schools. One man in his fifties said he had never been to any kind of museum. The man said he could not relate either to art or its enthusiasts. "They're into that type of stuff," he said during questioning by a defense lawyer, Marc D. Megibov. "These people are in a different class. Evidently they get some type of satisfaction looking at it. I don't understand artwork. That stuff never interested me."

The lesson: We are a nation without effective arts education. Our major conduit for arts education—the public schools—do not, at present, educate a population who knows or cares about art. The prosecuting attorneys in Cincinnati knew that the forced marches of school field trips to museums do not count. They tried to keep out of the courtroom adults who draw, collect, or go to museums—anyone who might understand art as invention rather than report, who might argue that the seven offending Mapplethorpe photographs on display at the CCAC were part of a larger body of work, or who might understand that to exhibit is not to endorse, but to invite response. But the attorneys can rest assured—at most, only three out of fifty Americans are that dangerous!

I refer to the alarming statistics of the NEA report "Toward Civilization," prepared under former Endowment Chairman Frank Hodsoll:

- 53% of Americans have never had a basic music lesson.
- 75% have had no lesson in visual arts.

- 84% have had no lessons in ballet.
- 82% have had no lessons in creative writing.
- 84% have never taken a visual arts appreciation course.
- 80% have never studied music appreciation.
- Only 9 states require art classes for high school graduation; another 7 require them only in a college preparatory program.
- At the time of the report, 61% of all Americans had not attended a single live performance of jazz, classical music, opera, musical theater, or ballet during the previous 12 months, nor had they visited a museum or a gallery.

"How do you get people to pay real attention to music again?" composer William Bolcom once asked. "People become interested in activities in which they have participated even reasonably well . . . Even though a person's participation may be far in the past, there will always be an affinity."

That makes enormous sense to me: How do you know you like it unless you taste it? It is quite possible for older adults to find a new love for the arts as viewers and supporters, but direct involvement in the materials, risks, and dangers of the arts at an early age provides the most profound basis for understanding. There are many explanations for the decline in arts audiences in the eighties, the first such decline since the fifties. Surely the progressive inattention to public arts education is one of them.

The arts became part of the common curriculum at the turn of the century, reborn from Europe as practical and publicly available. That the arts, as a kind of skills capital, were given a place in the curriculum at all was significant. But the bargain had its Faustian side: The arts became part of common schooling but consequently lost their distinctiveness as a form of knowledge and set of practices. The arts, like arithmetic or history, succumbed to an exercise-driven approach to instruction that gives us, to this day, art and music textbooks with numbered objectives and printed requirements for time and materials—instead of offering authentic problems and projects confronted by artists, composers, dancers, or designers. In a fascinating essay, "More than Minor Disturbances: The Place of the Art in American Education," Dennie Palmer Wolf and Mary Burger note:

High on a wall in a high school art studio, as late as 1970, hangs this list of criteria on which student work will be evaluated:

1. Work is turned in complete and on time.
2. Work is neat.
3. Work spaces and materials have been taken care of.
4. The student has cooperated with others.
5. The student shows evidence of having tried the techniques and problems that were introduced.
6. Work is original.

With the possible exception of number six, these could be criteria for an electronics assembly line or for training at an insurance firm. Nothing here argues that artwork demands attention to unique dimensions of process or outcome. There is no call for invention, for handsomeness of craft, for resonant meanings.

In the past two decades, however, a revolution has taken place in our understanding of human behavior. Often called the "cognitive revolution," this shift stresses the mind's ability to deal in rules, concepts, symbols, and representations; it emphasizes the role of invention, inference, and imagination in human life. It stems from fresh interest in the mind itself, it's capacity to entertain multiple worlds, to rework impressions and memories, to think about thinking. In this light, the arts have been reenvisioned as powerful ways of knowing and doing, out of which emerge radical methods of education.

Recent back-to-back issues of the *New York Times* featured informative articles about arts in education. The dire—"As Schools Trim Budgets, the Arts Lose Their Place"—and the hopeful—"Creativity vs. Academic Study, How Should Schools Teach Arts?" In December 1992, the new Secretary of Education, Richard W. Riley, gave an encouraging speech, calling for the building of broad-based coalitions to serve children and youth through "fundamental changes in our attitudes and our approach to education." In Riley's home state of South Carolina, schools that have experimented with the arts as a way to teach kids how to better read, write, and calculate became academic success stories.

Jerrold Ross, director of the National Arts Education Research Center at NYU, concludes that arts education has demonstrated significant impact on academic achievement in a variety of settings and population groups, ranging from the barrio of Los Angeles to the upper echelon of suburban New Jersey. He speaks of the "naturalness" of the arts to childhood: "The symbols of the arts in sound and sight are things that children deal with and respond to automatically. Students have a natural and immediate link to the things that arts are made of." He goes on to say: "I don't see how you can teach mathematics, for example, without visual representation of what mathematical concepts are all about. It inevitably leads you to figures, shapes, forms, which are best illustrated through real art."

The call is for the development of skills in and knowledge of the arts within the schools. The call is also for school instruction to be combined with the highest quality arts experiences in professional theaters, concert halls, and museums. Artistry-based education insists that students engage directly and personally with the works of art and with artists.

We are looking down a ten-year road to the building of new people and, in a narrower way, to the building of new audiences—to the preservation and extension of our arts institutions. Students learn to think about what they behold and experience. We have to be there for them, if we expect them to be there for us. We have to make the path together.

In December 1987, Bill Moyers produced and hosted a PBS series called *God and Politics*. One segment, "On Earth As It Is in Heaven," focused on Christian Reconstructionists. According to Moyers, the Christian Reconstructionists believe it is the moral obligation of Christians to recapture every institution of society for Jesus Christ. And they're committed to a long grassroots campaign. "They disagree on many things," Moyers explains, "but on this they agree: Every area of American life—law, medicine, media, the arts, business, education, and, finally, the civil government must one day be brought under the rule of the righteous."

We watched them operate, led by Jesse Helms, coming up for reelection, Donald Wildmon, leader of the American Family Association, and, surreptitiously, Pat Robertson, evangelical host of the 700 Club and 1988 presidential candidate. After a rapid succession of startling events in 1990, challenging and changing the relationship between our government and the arts, we watched them again at the 1992 Republican Convention in Houston, as Pat Buchanan and Pat Robertson dominated both the party's platform and the candidates themselves.

They are still at it. Emboldened by the furor over President Clinton's proposal to allow homosexuals in the military, conservative and evangelical Christian groups are furiously preparing for the battles to come. "It's a bonanza for building organizations and raising money: The fundraising letters are already in the mail," John Green, a professor at the University of Akron, who is an expert on the Christian right, told the *New York Times*. "I've been talking to several of these people, and they all say that they could not have scripted Bill Clinton's first weeks any better."

In 1990, for the first time in history, an American museum and its director were brought to trial on criminal charges of pandering obscenity. For the first time in its history, The National Endowment for the Arts was mortally threatened because of the kind of art it had, in a minuscule percentage of its grants, supported, a battle marked by distortions, divisive actions, and inflammatory rhetoric. In yet another first, the NEA's relationship with its own constituents in the arts community was eroded by the grantees' required signing of "obscenity oaths," which many refused to sign, so sacrificing much-needed grants. Also for the first time, artists and mainstream arts institutions sued their government patron—and won. The relationship between arts and government has been forever changed by these events.

Why were the attackers able to wreck such havoc? The political Far Right, strengthened and highly organized during the eighties, found itself without a unifying issue. When Helms threw down the gauntlet, the Religious Right generated an outpouring of letters nearly sixteen-to-one against the NEA. As the debate grew more strident and pro-NEA forces began to organize, testify, and editorialize in favor of reauthorization, the public's response shifted somewhat. A number of senators and representatives, however, viewed this shift with cynicism. One member quipped, "Most of my favorable letters are coming from actors and artists and very few from real people."

As we begin to make a path by walking, hoping to save our institutions and ourselves, it must be admitted that—decentralized, unprepared, and politically innocent—we provided a convenient, juicy target. We must confess that we are out of touch with those who will determine the economic future of our institutions: the people themselves. We have lost touch with their elected officials. We have failed to convince society that the arts are essential to life, giving meaning, color, and clarity to all the rest. Protected from "getting our hands dirty in politics," we are learning the price of our clean hands.

We need to develop strong coalitions within the arts and with citizens' groups outside of the arts. We need to establish and then tout our relevance to our communities. We need to assemble and disseminate a barrage of materials evincing the arts' relationship to quality of life, jobs, economic vitality, education, and the definition of national values.

The new Chairman of the National Endowment for the Arts must be a healer: both a spokesman and an ombudsman for America's art. It's a job that requires enormous skill and wisdom. We hope for the right choice.

But the battle for integrating the arts into American life belongs as much to us as to our leaders, belongs to every one of us who cares. An opinion poll reported just this month by Research and Forecasts, Inc. indicates that while Americans have an overwhelmingly positive view of the arts, they feel little connection with them. Ninety-one percent of those questioned said that the arts and humanities were important to freedom of expression; eighty-seven percent said they were life-enriching. Fifty-seven percent, however, said that they played only a minor role in their own lives. We must find ways to connect this generalized feeling for the arts to direct involvement with them. We must ask, "What is the soul of this country?" and answer, "The arts and humanities."

Remarks for the Cosmopolitan Club, March 10, 1993. Located on the Upper East Side of New York City, the club has for more than one hundred years served as a meeting place for women to pursue interests in arts and letters, public affairs, and current events.

THE PROFIT IN NONPROFIT

(2000)

There's a new and seminal thought bubbling up in American theater, embracing both its for-profit and nonprofit forms. The thought is that the differences between the two have become blurred, that the survival of each depends on increased collaboration between both, and that past resentments, one toward the other, are too expensive to harbor. "Hang together or hang separately" is the gist of it. Because the nonprofit theater arose in protest against the habits of Broadway, which has looked upon the rest of us as farm teams, this is an historic development.

Gerald Schoenfeld, chairman of the Shubert Organization (whose foundation generously serves the nonprofit theater), notes: "You cannot afford the luxury any longer of thinking of two distinct isolated worlds of theater. Economics has been the driving force between profit and nonprofit, or taxpaying and non-taxpaying, as I call it." Several alarming trends in the nonprofit arena probably drive his thinking. These include: our theaters' increased concentration on the bottom line, the development and selection of plays and musicals with an eye to Broadway transfer, and the adoption of practices—not to mention *vocabulary*—from the profit world. (Anyone who has attended a recent board or staff meeting will recognize such terms as "cost effective," "branding," "entrepreneurial," "leveraging," and "market share.")

Rocco Landesman, commercial theater producer, underlines the idea that the profit/nonprofit dichotomy is obsolete. "We on Broadway look like the nonprofit theaters, and they look like us," he observes. He notes, rightly, the increasing power of managing directors and boards vis-à-vis artistic leadership, as risk and experimentation become more costly. Assessing the nonprofit theaters as a group, he concludes: "What had been a cause seems now to be mostly a marketing campaign." Even Ben Cameron, executive director of Theatre Communications Group, the service organization for the nonprofit field, invites a "new spirit of candor and cautious collegiality." The world has changed, he says, and "we are now being drawn together in numerous ways." He expresses the hope for healthier working relationships and "perhaps the identification of one common cause that we might continue together."

Why the speculations, and why now? It's prompted, I believe, by the lurking feeling that we're sliding backward—all of us—in the acquisition of new audiences, the battle against rising costs, the development of young talent, in the art-based education of our young, and *especially* in our ability to articulate why and how art is a way of knowing reality and, therefore, must be free. Behind this feeling (maybe in front of it) is the logic of interlocking need: Money from foundations and government flows less freely, for which Broadway might provide some replacement funds; and Broadway is hurting for product, something the nonprofits can and do provide. A symbiosis à deux.

Additionally, by means of extra "enhancement" funds to a collaborating regional theater, a Broadway producer can lift a production to a more commercially viable level than the theater alone can. This may mean higher salaries for some actors, more musicians, a more lavish set, or a longer rehearsal period. In turn, the theater gains a participation, albeit minor, in future profits, program credit and, probably what's most important, the visibility of being associated with what might conceivably be a Broadway hit. Boards of directors like this, as it stimulates future fundraising and elevates the theater's standing in the community: a kind of gilt by association.

In exchange for these benefits, the theater opens its doors and offers its stages and physical facilities, its technical and office staffs, its less costly production methods, its subscribers and single-ticket buyers, its marketing budget and, in a more intangible way, the entire culture—both aesthetic and managerial—of its institution to the pre-Broadway, for-Broadway, for-profit process. Production at a non-profit theater has replaced the out-of-town tryout of earlier years.

The theater may be assured that artistic control will remain with them, but it can be difficult for this control to be exercised in an empirical, day-by-day manner, since the project is clearly not being grown for home but with the artistic/economic eyes on some other target. And under the pressures of time, hasty changes in text or personnel, the impending visit of New York critics and the natural power of the piper with regard to the tune, the theater can easily feel taken over by an outside force rather than engaged in creating something of its own to share with its community.

I'm sure there are occasions when this kind of relationship has proved to be harmonious and synergistic, and co-partnership has continued on to the hoped-for commercial and artistic success. But sometimes the theater is left in disarray, its powers depleted, its morale diminished, wondering what, in the end, the gain really was. Perhaps, if the truth were told, they wouldn't even have chosen to produce this play in the first place—but the incentives proved irresistible.

Actually, this enhancement phenomenon has not been widespread, but its significance outweighs the number of its examples. The larger impact of these *quid pro quo* arrangements is attracting attention, as shown by the call for the recent Act II Conference in Cambridge to discuss, *how* and *if* to join hands more tightly on this and other issues across the Great Divide.

Gerald Schoenfeld believes that this Great Divide does not exist. If he is right, it would be better if he were wrong. But if he is right, and Rocco Landesman is also right, then the nonprofit theater world has to hear this in a non-defensive, self-critical way. We in that world have to decide what price we are willing to pay for survival. Many vital issues call for joint action, and all of us should engage them together. Nonprofit theater, for-profit theater, opera, ballet, symphony orchestra, museums, and all individual artists and intellectuals must confront the strong and united anti-art forces of our times. But this action stands apart from the danger to the nonprofit theater of redefining itself—transforming its basic values—under the pressure of economic need.

Question number one: Is there, indeed, no difference between us? Is Landesman right that "we on Broadway look like the non-profit theaters, and they look like us"? Of course not. He exaggerates (deliberately, I suppose) to make his point. In thriving communities all over the U.S. there are theaters of all kinds—African-American, gay and lesbian, Hispanic, rural, and more—developing new talent and providing an alternative to the commercial theater. The repertory of theaters in every state recognizes that our human history is but a blink of an eye in archaeological time—Shakespeare (and Ibsen and Strindberg and Molière) are, in fact, our contemporaries and must be shown over and over again for their revelations about the human animal. Of course, we are not Broadway; Broadway is not us. Else what use would Broadway have for us?

In the exaggeration, however, there is some truth. What the "nonprofits" have to remind themselves in order to stand strong in their unique purpose is that the word *nonprofit* doesn't define them; it only describes how they are situated within an economy based on money. In relationship to money, yes, they are a *non*. But in relationship to other values, they are a *for*. Our theaters do not exist for economic profit; they exist to generate a profit of a different kind—a social profit and a profit earned from the examination of reality by means of theatrical art. Our reason for existence lies in this sense of "profit."

It's precisely because the profit that nonprofits make is of a different kind—and at the time we were granted our nonprofit charters an *unfamiliar* kind—that it has taken so long to make it clear to foundations, the government, and private philanthropy that our *profit* would—Surprise!—create an economic deficit, a deficit that society must be willing to underwrite, since the values we are creating are beneficial to all. By this route we arrived at our tax alleviation, while those whose primary business is to create wealth (however desirable it might be to create good art along the way) continue to pay taxes. Broadway is wrong to express our differences as *taxable* vs. *nontaxable* and leave it at that. We are different at the root—or should be. If we are not extremely aware of how differently we and Broadway make art, this blurring of intention (in our desperation to survive in the face of increasing societal indifference) may cause us to generate less and less profit, either way you define the word.

The more people who see good theater, the better. And earning money is always easier than raising it. But it is a good idea for all of us to remember that while *to experiment* means to test or to try, *to try* is not at all the same thing as *to try out*. Our theaters are destinations in themselves, crucibles in which to test a vision of the world that is ours, not someone else's. All art is personal, an expression of one's perception of lift, through imagination, intellect, emotion, and what we call the soul. This should be as true of an arts institution as it is of a painting or poem.

I'm looking at an ad by Lexus, a company "proud to be a lead sponsor of Lincoln Center Festival 2000." There are two dancers: one on pointe, the other with a leg outstretched, arms of both held wide. What's the problem here? The ankles, shoulders, knees, elbows, necks, and even portions of the two heads—and now I notice the hearts as well—are not bone and muscle, but automobile parts! Beautiful and sleek. Lexus says, "Our passion for excellence is clear." No one can dispute the creative pinnacles of Broadway, achieved along the path of commercial gain. Broadway can still provoke inspiration and aspiration. But we should dance our own dances and make them as we think they should be made. Or why are we here at all?

Published in *American Theatre*, December 2000.

WHITHER (OR WITHER) ART?

(2003)

U p and down, back and forth, move ahead and drop back, no straight staircase to the sky but growth in a kind of spiral: success, success, success, then failure and disappointment, then the struggle to get unstuck and push ahead, to keep on keeping on, and the one who finishes last wins. Brecht has Galileo say: "As much of the truth gets through as we push through; we crawl by inches."

Over the holidays, I had time to catch up with the October, November, and December 2002 issues of *American Theatre* Magazine and was astounded by the thought-provoking riches I found in them. Serious questions were posed about the very form and nature of what we have come to know as the "institutional theater"—a kind of theater that in the past half century has transformed the way we produce (bring forth) our art. We are pushed to think about whether these institutions do or do not—did but now don't—nurture the art and the artists. Since those who challenged and warned are our friends and colleagues, and raised their voices not only out of anger, disappointment, and frustration, but also out of love and a sense of responsibility, I took their queries very seriously. Here are some personal ruminations.

I cofounded Arena Stage in Washington, DC, in 1950 and was its producing artistic director for forty years. I left Arena Stage in 1991, and much has changed since then. It has become increasingly difficult to keep a theater pressing forward in a creative way. In my several years with The Acting Company, Margot Harley's spirited young ensemble that tours the country with classics and new work, I continued to learn about the aspirations of young talent and about the amazing audience across America that is hungry for theater. Now chairing an intense actor-training program at the Tisch School of the Arts at New York University, I've been taught how the weight of a highly structured, top-down institution actually feels; I have a deeper empathy with the artist's sense that the largest issues are decided above. I speak in this essay as a representative of what has come to be called the "institutional theater," now under scrutiny, if not attack.

What are the critics saying to us? What do they suggest as the next crusade? What have they misperceived, and what enlightens us? What is feasible, and what is pie-in-the-sky? And the big issues: a new generation of founders? Challenge the power of our boards? No longer an alternative theater as we were founded to be. Pass the torch to the new alternatives? Fold up our expensive tents and silently steal away? These are provocative questions, indeed! How do we respond to them? Jaan Whitehead (*American Theatre*, "Art Will Out," October 2002) acknowledges that not every theater or board or mission statement is like every other, but feels that the pressure of institutional art (emphasis on "institution") is widespread enough to warrant alarm.

What does she mean by "institutional art"? The following, I think: Art that is made with the right eye on the dollar, the left eye on the stage, with the right eye dominant. Art that doesn't fly because it's tethered to the bottom line. Formulaic art—this was a hit in Cleveland (Boston, Milwaukee, on or Off-Broadway), this could attract a star, this one got a Tony, this one would be great for group sales or students or at Christmas or for spring vacation, St. Patrick's Day or Rosh Hashanah, etc.—a sense of uniformity, predictability, a sense of low-grade depression. Where is astonishment, derring-do, originality, hoopla? Is our programming one from Column A and one from Column B or intentional and brave? Which comes first: what we think subscribers want or what quickens the theater's artistic heart?

Ah, what the subscribers want! The circle the critic traces really exists. I've felt that circle close around me, and it's a circle from hell. To stave off death, the maw of the box office must be fed. We count on subscribers who make up one-half (or one-third or two-thirds or ninety percent) of our audience to feed it. Indeed, if we appear plump and chipper, other sources of nourishment may open up; no foundation or corporation wants to feed a dying theater. If things work well and we give our subscribers what they want (and, of course, what we can afford), they'll be back next year, and we'll face another season with a full stomach. While there's life, there's hope!

This looks like a fair exchange, almost too good to be true, but we become suspicious and look around. Aha! The audience is running the theater! No, the box office is running the theater! No, it's the board and the executive director and his PR and marketing colleagues! No, the institution is running the theater! That's it. We've abdicated our creative freedom—that which defines us and for which we struggled to be born—so as not to bite the hands that feed us. And where does that get us?

A theater gets the audience it signals to and deserves, and repertory is destiny. Are we underrating our subscribers? Why should their taste, curiosity, and capacity to chew hard on tough thoughts or forgive a well-intentioned miss be less than ours? Presumably, deep down they're very much like us, despite differences in ethnicity, age, range of income. They come to the theater to be awakened emotionally, psychologically, even intellectually and politically. They come to have an adventure, to identify with a life that's similar enough to theirs to recognize, even as it plays out in different circumstances. Would their numbers increase if we shared our own personal tastes more fully, if we opened up, through our work, our deepest concerns. And how do we know what *they* want if we don't offer what *we* want? How do they know what they want when they haven't seen it yet?

Furthermore, what if the real audience, the one we need to complete our work, drifts away, replaced by another audience that is satisfied with less? Audiences are not interchangeable integers. Do we think that when the world turns—which it will—and the zeitgeist changes, we can return to what we really want to do? Recover the audience we've lost? The future grows out of the present while the present seeps up out of the past. The choices we make today describe the theater we'll have tomorrow. It's possible for a theater to die of starvation and, that, of course, is very sad. It's also possible for it to wither away, and that is ever sadder.

Whitehead invites us to consider the relationship between institution and art. I think of an institution as a cradle and the thing we call art as the baby. There is reciprocal need: The baby needs the cradle, but the cradle is an empty, useless piece of wood without the baby. The cradle/institution's function is to provide comfort and stability; opportunities for growth; an empathetic, responsive face; respect for organic creative process; tolerance of behavioral slipups (like flops!); and pride in high jinks (the baby's). The institution accepts that the baby will develop according to its own internal gifts and dedicates itself to providing the environment to encourage that.

Or this metaphor: The institution is not the main event; it's the Big Top, and the main event happens under the tent where performers of magic and daring gather together with an audience of empathy and imaginative belief and breathe the same air at the same moment. They are all grateful to management for making sure that everyone has been paid, that the seats are filled and the lights on, that the event comes in on budget, and that the tent doesn't leak. The board president and other board members have the best seats, as they deserve, and will later throw a party in appreciation of the audacious circus troupe. In threatening times, the clarity of this relationship is harder to maintain, because the board, responsible for the survival of the institution, can become excessively interested in what goes on in the tent, and not just how much it costs.

Because one thing is true, it doesn't necessarily follow that the opposite is not also true. The artist must have freedom to play, but he also shares responsibility for the fiscal health of the institution. Production departments struggle to stay on budget and are proud when they do. Actors extend themselves to build audiences. As an artistic director, I have always celebrated the box office. The dollars that come to us through the box office are twice blessed: once for the goods and services they buy, and once for the vote of confidence they confer— confidence that buys us freedom. The link between creativity and fiduciary responsibility is unbreakable. That said, we must always remember that while theater is a business, its business is art, not business.

Here's one from the Dinosaur Age: President Eisenhower had moved into the White House, and the Republicans moved into Washington with him, buying the houses from the Democrats who were moving out. Our audience at Arena dwindled; it would take several years to cultivate another. In that first Republican year, we lost ten thousand dollars at the box office—a large amount on such a small budget. Edward Mangum, my teacher and Arena Stage cofounder, had moved on, so, at the season's final board meeting where the loss would be explained and justified, fingers pointed only at me. I did my best. The board members were my friends, handpicked by Ed and me and executive director Tom Fichandler for their love of theater and their willingness to kick in a thousand dollars each to get this idea off the ground.

After I spoke, there was a fraught silence and then the chairman spoke up—heavily. This was the gist of it: "Of course we're committed here to a balanced budget and no red ink and so we regret the ten thousand dollars that was lost in this year's operations. Zelda has explained how this happened. With the expectation that this was a one-time circumstance and that she will be able to guide us to a balanced budget next year and the years following, we accept the explanation and the loss." The chairman then asked the board to give me a vote of confidence, which they did. This was very sweet of them, and I appreciated it. But I chiefly remember the gesture as a moment of profound and unexpected learning, as I had not for a minute anticipated that a vote of *no*-confidence was anywhere in the cards.

What I learned: I was entitled to enjoy the freedom to fail, but I mustn't indulge in it too frequently. Further, it would prove more comfortable for me if the failure could be attributed to some outside power—Republicans, snow, a flood from the Potomac River—and not to my own bad judgment or creative missteps. The *vision thing* was fine as long as whatever that vision generated by way of art paid for itself by way of money.

Not this *or* that but this *and* that—Money *and* Art, Art *and* Money. I lived through my long tenure at Arena Stage with this unresolved dialectic. At first, it was imposed by the institution; in time, it became internalized. Since the late eighties, as financial support has dwindled, the balance has become more difficult for artistic leaders to maintain.

Whitehead asks us to cease looking outside and turn our gaze inward—inside our institutions—for the source of our sense of oppression and ways we might free ourselves from it. Indeed, we must do that. But *outside* is the primary dimension within which our theaters live. A theater is an organism, an artwork in and of itself, and the person who holds the vision is its primary artist. It's her angle-of-viewing that animates all the rest. (Ralph Waldo Emerson wisely noted that "an institution is the lengthened shadow of a man." For "man," read "person.") As she confronts her time—the sounds, sights, rhythms, political conflicts, scientific achievements, timbre of human relationships, status of minorities and women, contemporary forms of theater and other arts, and, especially, systems for economic support—her vision for a theater forms itself. An artistic director belongs to both worlds—one foot inside the institution, one outside. Consciously or unconsciously, a personal vision is born in reaction to a world.

Just imagine how the artistic director's vision would expand and her heart lighten if a sudden, generous infusion of funds made it possible to pay for everything that she and the artists gathered around her had ever dreamed of. The tension between art and money could then resolve. The relationship between institution and art would then become crystal clear, unclouded by the pressures of survival. To think this way is to play with fantasy, of course, for the Great Benefactor has retired and departed on a long tour of the universe, and we don't expect him back. It's a beneficial fantasy, though, for it helps us perceive the difficulty of artistic freedom in a culture defined by marketplace success. "He who pays the piper calls the tune" may be an overstatement, but the notion threads through all aspects of our institutional life.

But let us imagine that the Great Benefactor does, indeed, return with new perspective on the Good and Beautiful and, particularly, on those needy arts institutions, impeded in their flowering. Could he lull our anxieties or endow us with the talent and wisdom that isn't already ours? Of course not. Take away our heartaches, help us to sleep more soundly, provide more time with our families? Not a chance. Attract collaborators who will stake their creative fate with us? Show us how to build acting companies and use them well? Teach us how to be diplomats, fundraisers, problem solvers, writers, speakers, psychiatrists, and still be prepared for rehearsal? No way.

Could he show us how to bring old friends like Molière and Chekhov into the contemporary world without betraying them, or how to read a new script in an unfamiliar form and imagine it living onstage? Endow us with humor, tact, and wisdom? With the capacity to infect others with our exhilaration? Make clear to us the language of budgets and balance sheets so that we know how to match expenditures to a value system and spend money without wasting it? Sharpen our judgment and broaden our taste? Awaken our capacity for attention and support to all the work, not just our own, and to all the people doing it? Keep us on the pulse of our community so we can fathom our neighbors' deepest thoughts, maybe even before they themselves are aware of them? And keep us in touch with our world so its preoccupations can be reflected on our stages? No, he can't. Of course he can't.

I've just set down a job description for artistic leadership—the artistic director and his comrades who share the vision and contribute to it with their own skills. And that was the short form! So, what *can* Mr. Great Benefactor do for us where Whitehead suggests we are remiss? Planning for the future would cease to be merely a function of budgeting and become one of dreaming. We would be able to plan out of the images in our minds rather than within the vise of this year's (reduced?) budget and/or the nagging weight of accumulated debt. What else? He could lift from us the fears that repress the creative spirit. For it's fear, I suggest, rather than lack of talent or imagination or good will that leads to making what Whitehead calls institutional art. Which one of us wants to be the one to fold up the tent?

Fear encourages caution and conformity, and caution and conformity are antithetical to what we refer to as art, since art is always a personal and original way of knowing the world. Creativity is born out of the capacity to play, and it's the very capacity for meaningful play that defines us as human beings. We can play with political ideas, with scientific hypotheses, with new forms in literature, with bodies in space. We call a theater production a play, and we play the piano and the violin. The notion of a play is indissolubly connected to the idea of freedom.

I left something out of the job description: It's the artistic leader's role to create a quiet, concentrated, and nonjudgmental environment, so that the entire community can play within it without fear. Benefaction can help her with that. I'm not sure the connection between funding and fear is fully understood by those who are pointing to our lapses, unfulfilled commitments, seeming inhospitality to artists, etc.

In addition to Whitehead, I must respond to Todd London, "The Shape of Plays to Come," and P. Carl, "Creating the Swell," in the November 2002 issue of *American Theatre*. London bravely opts for a new generation of artistic directors and theaters. For the companies and playwrights within them, he calls for not just a place at the table but the table itself. "Where is a new generation of writer-founders, of playwright-managers?" he asks. That's a rousing manifesto, and certainly anything imagined has the potential to be born. Let some talented, courageous new leaders come forward and hitch themselves to the wagon. They will be warmly welcomed into the field—and gently warned. Founding today is very different from founding yesterday.

More news from the dinosaurs: In the fifties there was a blank slate, and only a few of us were scratching on it. No models, just us, hanging on to skyhooks, with an almost primitive instinct for improvisation.

"What is to be done?" (Lenin's title!) and "*How* is it to be done?" were the subtext of our lives. At Arena, we sketched as we went, rapidly producing one thing after the other—seventeen shows the first year, because the audience was very small, and we had to turn productions over quickly. Poor, so poor! Tireless—no, tired!—we lived play to play. The future was right now. Modestly, slowly, the audience grew. Unexpectedly, foundations (circa 1957) and the NEA (1965) found us. (And, later, corporations and our own community.) They gave us money, but better than that, they gave us respect. We seemed to matter to the culture of our country. It was a heady ascent during those middle decades.

A kind of promise was made to us, not in so many words, but a promise: These agencies would continue to be there for us and would participate in our future, caring that we survive. For years the promise was kept, deepening as we evolved artistically. We enjoyed knowing that if we came up with an innovative idea—artistic or organizational—it stood a chance of being funded.

Then, for reasons you know, the promise was broken; the official culture turned its back. The final signal for me was that during her term as chairman of the NEA, Jane Alexander was able to pin down only one private meeting with Bill Clinton, which lasted just twenty minutes and offered no assurances. There was no longer any political capital for a sitting president to support the arts.

Pioneers will come or not come without our intervention. I salute the work of avant-garde theaters, community-based theaters, ethnically diverse theaters, ensembles of form-seekers, playwriting collectives and all forms of socially based theaters. I admire their creativity and freedom. I've watched them proliferate since the sixties.

But while we come from the same line, the same root, these theaters are not "an alternative" but "a parallel" to the institutional theater; they will neither replace nor inherit it. Nor do we need to choose one form over the other. We are on different paths, variants of the same species, each a vital and essential part of the wonderful variety-within-unity that is the American theater. These parallel theaters are in great need of increased funding, which their flexibility and very variety make it hard for conservative funding agencies to categorize and, therefore, to support. That's a great injustice.

There is an old Russian saying: "Circumstances alter cases," which I take to mean: "Depending on where you sit, is how you see it." It's about relativism and the subjective nature of truth. Institutions feel betrayed by this spate of critical articles in *American Theatre,* kicked when they're down—"After all we've done for you!" The artists are frustrated and angry and prod the institutions to include them.

The institutions are justified. Since the mid-twentieth century, they've been the primary developer of talent for stage as well as film and TV. Go to a movie, turn on the tube, get tickets to a Broadway or Off-Broadway show; there are our artists are. Taken all together, our theaters constitute a kind of national bazaar where Broadway producers shop for next year's product and next year's Pulitzer playwright. Where else can our new playwrights and their plays be developed but with us?

And we've created the possibility of a new way of life for those who want it. Actors, directors, designers, playwrights, can move from theater to theater, in dialogue with intelligent audiences, often evolving a sense of belonging with one or several theaters. With these "theater gigs"—plus film. TV soaps and commercials, voice-overs, designing or directing for opera, teaching—an artist can have a respected, even fulfilling life while building funds for retirement. Besides, say the institutions, artists don't really want a home; it's hard to pin them down even for one project.

What's wrong with this picture? Nothing. If everybody's satisfied with it.

But there are other voices, speaking up loud and clear. They ask for involvement, permanence, and continuity, the sort of emotional security and ebullience you feel in a personal relationship. They want their work to add to the overall work of the place. They want to belong to an idea they can believe in and serve. They want self-determination *and* a role in defining the institution.

In the manufacturing industry you get paid for the number of "pieces of work" you turn out; how many you make is the measure of things, not you. "Jobbing-in"—theater's word for piecework—can make one feel devalued: You may be moving—from "gig" to "gig"—but not evolving. If an actor is always cast because he's "right for the role," with no consideration for the development of his range and versatility, if with each role he starts over again with a group of strangers who have no collective experience to draw upon, if he senses himself as a commodity and then, "Time's up, thanks!" what are we saying to him?

Of all the artists, playwrights get the most focused attention from institutions. That's been my experience and it's what I observe. (See Lenora Inez Brown's article, "The Real World," also in *American Theatre*, November 2002.) But the number of productions she receives may not be the main point. What might weigh more than that is to know that even if this one fails, the next time she knocks, they have to let her in.

There's a tendency to romanticize our beginnings, as if we were an early Ideal Community. The beginnings weren't romantic—they were exhausting, impoverished, and full of anxiety. Yes, there was a specialness, because our intention was so clear. Each of the small band of beginners, flying blind in our separate air spaces, struggled to create an artistic home: a company, a collective, living and working in one place over a period of time, all with the same notion of why this was important. We had compatible skills and world views about the role of art. We all used theater to engage in a dialogue with audiences. We weren't conflicted. It all seemed entirely natural, inevitable; we didn't need to elaborate in manifestos or mission statements. What else could a theater be? How could you call it a theater if it wasn't a *place*? Who else but artists could define the culture of a theater? Define its style? Didn't a collective art form require a collective? Weren't we here to protest and replace the one-shot system of Broadway?

We emblazoned our earliest banners with: "Not a Hotel for Theater, but a Home!" As years went by, other slogans came into style:

"Professionalism! You Can Count on Us!" or "Good Plays, Well Done, That's the Ticket!" or even "Eight-for-the-Price-of-Six!" Until I picked up my recent issues of *American Theatre*, I thought that no one objected to the way things had become except some of my actor friends and former students, who trained for and want to be in companies, but have not been able to find them.

That artists are angry and disappointed is not necessarily bad news. These feelings indicate insistence, energy, and commitment; these artists want in. They want to become part of the warp and woof of institutional life or, as London puts it, to *occupy* its center. But they find institutions inhospitable or closed. How many artists feel this way? Six? Six hundred? Six thousand? If we threw a party, would they come? And is it true that the institutions are inhospitable or closed to artists? These questions need to be answered in practice. And the theaters need to make the first move.

Audiences come to the theater to partake of the work artists have made. It's art, I'm suggesting, that makes the money and not the other way around. What else might we do? One gesture more than any other will signal where the artist stands in relation to recognition and power: Pay mature and committed artists the top salaries within the institution—at least equal to that of any (other) fundraiser or audience-builder. In the deepest sense, artists are teachers—out of darkness, they bring light—and their salary should be pegged to what a full professor makes at the university in the theater's community. In some smaller communities, that may still not be enough, so that allowances should be made for commercial time-outs. (Time-outs for creative refreshment need to be possible as well.)

Artists should be invited into the total life of the institution, to provide it with their special knowledge and to have their say. I've read that while Ingmar Bergman was heading the Swedish National Theatre, he established a five-member artists' council that he consulted about repertory, casting and the like. I don't know how this idea would play out in America, though I wish I'd tried it myself.

Board positions should be set aside in the theater's bylaws for artists to occupy. This important change must be pressed for. The presence of artists at board meetings would transpose a bottom-line, market-share, brand-conscious, focus-group lingo—brought into the boardroom from for-profit culture—to a language of emotional meanings, thus bringing the board closer to the heartbeat of the theater and unifying everyone around the ideas that underlie what we do. Artists are smart; planning is the strategy by which they bring art into the world, including the ability to juggle an animating idea with time, money, and materials. They have much to contribute to the deliberations of a board.

To keep the artist outside the business of the institution (with which he's deeply engaged) is to romanticize him ("Artists are above business") at the same time that it miniaturizes him ("Artists are fanciful, unworldly creatures with no head for it; we need to take care of them"). Why has it taken so long to see this?

There are myriad ways for the institution to build relationships with artists that create a sense of home, in which each can be for himself and also for the other, in which all are for the work. Both Whitehead and London suggest some of these.

The creative courage of the artistic director will inspire artists; they, in turn, will support the risks she takes on their behalf, whether or not they succeed. The transparency she fosters, so that information—good or bad—is available to everyone in the building, will deepen mutual respect and the sense of communal destiny. She will see to it that no one feels intimidated to speak up; in story and myth, the figure of Death is always silent. The artistic director's acknowledgment of ambiguity, second thoughts, and struggle behind difficult decisions will draw the artists closer. The blinding glare of certainty always reduces the intimacy and trust.

Eventually, all of us must understand more deeply the nature of that organism we call a theater. I hold close Aristotle's statement: "What a thing can be, it must be, whether it be a horse or a man." Or a theater, he might have added. At some future point we'll judge ourselves by whether we insisted strongly enough on becoming what we can be and, so, becoming it. We will have to agree that artists *are* the theater, and that administrators who protect and advance the artists' work are also the theater. As is the board, which volunteers time, money, and care for a profession that can seem a total mystery, operating as it does on hunches, gambles, and the unknown.

What else is a theater? The repertory is a theater, its very flesh and bones. A theater is ticket prices, brochures, ads, and newsletters. It is spaces, even if they're humble, the intimacy of people pulling for the same thing, respect for the intelligence of the audience, restlessness and unceasing workload, and so on. Even the way the fair air hangs off the walls tells a stranger what kind of a place it is. All of these are a theater—everything tangible and intangible, everything a part of everything else.

A theater is a refracted image of life, and "life is all one," as Major Barbara exultantly discovers in Shaw's most revolutionary play. Being "all one," a theater must organize itself in circles—concentric circles, not vertically like Enron, but rather like the rings of a tree trunk, with the artist director and her artists in the center, yes, but what's a center without a circumference? The outer border of the cell guarantees the integrity of the nucleus. What is a theater building but a cell, the enclosing of an idea?

While our institutions may not currently be satisfying all the needs and expectations of artists, it's only through and with them that there's hope for growth. In both a Marxist sense and a practical, theatrical one, only the institutional theaters possess the "means of production" necessary to carry the work forward. Acquiring these institutions took labor, love, grit, and guts, as well as an act of large imagination sustained over a long period of time. Transformation via contagion is the evolutionary pattern of the resident theater movement. There is accumulated wisdom there.

Of all the theater's artists, our playwrights seem to be most angry, the sense of exclusion, of disempowerment, strongest among them. A deep source of creative power lies beneath "the rage of powerlessness," noted in one of the articles; it can be released by opportunity.

And so, I send out a Call. I call out to a leading American playwright whom the world admires and trusts to step up to the plate to take on the responsibilities of the artistic directorship of the next theater that's looking for one. A director, designer, or actor as artistic leader can provide this opportunity, and each has done so. But a playwright-leader can serve with a special understanding. The playwright whose authenticity is established and empathy assured would carry a natural authority with other playwrights.

Since the playwright's art is seminal to theater's other arts, if it can be empowered to flourish, the others will bloom with it. The playwright provides the scaffold of meaning and intention to which all the other arts attach. In performance, the actor is at the center. Through the flesh and blood of an actor, the playwright comes alive, no matter when she lived. Anton Chekhov wrote to the company of the Moscow Art Theatre: "An actor is a free artist. You must create an image different from the author's. When the two images—the author's and the actor's—fuse into one, then an artistic work is created." Could it be that the playwright, actor, director could come together in a place in such a way as to form a dreamed-of golden triangle?

There is a level of fantasy to my line of thought. What established playwright who would set aside his own writing for the arduous, time-consuming life of an artistic director? A playwright is the most solitary of all theater artists, while the artistic director belongs to the entire society of the theater, last to herself. There needs to be but one of you who hears my call. What follows is up to the others.

For Christmas I was given Mel Gussow's book *Conversations with Miller*. Here, from a 1986 conversation, is Arthur Miller:

> If I had a theater that I was connected to, a theater of my peers, a working theater with a good group of actors, I probably would have written a number of more plays. I had one experience like that in my life and that was before Lincoln Center collapsed. I had done *After the Fall*, and Harold Clurman came to me and said, "Look we've got to have another play. Do you have anything else?" And I wrote *Incident at Vichy*. And it worked out magically; there was a part for every actor in the company. That never occurred to me. There was an excitement about it. You didn't have to run around finding producer . . . It's very important. It's a defense against the outside. "We're all in this together."[1]

Yes, we are.

---

1. *Conversations with Miller* by Mel Gussow (New York: Applause Books, 2002).

American Theatre, May/June 2003.

Articles referenced: Jaan Whitehead, "Art Will Out," *American Theatre*, October 2002. Lenora Inez Brown, "The Real World"; P. Carl, "Creating the Swell"; Todd London, "The Shape of Plays to Come"; all in *American Theatre*, November 2002.

THE COMPANY YOU KEEP

ROBERT PROSKY: AT TWENTY

(1977)

Dear Bob:

I hope you don't mind that I say these things, some of them private, in public. Twenty years of your artistic life have coincided with—indeed, in many ways *described*—the major part of Arena Stage's history. You are not only a personal artist but an American phenomenon, an actor who has staked his professional life with, and evolved his art within, the resident theater outside New York.

We met in New York, at a crummy hotel, the Piccadilly on 45th Street, I think, in the fall of 1958. You auditioned for the role of the Sheriff in *The Front Page*. (You got it—and deliciously repeated it a couple of years ago.) You were a good actor—facile, gifted, energized, funny. But who would have thought that the man I met then (already with white hair and a "character face," though not yet thirty) had in him so much originality, perception, passion, force, extravagance, courage for self-exposure, and capacity to transform both psychologically and physically that, two decades and one hundred and twenty-one roles later, audiences, directors, and fellow actors would expect all this from him as a matter of course and, indeed, assume you'd arrived in full flower? Where did all this come from and how did it grow?

Let me interrupt myself to celebrate some of the things you have given me. In no particular order, I thank you for:

- The silent clown, aggrieved and self-mocking, in *He Who Gets Slapped*; the first time, I think, I recognized that you would become a first-rate American actor. All good actors are good in their "big" moments. It's the special actor who communicates in stillness, in silence.

- The zany Russian ballet master in *You Can't Take It with You*—outrageous, self-affirming, *joie* personified. In the same idiom, but with a difference—the lusty, lecherous, sponging Sir Toby Belch, conducting revels with relish and a concealed, complicating hostility.

- Baffled, self-deluded, a bluffing child living out death and refusing to die—Sergeant Cokes in *Streamers*. And, yes, the wad-chewing, racist, small-town, big-city, slow-talking, slow-thinking, world-making Sheriff of *The Front Page*. It astounds me that two such opposing images could be made of the same clay.

- *Our Town*. They stood and cheered you in Moscow and Leningrad, and the press took long paragraphs to describe your performance as the Stage Manager. Laconic and involved, compassionate yet dry, full of tenderness for the vicissitudes of humanity and at the same time angry at its blindness and carelessness. A new embodiment of an old role and the best one I've seen. I treasure the photograph of us on the stage of the Moscow Art Theatre, receiving flowers at the curtain call.

- And its companion piece *Inherit the Wind*: Matthew Harrison Brady, stuffed with dogma and revealed truth, a little fear behind the eyes, preening in the courtroom, sunning himself in the love of the crowd, withering when the sun went away, lonely child under the Big Guy bluster. You took a role that could have two dimensions and gave it eight or ten.

- Jacob in *Awake and Sing*. My second confirmation of the size of your talent. The grandfather with his Caruso records and his books, the proud Jewish patriarch, now merely tolerated in his daughter's house. You managed the tension between silent rage and pride, between the docility and uselessness of old age and the revolutionary spirit that kept him young. "Life shouldn't be printed on dollar bills." You made me weep each time you said it.

I had better stop the list. There are, after all, one hundred and twenty-one roles to remember. I have to add two more, though, because they represent two of my most fulfilling experiences as a director: Dr. Stockmann in *An Enemy of the People*—high intellect and whirlwind energy. I wasn't sure you had that much sheer physical strength, but we built that role as if for an athlete. And Willy Loman in *Death of a Salesman*—you were a raging, wounded dinosaur, refusing extinction. What an experience that was! We had talked for years about when you would be ripe to play that part. Finally we decided, and it was worth the wait.

Where did it come from, and how did it grow, this actor's range and power? From many places and in many ways. It came first from your own talent. It came from those places of curiosity, observation, imagination, belief, mimicry, and physiology that live in the body and psyche of any actor who is to be important. It came from your "divine restlessness," something all highly creative people share. I have learned that for you this is always a part of the process of embodying a role. Self-dissatisfaction. Hanging between "I can" and "I can't," as the pieces refuse to come together. Arguing with yourself (and the director) as you chase the text down this alley and that, over a hill, through the stile, around Robin Hood's barn. I love working with you, Bob, but oh, how you worry! For twenty years, you've worried yourself into every role, and the longer you work, the more you seem to worry. And so you've grown—through industry and not letting yourself off the hook, by facing your fear of the dark.

Finally, I believe you have evolved into who you are because you have had a creative home for the continuous exercise of your skill. From play to play, season to season, it has been possible for you to examine the building blocks of your craft—its laws of inner technique and physical embodiment, and the relationship between the two, in a systematic, progressive way. You have been able to incorporate and use what you've learned—immediately, not later, when the learning has already cooled. You have had the privilege to be the continuous and conscious maker of your own instrument.

The discontinuity in an actor's life not only eats away at his sense of self, his ego, which is the raw material from which all else is made, but it prevents him from "putting it all together." His body forgets from one experience to another what it has found out. You have avoided the waste of discontinuous creative work.

The negatives. We've talked about these too, Bob.

The need to get off the treadmill. The need for the diversity of film, television, other theaters. The need *not* to work for a while, to vegetate, to be silent, to have things come together unconsciously. The need for creative change and creative goofing-off.

And the need for higher salaries. We'll never compete with media, but something roughly equivalent to what a full professor at a leading university earns would do nicely. I not only understand these needs, I share them. We have to address them in a practical way if we wish to keep longtime creative members of our companies like you.

Then there is the problem of what you call "anonymity." Without films or TV, even without Broadway, with its smaller audience, but its lingering aura of high prestige, you have felt very big in the Soviet Union but not so big in your own land. It is good to be recognized in the supermarket, but every artist wants the largest possible circle of social love, that elusive thing called "recognition." I don't know how to answer you on this point. It is a problem in search of a solution.

You may not know this in the deepest part of yourself, but you are not only one of the leading actors in America; more, you have also been at the heart—have *been* the heart—and part of the conscience and mind of a new form for theater in our country. It's hard for us to know that, even as we work, a new fabric is being woven. We are changing the way things are and are going to be. By staking your creative life here in Washington at Arena Stage, you have made new stuff that wasn't here before you came.

The high point of a conference I recently attended on "The Future of the Performing Arts" was an address by Martha Graham. This great form-giver of contemporary dance spoke personally and movingly about her life and the meaning of her art. She described a woman who came backstage after the performance of *Lamentation*. The woman had witnessed her own child being hit and killed by a truck. For years she had been unable to cry. At this performance she finally wept.

I said I would speak to you personally, though in public. You have given me much joy and much insight. Most of all, you have tapped the unexpressed anguish we all share. You have given me the ability to weep for lost things. As long as I live, Bob, you will never be anonymous to me.

With much love,
Zel

In December 1977, Robert Prosky appeared as Azdak in Bertolt Brecht's *The Caucasian Chalk Circle*, thus marking the start of his twentieth consecutive season as a member of the Arena Stage acting company. Zelda had first engaged him in 1958 for a single-role, eight-week contract. Here she celebrates his anniversary with the Arena community.

A TRIBUTE TO ALAN SCHNEIDER

(1984)

Can you name any other man who could go on a honeymoon, leave his bride alone in Niagara Falls, and still make a production of it? That was Alan.

It was the summer of '53, the opening of the Stratford Ontario Festival Tent, and Jeannie's[1] passport was not acceptable for Canada. The nearest point to the border, and the closest to the aura of a honeymoon, was Niagara Falls. There was Jeannie ensconced in a room, while Alan, Tom, and I, and our friend Berky continued northward. Alan simply had to be at that opening; he had to see what was going on.

We arrived toward dusk. A man in a white suit tipped over on his bicycle. Alan righted the bike and helped him back onto it. The man was Alec Guinness. A larger, raw-boned man with a washtub full of props tried to get over a fence but couldn't quite negotiate it. That turned out to be Tyrone Guthrie. Alan held the tub while Sir Tony hoisted himself over. With Alan as scoutmaster, we crawled under a flap of the festival tent and snuck-watched some last-minute rehearsals, making ourselves as small as possible in the hot shadows.

1. Schneider's new wife, Eugenie Muckle Schneider.

The next day we found out that by some error in the PR department *New York Times* critic Brooks Atkinson's seats were behind an eight-inch tent pole. Alan got hold of Tom Patterson, the Festival head, and we swapped seats, saving the day.

It was the first time we had met Brooks, and we invited him to one of our rooms for a drink. Alan delegated himself to round up the booze, only to find the sleeping, unexpecting town was dry. Never mind, the scene could be improvised. Jeannie had emptied a small bottle of cough medicine and filled it with worthier stuff for our journey. But the bottle was small, and there were four of us—now five. Just as the guest was due, Alan served the rest of us tap water with ice, directed us to get progressively more heady and loose-tongued as we socialized, Brooks got the Stolichnaya, and the scene came off as directed—the talk made intoxicating by water-on-the-rocks. Ten years later—maybe more—I told Brooks the story as we walked in the rain one night in Washington. He said it was the best scene he'd ever played in.

"Now is the winter of our discontent / Made glorious summer by this sun of York." Guinness as Richard III, the first words spoken on the inner above of the Festival stage. Behind the post, Alan squeezed my hand. He took such childlike delight in the magic of the theater and in the achievements of others, such joy when someone, anyone, anywhere could make it happen.

He squeezed my hand the same way when he came to see *Candide* at Arena last June and beelined around the building, peeking into all the spaces to see what was going on. He took such joy in it all. The joy, I think, made him sleep well at night after whatever ravages of the day might have kept the rest of us awake. Alan's demons always went obediently to sleep at the appointed hour, calmed I think by the pleasure of knowing they had served a good cause and deserved the rest.

We opened two theaters together (both times it was a race to get the building there ahead of the production), did forty productions together. We turned *Our Town* into Russian in a two-day, nonstop session of simultaneous translation for the opening at the Moscow Art, scurried around Moscow and Leningrad—shopping, seeing, meeting people—with a group of seventy-one and a monkey from *Inherit the Wind*—did victorious battle with Madame Furtseva, then Minister of Culture, to open up additional performances for theater people unable to get tickets, received and made toasts, heard and made speeches, performed, traveled on trains and buses and planes, saw reporters, went on television, went to late parties, and sang and danced. Alan was the only one who was never tired. He was endlessly frustrated, endlessly dissatisfied with the resistances, large and small, of that universe, but the boundless joy in it all kept him from fatigue. How I envied and loved him for that limitless creative energy.

Last year, at the first public dress rehearsal of the Beckett plays, a light cue went wrong. Alan stopped the rehearsal and spoke to the audience: "I'm going to stop and get this right; I hope you'll stay with me." He was irritated—his eyes flashed and his nostrils flared. He crushed his cap in the Alan Schneider way, but he was also affectionate and teasing, present with every bit of himself. He was going to stick with it until it was the way it damn well ought to be.

In an unremitting battle with Murphy's Law that if something can go wrong it will (a law he first pointed out to me), Alan made things in the theater the way they ought to be more times than anyone I have ever known. People think this is about something called "standards," but it is really about the man himself. Alan raised our national theatrical standards, not out of any abstractions of "professionalism," but out of what he believed in and what he saw. Wherever he worked—a school, a resident theater, Off-Broadway, on Broadway—he had but one aim: to uncover the vision living inside the play by the most vivid theatrical means available, so that others could see it with him.

How many of us has he taught? Alan started me off, gave me the first insights to build upon. I'm so glad I had the chance to thank him for it.

> Oh, oh, oh! Six o'clock and the master not home yet. Pray God nothing serious has happened to him crossing the Hudson River. If anything happened to him, we would certainly be inconsolable and have to move into a less desirable residence district.

It was Frances Sternhagen, a glorious Sabina in the 1952 production of *Skin of Our Teeth* at Catholic University, who told me that Alan suggested she play this opening monologue like someone going down a steep hill on a bicycle with no hands—and no brake. From this, I first latched on to how much more evocative images are than instructions to release an actor's imagination. I've never stopped using and exploring Alan's idea.

Also at Catholic University, even earlier, 1948: student actress Teddy Kinsey's boldly extravagant, mimed reaction of horror and guilt when Jocasta finds out her real relationship to Oedipus. The moment lasted, in silence, for more than a minute. It said all there was to say about the tension between reality and style that is the basic subject of the art of theater. After thirty-five years of seeing and making theater, the moment is still with me.

The sound of billiard balls clicking offstage, randomly ricocheting off each other in the ballroom scene of *The Cherry Orchard*, masterfully blowing open the text: "You do nothing, Fate simply flings you about from place to place, and that's so strange—isn't that so?"

Fate simply flings us about.

Alan always believed this to be true. Like two good Russian souls, we had many talks over the years. But whatever the subject, whether funny or sad, his encompassing theme was always that life is unpredictable, that forces are at work we can neither count nor counter. He answered them back with his sweetness, his compassion, his love of young things—people or theaters or simply a new day. And with the gusto of his creativity.

"Well, what are you going to do?!" he would often ask. It wasn't meant to be answered; it was said ironically, lightly, a way to wind up a topic that had played itself out. It had as subtext: "Well, what now? What's the next thing? Let's get on with what's still left, with whatever else has to be done, looked into, discovered, fixed up, turned upside down, made into something else, or put on the stage."

It was deeply connected to his sense of life, the other side of his awareness of the Infinite Caprice of all things. "Well, what are you going to do?!"

What are we all going to do?

Zelda delivered this eulogy as part of a memorial for Alan Schneider held at Circle in the Square Theatre in Manhattan on May 22, 1984, nineteen days after the director's sudden death in London; he had been hit by a motorcycle while crossing the street.

JANE ALEXANDER

(1994)

Dear Jane:

Memory alters history. But as I remember it, I got a letter from an Arena Stage subscriber in the early sixties bringing to my attention "a remarkable young actress" playing Nora in *The Plough and the Stars*—for some reason I think it was in Scotland. I saved the letter. In the mid-sixties Ed Sherin and I auditioned this remarkable young actress in the offices of Theatre Communications Group, which then had a casting service. I remember you did Nina from Act Four of *The Seagull*, a fire-and-ice soliloquy that blew us away.

With your little son, Jason—now actor Jace Alexander—you trundled down to Washington for a three-year stay, launching it, at twenty-four, with Shaw's *Saint Joan*. My office was perched above the stage door, and I could see everyone checking in for the day's rehearsal. From there, I could keep track of the human life of the theater. Often you rode a bike to work and wore a red coat, with a long scarf flowing behind. One day resident director Ed Sherin got up from my gold Naugahyde Herman Miller couch—we were planning the next season—and peered down at you, Jane, locking up your bike, and murmured, "That's the most magnificent woman I've ever seen."

Now you and Ed have been married for twenty years, often working in creative collaboration.

Jane was infinitely talented, versatile, a wonderful community member—and tenacious. When she wasn't cast as the young girl in Ionesco's *The Lesson*, she came up to the office and protested, arguing and asserting her creative rights. Ed and I reversed our decision. And she was wonderful in the role. She got what she wanted. She went for what she wanted. That was but a tryout. Now she can go after it for real—with Congress!

As Katrin in *Mother Courage*—mute, without language, a casualty of the unending war—she had only a drum to bang on to wake up the land. Now she has a drum, *and* she can speak up! Aren't we all the lucky ones that she can! And will!!

When I sent your picture to Howard Sackler in Spain, to ask for approval to cast you as Eleanor Bachman in his *Great White Hope*, he wrote back: "That's my Ellie, don't look further." And so, opposite James Earl Jones, as Jack Jefferson's "white wife," you opened in Washington on December 7, 1967, and your wider career was launched: Broadway, film, television, and all those Tonys and Oscar nominations and Obies and Drama Desk Awards and ecstatic reviews. You continued to work as an actor in our nonprofit, community-rooted institutions. You always came back to the stage. You were onstage—in Wendy Wasserstein's *The Sisters Rosensweig*—when the nomination as head of the National Endowment for the Arts came. The standing ovations grew louder. They wanted to be heard in Washington, I think.

If ever there was a role model for young actors, Jane is it!! Recently she said, "My dream was to be like the great American actress, Katharine Cornell, and do a play a year on Broadway, and then tour around the country. But that kind of theater had dwindled."

Jane's artistic choices reflect her strong social conscience. We remember her as Eleanor Roosevelt in *Eleanor and Franklin*, as Miss Rose in *Playing for Time*, as the young mother in *Testament*. She has tackled issues ranging from racial discrimination and nuclear war to ethics and integrity in politics. "The stories I'm drawn to are those about women who are doing rather extraordinary things that have to do with some kind of social consciousness," she explained.

Her characters are always invested with complexity, depth, originality, and deep humanity, as she transposes parts of her most intimate self to create the life of another. "Art is the expression of one's perception of life, made manifest through imagination, intellect, emotion, and what we call the soul." She has said that, and she has shown that.

For your spirit, for your talent, for the force of your example, for your deep sense of national service, it is the greatest honor for me to award you the John Houseman Award for 1994. Jane Alexander—citizen/artist.

Delivered at The Acting Company Benefit, May 22, 1994. Zelda was artistic director of The Acting Company in New York from 1991 to 1994. The award Zelda bestows on producer Jane Alexander here is named for John Houseman, who on the occasion of graduating his first class as founding director of the Drama Division at The Juilliard School, cofounded The Acting Company in order to keep that class working and performing together.

ROBERT ALEXANDER
(1996)

On the occasion of its thirtieth anniversary, I'm here to celebrate Living Stage and its creators and descendants; the company, its board and contributors; the electric piano and conga drum; the hats and blocks of furniture and flat open spaces of their deployment; the jamming; the dancing and singing; the warm-ups; the living sculptures; the wonderful audiences of children, parents, and teachers; men and women in prisons; blind, deaf and physically disabled children, men, and women; the senior citizens. I celebrate all the people in the workshops who had the curiosity, strength, and will to overcome fear and inhibition to explore and express their inner life.

And I'm here to celebrate Bob Alexander, whose vision and labor are the fount from which all of this came.

I have just reread some of Bob's writings. The first thing that struck me was the intensity of his rage and the passion of his beliefs—the heat and depth of them and their duration decade after decade. In Brecht's parable play about the Thirty Years' War, Mother Courage says to the Young Soldier: "Yes, you are angry now, but how long can you stay angry: a day, a week, a month, a year, several years? Can you stay angry for as long as it takes?"

Well, Bob is still angry and still passionate. I asked for his favorite poems and, dwelling on one by D. H. Lawrence, he wrote:

> You know, one has to believe that the fire is always there, that the pilot light never goes out until one is dead; and that belief in the grandeur of the human spirit is what I, what my work, has been about and what I tried (and sometimes succeeded) to help others understand when in the presence of children . . . unconditional love, no matter what. And in order to be able to do that you have to believe in that pilot light of love and compassion and beauty that burns in everyone, no matter what! And not to give your life away to people who do not care about you, people who really do not love and admire you—and quoting Lawrence—"not to give your life to the living dead, not the tiniest shred."

I never really understood until reading his speeches why Bob repeated adjectives rather than find new ones, ones that were cumulative or descriptive in varied and surprising ways. Now I get it. His repetitions are meant to be intensives, pushing the image deeper and deeper into our awareness, or *expansives*, opening the vista of his idea of infinity.

In one speech, *Healing Our Society Through Creativity: Understanding Your Birthright as An Artist*, he says:

> Talent is the ability to penetrate or embrace the environment. You're not a leaf that's blown in the wind hither and thither; you're not going with the flow. You're rooted and you make a move, an aggressive move, out into your world. Then you're strong enough to be soft enough, to be sensitive enough to be affected deeply.

"To be affected," Bob says, "you have to be very, very, very, very strong." Note: Not just very strong—that won't be enough talent—you won't make anything happen that way—you have to be "very, very, very, very" strong. Because talent is that important—and that transformative!

"The human being was born to think, to learn, and to create," Bob tells us. "It's our natural, biologic state. Whether or not you're in touch with your artistry, that is something else. But that pilot light is still alive. Maybe there's a lot of garbage heaped on top of it and maybe it's very, very, very, very, very, very dim, but it's never extinguished." Note: how deeply, terrifyingly "dim" all those "very"s make it! Bob expresses his total, rock-bottom faith in the resistant, irrepressible pilot light of creativity by accumulating this one word. He built a life's work around "*very.*"

Bob's rules of living are strict and, in some ways, awesome. He speaks of softness, but this softness is the softness of pliancy in the interest of ultimate survival, ultimate power. "No compromise," is his credo.

> If a redwood tree compromised, it would fall over dead because the roots would be cut. That's what it means to compromise: your roots get cut. If you are an artist and live your life as an artist, you do not compromise ever, ever, ever, ever, ever, ever, ever, ever, ever, ever, ever, ever, ever, ever, ever. (You can enter into agreements, but you can't compromise your ideals. You can't compromise what you feel is the life quality in yourself, in anyone else.)

Fifteen "evers." That's a long time. As long as Lear's five "Nevers" over the body of his dead daughter Cordelia: "Never. Never. Never. Never. Never." Like nails in a coffin.

That same inexorability. That same *gravitas*. That same weight. That same system of thought. We who have worked with Bob know how he can push at the bars of any barrier, press against them, bend them to his will. And keep on keeping on. And on. And on. God bless him!

And we know the ecstatic expansiveness of his spirit! From the same speech: "Your imagination is real. It's real. It's real. It's real. It's as real as this pen, this microphone, this glass of water. It's as real as I am or you are. It's real. It's real. It's part of us. Anything that's part of us can't be unreal. It's real."

All those who believe the imagination is real, say, "Aye"! The ayes have it.

Bob is a fighter, and Bob is a lover. Not just in the abstract sense, but in a very specific human way. As Bob has moved away from me professionally and then geographically, we've had to stretch a little to stay in touch. He once said to me over one of our rare dinners: "If you ever need to talk to somebody, even if it's two in the morning, call me up. You can do that." It went by me at the time. But I've been thinking that I really could do that, and it would be okay.

He sent me a Passover/Easter blessing, perhaps he sent you one too. "A summer's day / water shimmering in sun's sparkle / ocean as blue as sky laced with soft clouds / gentle wind, dancing trees / and I, content in heart, think of you . . . So in the week of Passover, the celebration of freedom, and Easter, the celebration of hope once more renewed, I say hello / send you my love and wishes for your heart . . ." And he quoted the poet Rumi: "Let the beauty you love be what you do. There are hundreds of ways to kneel and kiss the ground."

Hundreds of ways to kneel and kiss the ground. To raise a child, to plant a tree, to embroider a shawl, to make a table, to cook a dinner, to nurture a friendship. To create and sustain a theater company that would turn each person on to his/her own creativity; empower them with awareness of the living process, including the possibility of change; give them the courage of their own thoughts and feelings and the hope that courage brings; educate them—that is, lead them out, from the darkness into the light; and, finally, give all of us the understanding that art is dependent on life, derives from life, and therefore our artworks are not idle creations, but instruments by which life is illuminated and enriched.

A quote of García Lorca's that Bob and I have passed back and forth over the years: "The poem, the song, the picture, is only water drawn from the well of the people, and it should be given back to them in a cup of beauty so that they may drink—and in drinking understand themselves."

The Living Stage will go on. There will be only one Robert Alexander. I'm very, very, very sure of this.

Tribute on the occasion of the thirtieth anniversary of Living Stage, April 29, 1996. Under Robert Alexander's leadership, Living Stage led workshops and performances with children, seniors, incarcerated youth and adults, and people with disabilities. Founded in 1966 as part of Arena Stage, it held its first performance the following year in the prison at Virginia's Lorton Youth Center.

LIVIU CIULEI

(2003)

A question: With all the inventions credited to the imagination of humankind—the computer chip, the PET scan, the Palm Pilot that sees, even the lowly microwave that bakes a potato from the inside out, the 737 that masters the friendly skies, the smart bomb that depersonalizes warfare, the astounding science of quantum mechanics which promises to unlock the mystery of the universe itself—how come nobody's figured out how to get the genie back in the damn bottle?!?

That demon, that spirit—once he's gone, he's just gone. The past just won't return; the world only turns forward. That word *genie* is only a couple of letters away from *genius* and, in fact, *comes from* the Latin *genius* and, what's more, *genii* is a plural form of both genie and genius. (What you learn in high school is yours forever.) If we could put the *genii*—or the *genius*—back in the bottle, snap on the cap, then we'd have Liviu Ciulei with us forever more. He wouldn't be able to get away.

You see, Liviu and Helga[1] are returning to their ancestral home, and I'm sad about that. Despite the extraordinary talent gathered in

1. Ciulei's wife, Helga Reiter-Ciulei.

and around the Graduate Acting Program here at NYU, I know that Liviu Ciulei is the only certifiable, universal, international genius I have been able to offer the students or, for that matter, earlier, the acting company and audiences of Arena Stage, which is where he began his American career.

Here is Liviu: with his courtly European manners—who else kisses your hand, other than in a period play?—his quiet charm, his sartorial chic in black leather jacket and gray flannel trousers, his ironic sense of humor, his worldly wisdom—been everywhere, done everything—his observant eye with its unerring visual sense. His wonderful stories reveal human beings with their foibles and fates, viewed from his own distinctive angle. His compassion is real but never sentimental, always somewhat objective. "Sometimes these things happen," I've heard him say, ruefully but dryly, more than once.

The life of any genius is complex. He has had a fascinating and unique life. When he was twenty-three his father, satisfied that Liviu was both talented and serious, built him a theater to run, with several stages. Imagine that for yourself. Things go well at school, and your mom and dad take you to dinner to celebrate. Over dessert they give you a present—a theater building and the means to run it. Liviu was evidently ready for this responsibility—he took it on and made it fly.

Parallel to and entwined with the political upheavals of Eastern Europe—into communism and on the torturous path out again—his creative leadership defined the theater of post–World War II Romania. Actor, director, designer, architect (he was the technical architect for the four-theater National Theatre of Romania), artistic director— his Bulandra Theatre and his own work within it became celebrated throughout Europe. Indeed, he has directed on five continents.

Knowledge of his work, wafted to America by visitors, reached me in Washington. A production of Gogol's *The Inspector General*, a nineteenth-century Russian play that pointedly satirized bureaucrats and the system that gave rise to them, touched too close to home. The Bulandra, victim of political censorship, lost Liviu. And so began the possibility of a career in the U.S., England, and elsewhere.

Liviu has had to remind me of our first meeting. It went by me. In 1962, about to rebuild the Bulandra, Liviu visited America to see a number of theaters in the early stages of construction. One of those theaters was the then-new Arena Stage. Many people came by in those early days—Laurence Olivier, was very vocal about not liking the in-the-round form: "No place to hide," he said. Charles Laughton, in town to film *Advise & Consent*, inaugurated the stage even before the seats were in with *Henry V*'s "O for a Muse of fire" speech. Liviu must have been with a group and, always discreet, came and went without pushing forward to meet me. It was ten years later before I really knew him. My Arena colleague, the major director Alan Schneider, had seen Liviu's work in Bucharest and urged me to invite him to Arena, which I did, for the 1973–1974 season.

Liviu's production of Büchner's *Leonce and Lena*, which he both directed and designed, was a landmark in the history of our theater, a so-called "avant-garde" production of the sort our audience wasn't used to. It gathered momentum from the first preview, at which the audience was confused by the nonlinear style, to the opening, when it became a standing-room success.

In my maternal, and, I hope, aesthetic view, we had a fine acting company. It had just been acclaimed in Moscow and Leningrad, the first American company invited to play the Soviet Union under State Department auspices, and I was proud that Liviu appreciated our actors. It was for me a validation, like no other could be. For Liviu has always been for me the standard of creative achievement.

The productions Liviu did for Arena between the 1973–1974 and the 1996–1997 seasons (the last three after I had left Arena) marked the evolution of that acting company and also how the Kreeger Theatre, an end-stage house we opened in 1969, came to discover its scenic possibilities, largely through the half-dozen productions Liviu directed in that space. His rebuilt Bulandra Theatre was, Liviu tells me, in turn influenced by the Arena space, opened in 1961. So, our creative lives have been intertwined for more than forty years. You can see why I long to put the genie back in the bottle.

Among American theaters of its kind, Arena is—if I may say so—a really good place to work. But Liviu came from a theatrical culture altogether other than ours. I remember his saying, not boasting or demeaning us, but merely explaining: "In my theater, we had several Helen Hayes, two Spencer Tracys, a number of Cary Grants, several Katharine Hepburns, and so on."

In 1978, I asked him to send me what he called "data about the typical subsidized repertory theater" in Romania for a speech I was to make. It included, for example, the list of personnel: four directors, two assistant directors, three set designers, two assistant set designers, two literary managers, one librarian, seventy actors, four stage managers, two technical stage managers, two master sound technicians, two sound associates, two masters for makeup and wigs, two assistants for makeup, one hairstylist, six gentleman tailors, six ladies dressmakers, one shirtmaker, one hatmaker, one embroiderer, three warehouse keepers, one laundry person, thirty administrative jobs, and so on. The total company and staff numbered two hundred and thirty-two. The Bulandra operated two theaters, mounted eight to ten new productions a year and kept eighteen productions in repertory. Subsidy covered *all* the salaries, which represented about two-thirds of the total budget. The rest of the budget was covered by the box office, which needed to sell eighty-seven percent of the seats. Their season averaged six hundred performances in Bucharest (three hundred for each house) and thirty–forty performances on tour, usually in the summer.

Not with The Acting Company, where he has directed a number of notable productions, or with Theatre for a New Audience, not even at the Guthrie Theater in Minneapolis, where Liviu was artistic director for six years and which has always had the highest budget of any regional theater, could the Bulandra resources be compared in any meaningful way. Nowhere in America *then* (1978), nowhere in American *now*.

In an ambivalent, and always compromising profession, Liviu's intentions are absolutely and totally pure. To challenge himself: That's where he always begins. Since the day we first entered each other's lives, I've never known him to undertake a production anywhere for any reasons but his own personal creative curiosity, his attraction to laying bare the subtext—no matter how much money he could earn or what institutional need might be served. I've never known him not to drive himself crazy seeking perfection in the details through which to realize his vision—as anyone who has designed for him or acted within his company or worked with him in any capacity—will testify.

It doesn't matter if you're a second-year student actor or a long-standing member of an acting company like Bob Prosky or Dianne Wiest, a graduate designer or a distinguished set designer like Ming Cho Lee, or lighting designer like Allen Lee Hughes—it's perfection that he sees and serves, the Holy Grail of the theatrical art. It's the ultimate realization of the vision on the retina of his mind that obsesses him, from the very first moment to the very, very last. In NYU's Atlas Room, at the Lyric Opera of Chicago, or in the Royal Opera House of London, the same rules apply. He is able to engage on any level with a purse of any size as long as the intentions are pure.

Isolated memories flash across my awareness: Liviu, at NYU, with a budget of a hundred dollars, searching for discarded lumber on the street for the set of *The Lower Depths* with Ntare Mwine, Antoinette LaVecchia, and Boris McGiver; Ming Cho Lee's set for *Hamlet* at Arena, a dark warren of sunken tunnels and passageways, the walls covered in Mylar reflecting and refracting light, Ophelia going mad at a state dinner; Arena's *Lower Depths*, Santo Loquasto and Liviu, a multilayered set, some levels below ground, some above, a sense of squalor and crowded, confined spaces. The set he asked for and got required an unprecedented investment of labor by the small Arena shop. At a dress rehearsal, Liviu asks: "Tell me, Zelda, I trust your eyes, you think this central platform should be just this much lower?" His fingers measure three to four inches—that vision of perfection— and I have to say, no, the shop is too tired. *Six Characters in Search of an Author*—Stanley Anderson at his most profound as the anguished Father, the six haunted characters making their entrance through the large, heavy, metal shop doors backlit by Allen Lee Hughes onto a stage that represents a small proscenium Italian theater designed by Liviu. *A View from the Bridge*—Joaquin Torres as Eddie and a remarkable company around him, the best Miller I have ever seen. And *Andorra*— Josh, Gareth, Mia[2] and Liviu's concrete wall of shame and prejudice— maybe this is the most searing memory of all.

Liviu designs not the decor, never the decor, but always the space—the shape of the interior logic of the play. He gives form to psychology: meaning and motive, beat by beat. Also, however simply, however inexpensively, he gives form to the underlying thought—the germinating idea that propels the action. Now, a memory from *Blood Wedding* drifts up—at the opening, the women silently making lace at their wooden looms—an image that describes the world, the very culture within which the tragedy will take place.

2. Zelda refers to Ciulei's production of Max Frisch's *Andorra* at NYU's Graduate Acting Program where the cast included Josh Radnor, Nealy Glenn, Danielle Skraastad, Gareth Saxe, and Mia Barron. [T.L.]

Actors who may think at first that Liviu is narrowing their contribution by focusing on an exterior design will find out, if they permit themselves, that a rare thing is happening: Liviu is making a series of paintings or a moving architectural frieze or sculpture out of psychology and human intention. If the actor fills the moment with her real interior life, the audience will experience the highest of high art. I only know one Liviu who can do this like Liviu.

Liviu Ciulei is ferocious in pursuit of what he sees as necessary, but he is also a very, very modest and gentle man. He's recognized and celebrated on the streets of Bucharest as if he were a sports hero or a rock star. Cab drivers wish him a happy birthday, and parades are organized to celebrate him when he and Helga return to work there.

In this country, we haven't been able to fully answer his challenges, although, Liviu, it surely hasn't been for want of appreciation, recognition, respect, and love. Go, the two of you, in good health, and hang on to the green card, so we can hope you will come back from time to time. We want very much to have you with us.

Tribute in honor of Liviu Ciulei, NYU, April 21, 2003. Ciulei returned to Bucharest to work following the Romanian Revolution in 1989. He taught at NYU well into the nineties before returning home for good, where he was named honorary director of the Bulandra Theatre.

PETER ZEISLER

(2005)

" Look to the future. You are not expected to complete the task. Neither are you permitted to lay it down." So the Talmud tells us, and so it speaks to me of Peter Zeisler.

It started way back with him, the commitment that was to last a lifetime. It took many shapes along the way and had several tunes, but it had one long underlying action—like a well-made play. First, to find a place for himself within a new idea for theater, when he and it were very young. Then to become uniquely instrumental in securing the idea in American soil. And next, to preside over its needs—administrative, political, structural, *and*, *above all*, *artistic*, in the persistent way a parent presides over the ongoing action of a child's life to ensure that he flourishes.

With high optimism—and anger—both lusty in their hold on him, with infinite caring—and outrage—Peter held to his path and pushed and pulled us to get with him toward the place he was trying to reach. He was a true leader. I wonder if we totally understood the full scope of his leadership while we were imbedded with him.

It started with Peter the way it starts with everyone: with dreams, images of what could happen. And since all such dreams are young, no matter the age of the dreamer, and since Peter kept having them and never gave up on them—like a good Talmudic scholar, he never did lay down the task.

On this past January 16th, he simply released his dreams to us, hoping we'd grab ahold. Those dreams are his legacy, and if we mean to honor him, we're committed to making good on them to the best of our ability, even in the face of the overwhelming obstacles.

I have a letter dated April 14, 1947, that Lindy Zesch[1] gave me when I asked if there was anything in the files about Peter's earliest life choices. I sought a deeper understanding of him. The letter was sent from Bard College, Annandale-on-Hudson, where Peter was finishing up a college degree begun before World War II. He was twenty-three. It's addressed to Margo Jones, who was the first mother of the regional theater, with her 198-seat arena in an abandoned fan factory on the Dallas State Fairgrounds, her eight-member professional acting company, and her policy of presenting only classics and new plays, one of those being Tennessee Williams's *Summer and Smoke*, which launched his playwriting career.

Dear Miss Jones:

On the suggestion of Horton Foote . . . I wrote to you last spring to inquire about a job in your repertory theater in Dallas but was informed that you were not ready to start production at that time. I am now writing to you again after reading reports in the *New York Times* that you were actually starting production this summer.

My main interest in the theater is the type of work you are interested in doing in Texas. I never have had, nor do I now have, any desire to work on Broadway. Everything that I have heard of your plans . . . makes me most enthusiastic and eager to try to fit into your organization in some capacity . . .

The idea of taking theater outside of the narrow limits of New York, where I feel Drama has lost its integrity and purpose and has become another "business," is a definite challenge to me as well as the challenge of starting a permanent theater in a fundamentally nontheatrical section of the country.

1. Zeisler's closest collaborator Zesch was his associate and later deputy director of Theatre Communications Group during her twenty-three-year tenure there.

Additional paragraphs outline his credentials thus far, including some acting and directing stints, which I hadn't known about before this letter, and include the message that he could get away from classes on either April 25th or May 3rd for an interview in New York.

We know the plot of the Peter Zeisler story, and I don't want to recount it in these few minutes. But did we weigh heavily enough the artistic hunger, the longing, that lay under it and propelled it forward?

Looking back, it seems to me that the goal of Peter's heart did not stop with the decentralization of the American theater away from the magnet of Broadway—a goal that we universally identify with him—but extended to the creation of artistic standards for this theater that had never yet been achieved, not on Broadway then and not anyplace else in the country's history.

It was as if he were looking for the standards of perfection in theater that are found in the Big Five Symphony Orchestras, say the Cleveland Orchestra or the New York Philharmonic, under a conductor who could enable the ensemble to acquire a powerful personality that exceeded the sum of its parts: hence, Tyrone Guthrie. Where, by some mysterious alchemy, all the pieces come together—under a worldview—and all the arts that make up the art of theater form a unity that is perfection. Where artists work not just to please the audience but to please each other. An ensemble where the actors seem to be inside the same skin. An ensemble that would combine American energy, diversity, and freedom of spirit with the virtuosity of execution, the sense of tradition, the sense of style, of the European theater. Hence, the Guthrie Theater, which perhaps represented the most fulfilling segment of his professional life.

How proud Peter was that Jessica Tandy played not only leading roles but also a peasant in Brecht's *The Caucasian Chalk Circle*, and had gone to movement classes with the rest of the company. That was a symbol of achievement to him.

In 1963, a young George Grizzard, grown at Arena Stage, opened the Guthrie space with a vibrant American Hamlet; the next night came Rita Gam as Frosine to Hume Cronyn's lecherous Miser of Molière; then Hume again with Jessica Tandy gave us their own *Death of a Salesman*. And, of course, the unforgettable *Three Sisters* with members of that remarkable first acting company. I can still see Vershinin thrusting the memento of his pocket watch on a distraught

Masha (again Rita Gam), and Zoe Caldwell as Natasha, her long cross with a lighted candle claiming the space in the murky predawn hours of the fire. Four plays. In repertory. Stunningly brought to life. Peter Zeisler was a totally happy man. For here was a *theater! An artistic home!* Here was the dream come true.

These clues are the best I have to find Peter, sometimes elusive to me, screened behind a tangle of thoughts and plans and stratagems and the distraction of multiple tasks.

This is how I can best understand his tirelessness, his obsessiveness, and the radiating authority he brought to his work as executive director of Theatre Communications Group: Communication. Relationships—artist to artist, artists to unions, art to funders, art to free expression, artistic leaders to boards, board leaders to board leaders, arts to other arts, minds to the printed word, cultures to cultures—internationally and within our own borders. *Relationships as the means*, the web within which to capture and hold the prize—a new, surprising American theater that could be defined as high art.

Peter taught me a lot of what could be aimed for and achieved, even though Arena Stage was already thirteen years old when the Guthrie opened. He spurred me on to *know more* and to go for it. And when he would come to visit, he could define what he was seeing. He had an artist's eye.

"We'll hang ourselves tomorrow," Vladimir says. "Unless Godot comes." "And if he comes?" asks Estragon. "Then we'll be saved." For a number of decades, this upbeat, complex man felt to us to be our Godot who had actually come. We counted on him to save us, and in many ways he did. And we're so grateful. And we're so sad.

Memorial ruminations for Peter Zeisler, delivered February 28, 2005, Biltmore Theatre, New York City. Zeisler, a founder of the Guthrie Theater in Minneapolis (1963), served as Theatre Communications Group's executive director from 1972 to 1995. He died in 2005.

AFTER WORDS

THE ZELDA FICHANDLER AWARD

(2009, 2011)

This is my dream of an award.[1] Thank you so much. Not too heavy to get it home; not so bizarre it has to be hidden away some place in my apartment. An award that belongs to someone else each year— one of you, perhaps; or a colleague; or a talented child, maybe one of yours, aesthetic or biological; or some artistic leader ready to move forward. And the award will go on forever and ever, as long as there are arts to support, and there will always be. When the arts fade, so does the civilization from which they grew. We won't allow that to happen. We swear that to each other.

---

1. The Stage Directors and Choreographers Foundation established an annual award in Zelda Fichandler's name and unveiled the award in 2009, at the fiftieth anniversary gala of the Stage Directors and Choreographers Society. What follows is a combination of Zelda's remarks on that occasion, delivered in her absence by Jane Alexander, and the speech she gave in person at the Fichandler Award ceremony two years later at Arena Stage. The 2011 award was given to Blanka Zizka, then artistic director of Philadelphia's Wilma Theater; Zelda's speech was introduced by Jonathan Moscone, then artistic director of California Shakespeare Theater, who had been the inaugural recipient of the award. Because the two speeches cover much of the same history and use some of the same language, I have edited them together. What comes through in each of them—and I hope in this fused version—is Zelda's passion, maybe even urgency, as she recounts her movement's history as a benediction and call to action for its future. [T.L.]

I'm deeply honored to have my name attached to this award. This represents a story—a history. It celebrates the past, a vibrant present, and promises an evolving future, if we stay with it and solve our problems as we've always solved them—with tenacity, imagination, and hope. And if we can continue to be tough in the service of something that is tender.

I want to say what we all know, but what I want you to know that I know. I was there at the beginning—and am lucky enough to still be here while many are not—but I was not the founder of this movement. The idea for our kind of theater was there, ready to be found, at a particular moment in our history, post–World War II. Why just then I'm not entirely clear.

There are form-givers in every new style of art, form-givers in new scientific inventions, new medical discoveries, new technologies. There may seem to be *just one* in front but, like seeds under the snow, they emerge in small clusters and, if the plants are strong, they become widely absorbed into the culture.

So, then, I'm the chorus in *Henry V*, and for that I'm very proud to have this award in my name. It's the chorus who enlists the imagination of the audience to "think when we talk of horses that you see them" and "into a thousand parts divide one man." Well, I'm your man, and there are a thousand men and women with me. More than a thousand. Many thousands.

I think of them, I knew and know so many of them, I feel their presence. The founders: Joe and Gordon and Tyrone and Nina and of course Margo, who was truly the first; and Jules who I met when his daughter Amy Irving was still crawling around on the kitchen floor; and Herbert,[2] his partner, and all the others who came after them— using these founders as a model or finding their own way, each with his individual nature, his own inherent style and view of the world. And all the actors through all the years, all the directors— architects of our work—and the designers, and stage and production managers, administrators and artisans and board members, and

2. Joe Papp, Gordon Davidson, Tyrone Guthrie, Nina Vance, and Margo Jones were founders of the New York Shakespeare Festival, the Mark Taper Forum, the Guthrie Theater, the Alley Theatre, and Theatre '47, respectively. Jules Irving and Herbert Blau cofounded and led The Actor's Workshop in San Francisco.

fundraisers, and so on and so on—who have made this idea concrete. So many thousands. There's hardly room for me on the stage. I should move away and give room for the others. And, in my mind, I do.

Fans of Saul Bellow, our great master of the art of the novel, will remember a certain dog barking forlornly in Bucharest during the long night of Soviet domination of Romania. It's overheard by an American visitor in *The Dean's December*, who imagines these words as the barking plea: "For God's sake, open up the Universe a little!" And that's what we all try to do every day, what this Society has done and will do for the next half century, barking even louder: "For God's sake, open up the Universe a little MORE!"

I'm so honored to be chosen to stand in for the six or twelve who, almost simultaneously, asked the question: "Why is it that our performing arts are concentrated in New York, when people live all over the place?" We couldn't find a sensible answer, except the one we found. We'd make the arts in places where we found ourselves. Grow where we were planted, so to speak.

Why art? Why? The everlasting persistence of and seemingly bio-logic necessity for human creativity. We have always had our griot, our storyteller, who seeks to unravel the mysteries of the world for us, hoping to find hints, clues, by walking in the shoes of another, gathering up the cultural strands of time and weaving them into a tapestry of meaning, trying to pierce the opacity of the world and of our human nature in particular. Camus has told us: "If the world were clear, art would not be necessary. Art helps us pierce the opacity of the world."

It seems that we humans are creatures without defenses but for our creativity. Shakespeare's "poor fork'd animal" is subject to huge vicissitudes of fortune in the course of a lifetime. Despite our talent for denial, we are aware that those we love may die and that we ourselves will die, that, in the end, life's a failed enterprise. On top of these insults to our self-importance, we can't run very fast, and we lack the tough hide of the elephant, the long neck of the giraffe, the teeth of the shark. We're subject to a range of bodily and emotional illnesses. We are each of us isolated in our separate skin. Living outside of nature, unlike other animals, we find to our surprise and indignation that the world was not made for us at all. We only dwell in it for a time. The gods—or the one God, or our internalized consciences—exact a heavy price for the pleasures of life they allow us.[3]

For those of you who didn't live through the earliest years—say 1950 to 1965—the years the Ford Foundation finally gave in to the notion that our theaters would never, ever balance the books on box office alone—to those of you who believe "it was easier in the olden days," I respond with a different view. The problems of creating a theater institution or inheriting one and sustaining its development have always been insurmountable. Then we find a way to surmount them. Then new problems take their place, or old ones reappear in a new guise. It was never any easier and won't be. Isn't creativity itself the overcoming of resistances?

Things like getting actors to leave New York and L.A.—still difficult. I recall an actor asking me if you could get fresh tomatoes in Washington. Each contract was an act of personal persuasion. Subscriptions? Three hundred was a bunch! Single tickets? Don't ask! Boards? How to work with them smoothly and all-around happily was already a mystery. Sleep, recreation, time for personal relationships? Creating something new where there was nothing before has never been for sissies.

We need what we always needed and what every artistic leader needs in a country that doesn't provide sufficient subsidy or have genuine respect for culture: stamina to persist; capacity for a deep interiority on one hand and a practical manipulativeness on the other; concentration to hear one's own voice and courage to listen to it in the midst of a cacophony of other voices; and, again, toughness in the service of something that is tender, while you try to remain tender yourself.

Through art, we can confront the final core of uncertainty at the heart of things. On the whole, artists do this far more bravely than engineers or lawyers or politicians. In a culture of specialists, the artist is something else. When the students and faculty at NYU gathered

---

3. The previous two paragraphs are repeated from Zelda's 2002 speech, "Creativity and the Public Mind." Zelda often drew on earlier or other of her writings to continue thoughts or flesh out new ideas. I've often cut these repetitions; here I've kept this one because, as fate conspired, her 2002 essay and 2009 and 2011 speeches to SDC captured many of her late—or even final—thoughts about art, creativity, and the movement she led for so long. [T.L.]

with me after 9/11 to meditate on what it meant to be or become an artist in relationship to this terrible event, I could recall no play—no Greek or Shakespearean tragedy, no contemporary work of darkness and despair—that doesn't conclude with some stirring, however faint, of hope, even if that hope presents itself only as a recognition of the worth and dignity of human experience.

Václav Havel, playwright and former President of Czechoslovakia, writes:

> Either we have hope within us or we don't; it is a dimension of the soul; it's not essentially dependent on some particular observation of the world or estimate of the situation. Hope is not prognostication. It is an orientation of the spirit, an orientation of the heart . . .
>
> Hope, in this deep and powerful sense, is not the same thing as joy that things are going well, or willingness to invest in enterprises that are obviously headed for success, but, rather, an ability to work for something that is good.

It's an honor for me to be among you tonight and to speak of these things so close to my heart. I thank you for your attention. I wish for your flourishing.

Parts of this speech were delivered at SDC's fiftieth anniversary gala in New York City, November 8, 2009. Many who attended that night, still remember Jane Alexander's comic entrance as if she were Zelda, arriving late and disorganized or, as Zelda wrote in her "directorial" note to Jane, "a 'caricature' or 'charming busy.'" Zelda wrote the following intro for her impersonator: "Thank you so much—so much! I got locked up in the ladies' room and didn't hear the speeches . . . I hope you didn't praise me too much. What a wonderful way to celebrate my fift—I mean your fiftieth anniversary! There's nothing like a millstone to—MILESTONE, nothing like a *milestone*—I'm just flustered . . . to open up the future in a positive way." The rest of this edited version needed no direction, as Zelda was present to deliver it in her home space, Arena Stage's Mead Center for American Theater on October 26, 2011. [T.L.]

THE BEGINNING

In 2011 Zelda wrote: "Here's a story with a happy ending. On behalf of Arena Stage, I wrote a long document to the Department of the Treasury, supporting theater as an instrument of education . . . And therefore, deserving of tax relief. The document happened to land on the desk of an Arena subscriber! And was read into the Congressional Record. We've been nonprofit ever since; actually our profit is simply of a different kind."

This, then, is that document, dated June 1959. Nine years after the founding of Arena Stage as a for-profit theater, Zelda's paper represents a new beginning—maybe the *beginning—for Arena and the American regional, resident, repertory theater movement as a whole. [T.L.]*

A PERMANENT CLASSICAL REPERTORY THEATER IN THE NATION'S CAPITAL

(1959)

THE CULTURAL CLIMATE

The new recognition of the need to establish, throughout the United States, permanent repertory theaters is part and parcel of the new recognition of the need to attend to America's cultural resources in general. Wherever one turns, one reads or hears distinguished men, men who know, exhorting us to develop our educational, cultural, and artistic resources in order for the United States to take its due place in the international family of nations, creatively utilize the leisure of its citizens, and enrich its national life.

The signs in the air are so profuse and exist in so many fields—economic political, artistic, educational, scientific, journalistic, social—that documenting the above statement is more a problem of selection than of research. For example, at the groundbreaking ceremony for the Lincoln Center for Performing Arts on Thursday, May 14, 1959, President Eisenhower remarked that the Lincoln Center "symbolizes an increasing interest in America in cultural matters":

> At Lincoln Center Americans will have new and expanded
> opportunities for acquiring a real community of inter-

est through common contact with the performing arts . . .
American technology, labor, industry, and business are
responsible for the twentieth-century freedom of the individual—making free a greater portion of his time in which
to improve the mind, body, and the spirit.

He added, "The lives of all of us will be enriched," before putting the
event in its global context:

The beneficial influence of this great cultural adventure will
not be limited to our borders . . . [Here] will occur a true
interchange of the fruits of national cultures. From this will
develop a growth that will spread to the corners of the Earth,
bringing with it the kind of human message that only individuals, not governments, can transmit.

Previously, in his 1955 State of the Union message, President Eisenhower asserted that the "federal government should do more to
give official recognition to the importance of the arts and other cultural activities." He proposed a permanent Federal Advisory Council of Art to come under the Department of Health, Education, and
Welfare. In June 1959, Welfare Secretary Arthur Flemming told the
House Education and Labor Committee that passage of a bill to bring
such a council into being "would be in the national interest. There
is inadequate recognition of the fundamental importance of artistic
endeavor in our national life." Another reason he supported this legislation, Mr. Flemming went on to say, was "the national interest in
promoting educational, cultural, and personal development of our
citizens through a more widespread appreciation of and participation in the arts."

Recently there have also been renewed proposals for a Department of Fine Arts, headed by a leader of cabinet rank; for an Assistant Secretary of State for Cultural Affairs; for a United States Art
Foundation; and for a National Theater. A bill authorizing a National
Cultural Center has been approved by Congress and signed by the
president.

Senator Jacob K. Javits, in an illuminating article in the April 5,
1959 issue of the *New York Times*, notes that "'culture' only too often

has been a suspect word in the American language. At the very beginning of the nation, we acquired a reputation—now undeserved—for being crude and 'rock-ribbed.'" He continues: "The old traditions linger . . . This attitude has long tended to persist in the thinking of our government on cultural matters, and since the notes of a Beethoven symphony cannot be weighed and assessed, since the tread of an actor's foot on a stage does not rock the earth, our cultural institutions have been left . . . to shift for themselves. Whatever men and women have done in the arts, they have done largely on their own."

Senator Javits goes on to note that the sum total of our artistic accomplishment is not nearly what it should be in a country of our size. There are a few great orchestras, but large sections of the country are foreclosed to serious performances of music, dance, and theater—circumstances which, he believes, do not make for cultural adequacy. He advises that "in self-defense, if for no less selfish reason, we must be prepared to meet the cultural challenge of our competitors" and nurture all the talent we have and assure the next generation of every possible chance to develop its full potential. "If we are to measure up to the stature of leader of the free world, we must act as such; and a nation's civilization is equated in many places with its degree of culture."

Senator Javits turns his attention to all the arts—opera, symphony, ballet, and theater—emphasizing still more firmly that the majority of Americans around the country face a meager cultural fare. Indeed, they are blacked out of professional, cultural activities for a good part of the year. He contrasts this country's situation with that obtaining in England, Canada, the Soviet Union, Italy, France, and Austria, where a plethora of nonprofit institutions for the arts—covering opera, symphony, and ballet, as well as theater—serve the public, and where such cultural institutions are a vital part of the daily way of life.

"Last year Austria spent $5,800,000 on its four state theaters in Vienna . . . larger than the sum . . . paid to its entire foreign service. Imagine! $5,800,000 out of a total national budget of $1,500,000,000," Javits exclaims. He proposes a Federal Arts Foundation to assist private, nonprofit theater, opera, symphony, and other art groups, to help both professional, and amateur segments of the performing arts, to encourage performances of the best we have in large areas where little is available, and to stimulate widespread training and teaching of all the arts, so that more young people may receive guidance and direction in realizing their full artistic potential. For theater, in particular, he envisions as necessary and desirable the establishment, throughout the country, of professional companies able to support a full season of theater, the establishment of traveling repertory companies, and the provision of scholarships to some talented students from the more than four hundred colleges and universities that offer degrees in drama.

"Above all," Javits concludes, "so many neglected audiences of America could have the chance to breathe some of the cultural air they now lack. Who knows but that such exposure to the arts might stimulate the emergence of an American Mozart or Corneille?"

Senator Philip Hart of Michigan rose on the floor of the Senate recently to speak in support of the American National Exhibition of contemporary art now on its way to Russia. His remarks add dimension to these examples: "There are a great many people in the world who think one can judge a civilization and the soul of a people more clearly by looking at its painting and sculpture than by counting its plumbing and automobiles. The sooner we understand that fact the better it will be for us."

This awareness in our great political leaders grows deeper every day and its expression more articulate. It is a happy commentary on the American cultural climate, within which we propose a permanent repertory theater in Washington, DC, that a burgeoning interest in the life of the mind and spirit has, indeed, become so manifest in recent years. The scientist, the news analyst, the poet, the drama and music critic, the theater artist—all these support and extend, each in his own way and in his own area, the deeply held belief in the need to develop America's cultural life, as expressed by President Eisenhower and others.

In the January 1958 issue of *Foreign Affairs*, Lloyd V. Berkner of the President's Scientific Advisory Committee argues that the fundamental challenge of contemporary American life is the challenge of intellectual attainment. Military power, he says, has become absolute in its destructiveness and relatively easy to acquire. "Both the United States and the USSR have acquired the power to destroy a people and all its wealth by a single blow." Such absolute military power is so dangerous that it cannot be used as an instrument of foreign policy.

Berkner also eliminates, as an instrument of foreign policy, the use of national wealth, since the undeveloped countries are suspicious of both communist imperialism and foreign investment by the West. This leaves a power vacuum, he explains:

> Clearly the side that can effectively develop a new instrument will enjoy a powerful advantage. The Soviet Union seems to have found one in scientific and cultural achievement as a basis for claiming intellectual leadership. [The Soviets see] an opportunity for leadership based on recognized intellectual stature . . . Leaders of the Soviet Union are now capitalizing on intellectual leadership as a means of acquiring an essential element of what Milovan Djilas calls "the inherent need of those in power to be recognizable prototypes of brilliance and might."

The challenge, Berkner concludes, is not of maintaining or restoring the balance of military power, though that is necessary. The challenge is whether we can restore the intellectual greatness of the West, if not to its former preeminence, at least to a new equality. He calls for "an American renaissance." Walter Lippmann, in his January 1958 column in the *Washington Post*, seconds the idea, adding that "the renaissance will have to come from men of learning . . . men who know, because they live the intellectual life, what a renaissance would be."

Dorothy Thompson, the distinguished columnist, noted on December 13, 1955, that European theater audiences are much more sophisticated than American "for the simple reason that all European countries have a theater that is not wholly the instrument of commercial interests. The professional theater is not confined, as it is here, to a few streets in the national metropolis." Nearly every city of one hundred thousand or more, she informs us, and many that are smaller, has an opera house and theater playing the classics and modern operas and plays with companies that are seasonally employed. Miss Thompson writes:

> The houses and casts are subsidized, usually by the municipalities. In the larger cities they compete with commercial theaters but attract the best actors and, of course, create

great schools of acting, because they usually present two or
three different plays each week, and change their programs
numerous times during the season, thus calling on their
casts for a great variety of talent and industry.

The same is true of Russia where the theater is superb
and—contrary to what many people think—almost entirely
free of propaganda. More residents of Moscow see, and have
seen, the great Russian European operas and the great classic dramas, Russian, French, German, and English, than
New Yorkers ever have. The plain fact is that with unused
acting talent equal to any, were it not idle most of the time,
and with playwrights second to none in the world . . . America, in the great domain of the theater, is culturally behind
half a dozen small and relatively poor European states.

In a letter dated two weeks later, Miss Thompson noted that, as
America's cultural export program develops, we are likely to make
an increasingly poor showing "simply because in certain areas of culture, notably the theater, we are culturally backward." She airs her dis-
tress that "the poor Russkies—and they *are* poor—see more Shakespeare in any season than the New Yorkers do." And her regret that
the world's richest country "cannot afford financial support for what
from time immemorial has been a *fundamental* cultural institution."

Archibald MacLeish, Pulitzer Prize winner in 1959 for his verse
play *J.B.*, adds the voice of the poet to that of the scientist and the news
commentator. In his Gideon Seymour lecture at the University of Min-
nesota, he states that the greatest flaw of modern civilization is its
inability to "feel" and "imagine." "Far more than we need an interconti-
nental missile or a moral rearmament or a religious revival," MacLeish
insists, "we need to come alive again, to recover the virility of the imagination on which all earlier civilizations have been based . . ." He looks
to poetry, journalism, and the public arts to reawaken modern civilization and to fill the void created by "knowledge without feeling."

The arts' family, too, vehemently appealed for cultural growth.
Brooks Atkinson, dean of the American drama critics, writing in
the *New York Times*, voices his desire for more theater "that is not
so much show business as a form of culture," that will serve people
whose "attitudes toward the theater have been formed or influenced

by the universities, which for half a century have been graduating
thousands of young people who have studied drama, and who know
that for two thousand years the drama has shaped and been shaped
by the spiritual experience of mankind." Mr. Atkinson calls for the
growth "in numbers and influence" of theaters throughout the country that serve as "the custodians of civilized drama."

Also in the *Times* (August 1957), Playwright Marc Connelly, best
known for *The Green Pastures*, decried the absence of any government support for our theater. He blames this situation on both the
blindness of officialdom to "civilized man's need of the theater as a
therapeutic agent," and the blindness of many of the people themselves to "the theater's importance in a healthy society." Mr. Connelly
contends that "the theater will not truly serve us as it served Greece
and is serving other countries today until we recognize that it is the
duty of a democratic society . . . 'not only to eliminate material poverty but poverty of desire.'" He reminds us that the theater is "not
only a fountainhead of amusement but also a place where moral values are constantly reexamined and truth itself is sought . . ." And he
contrasts our lack of government support with the way it is supported
elsewhere:

> The Australians are at present running a $12,800,000 state
> lottery to finance an opera house in Sydney. Last February
> the Canadian Parliament established a council for the arts
> and endowed it with $50,000,000. Only recently announce-
> ment was made of generous grants to two Canadian reper-
> tory theaters. Compare our own financial starvation of the
> arts with France's annual grant of approximately $4,500,000
> to the Paris Opéra, the Opéra Comique, the Théâtre-Français
> and the Odéon.
>
> Many single towns in Germany spend more on music
> than the United States government. Long before the post–
> World War II Viennese had enough to eat they were plan-
> ning to rebuild their opera house, the present support of
> which is generous and above politics. The Scandinavian
> governments are constantly demonstrating their recogni-
> tion of the importance of the theater as part of a commu-
> nity's daily life. Denmark spends $750,000 annually for the

upkeep of its Royal Theatre in Copenhagen. Sweden's Opera, State Theatre, and Lilla Scena, an experimental adjunct, receive annual subsidies provided by a national lottery. And not only are the municipal theaters at Göteborg and Malmö aided by the parliament, but several smaller municipal theaters and touring theatrical troupes as well.

In June 1959, Ralph Bellamy, president of the Actors' Equity Association and star of *Sunrise at Campobello*, made another appeal for government funding. Mr. Bellamy spoke as a representative of two hundred thousand persons in the fields of music, drama, and dance. "They ask that their government officially recognize that the arts and those who practice them are a major asset to the country and subject of proper concern to its government," he said. Mr. Bellamy specifically supported legislation to establish a Federal Advisory Council of Art, as recommended by President Eisenhower, noting that legislation has been before Congress in each of the last five sessions. The theater reflects the "cultural development of the people," he added.

Dr. Tyrone Guthrie, the famous British director who was instrumental in bringing one repertory theater—London's Old Vic—to its present eminence, joined the charge in "Repertory Theatre—Ideal or Deception?" (*New York Times*, April 26, 1959). A permanent company doing a variety of plays is, as he sees it, "a consummation devoutly to be wished." Dr. Guthrie feels that a theater with three or four classical masterpieces in any given season is a necessity of modern life:

No doubt there are tens of thousands of citizens who could be persuaded that a repertory theater with a policy governed by something more respectable than the pursuit of financial success, and looking further ahead than next Thursday fortnight, is not a mirage shimmering in front of weary professionals, is not merely a perfectly practicable possibility, is not merely an amenity which it might be elegant, and even fun, to possess—but is a necessity without which no great metropolis can consider itself civilized; a necessity partly as a matter of prestige in the eyes of the world, but far more for the enrichment it can bring to the eyes and ears, wishes and dreams of those who use it with intelligence and love.

Miss Eva Le Gallienne has been a principal in two of the three main modern New York ventures in repertory—her own Civic Repertory Theatre (1926–1933) and the American Repertory Theater (1946–1947). She writes, regretfully, that "we still have no theater that can stand beside our symphony orchestras, our opera and ballet companies, our museums of art, and public libraries as a permanent and integral part of the cultural life of New York City, or any other city in our country." (*Theatre Arts*, September 1958.)

Such a theater would appeal to a different audience than the one that attends the Broadway theater, she believes. It would attract an audience "composed of people of modest means; students, workers, thinking people to whom art in any form is a necessity." She finds this audience "among the standees at Carnegie Hall, or in the gallery of the Metropolitan Opera House. These are the people who really use our museums and public libraries; and these are the people who would use a repertory theater if only we had one."

Since they are a discriminating audience, Miss Le Gallienne insists, they must be given productions of the highest standard. And since they are "anything but wealthy," they must be given these productions at very modest prices. "High standards and modest prices cannot coexist without subsidy," she concludes, noting that many people do not understand this attitude. They confuse "show business" with genuine "theater." She defends her point rhetorically: "Do our orchestras make money? Does opera make money? The dance theater? Without endowment where would our museums of art and our libraries be?"

Howard Taubman, dean of America's music critics, writing in the *New York Times* in December 1958, echoes these calls and summarizes their most important lesson:

> We must be convinced by cultivation and experience that the arts are a vital element of any civilized society. Only if we achieve this conviction and wisdom shall we go on to integrate the arts in the fabric of everyday living. Then we shall proceed to do the things that remain to be done.
>
> We shall insist that our artistic institutions have continuity. We shall make sure that their fate does not depend on the fluctuations of business cycles or on the whims of indi-

viduals. We shall not allow them to go about hat in hand like beggars. We shall work out techniques, using government or private initiative or both, to employ our artistic resources to the full, thus serving the artist and the community. We shall see to it that our creative and interpretive artists will have not only an honored place but a secure one. We shall continue to be generous in our acceptance of the best from abroad but shall learn to appreciate our own at their full deserts.

Our attitude toward the arts will undergo a change when we learn to admire wholeheartedly achievements of the mind that do not produce an immediate monetary gain . . . Let us learn from Europe—and from our neighbors to the south, as well—that some of our wealth and ingenuity should be employed to provide our people not only with the material comforts but also with the adventures of the heart and mind that bring compassion and exaltation into our lives.

THEATER AS AN ART

The effect of Big Business Theater on the art itself is the proper subject for an entire book, but a few general points should at least be touched on here. The Broadway theater is "hit happy." Only major smash successes can survive economically. The audiences whose tastes include but are not limited to the hits of the season simply have nowhere to go; after seeing *My Fair Lady*, *Sweet Bird of Youth*, and a few others, they simply stay away. For the in-between show, the show that is interesting but not a smash—and these shows must be the staple of any truly living theater—simply can no longer exist.

Classics have all but left the stage. Shaw, Shakespeare, Chekhov, Molière, Sheridan, Pirandello, and even the modern playwrights, whose works a whole new generation of people have not seen—Wilder, Williams, Elmer Rice, Maxwell Anderson, the young O'Neill—have been almost completely banished to the library shelves. Their plays are too expensive to produce at the level of ticket prices that the kind of people who want to see them can pay. The literature of the stage, which is the very fount of all the dramatic arts, lives in our American theater only sporadically and in limited runs and, even then, is usually presented Off-Broadway under impromptu conditions, on shoestring budgets, in unsuitable lofts and basements, and on a hit-or-miss basis.

Further, the production system of Boom-or-Bust Broadway is itself entirely and irreconcilably incompatible with the nature of theater as an art form. Theater is a group art, and its flowering demands permanence and continuity, the opportunity to build a tradition and evolve a characteristic method of work. Its artists must work together over time in conditions as free from stress as the creative process will allow, and they must work with the sense of effort flowing out of previous effort in a continuous and building stream. There must, above all, be time and permission for the essential elements of the creative process—maturation, experimentation, and failure. The conditions of Broadway forbid all three.

The very word "culture" implies "continuity" and "permanence." The word "Broadway" is antithetical to both. For Broadway's objective is not culture at all. Its objective is commodity.

Production on Broadway is a "one-shot" system. There is separate financing, separate bookkeeping, separate management, separate casting of actors, and separate hiring of designers, directors, and choreographers. Everything is assembled for a one-shot effort, and when that production is over, everything is broken up and sent away again. (Often the set is literally demolished and then burned, dumped, or used for scrap.) As it wastes artistic materials, Broadway completely wastes the knowledge gained by group association.

All this leads to an atmosphere of high-pressure buying and selling, with the objective being to make money rather than plays, no place for the creation of art. Broadway operates like a badly run business, where the "angels"—the men who put up the money to make it all possible—are the Magic Masters. Brooks Atkinson concurs:

> The Broadway theater has been slowly becoming a neurotic ordeal. The cost of production and operation has become so high that successes have to be fantastically successful and failures have become catastrophes . . . It is not art, but an unsuccessful form of high-pressure huckstering. There is almost no continuity of employment among actors, play-

wrights, and allied artists, and craftsmen. The whole business is conducted in an atmosphere of crises, strain, and emergency. Crisis is the normal state of affairs on Broadway.

The art of theater, whose true function for over two thousand years of human history has been the interpretation of man to man, has dwindled in contemporary America into nothing more significant than "a night on the town," or a method of achieving prestige by having seen approval-stamped bits. This economic framework has deprived the American stage of its core vitality and its dynamism—indeed, of its very place as a cultural and artistic force in the nation's life. One is reminded, by contrast, of how Hallie Flanagan, former director of the Federal Theatre, once described the early Greek theater:

> Once there was a republic where people used to get up early in the morning and take their bread and cheese and travel miles and sit for days looking at a stage. Why? Because what was going on there meant something to them: life, love, death. Things they cared about. Art to them wasn't just the frosting on the cake. It was the yeast that made the bread rise.

My full heart wishes that the American theater would immediately set about to discover how to revitalize itself as an art form, reestablish this same rousing relationship with its audience, and restore its ancient function of leading man to the brink of his own mind.

ANSWERS

The answer to the dilemma of the art of theater in this country is simple and readily turned into a practical, living reality: We must create more theater that, as Brooks Atkinson says, "is not so much show business as a form of culture." We can do this by increasing "in numbers and influence the theaters throughout the country that will be the custodians of civilized drama."

It is, indeed, toward this very end that we propose the establishment of a permanent classical repertory theater in our nation's capital.

THE PERMANENT THEATER COMPANY

A theater in Washington, or in any other city in America, must be a home and not a hotel. It must have the permanence and continuity that define similar institutions of culture and education—schools, libraries, art museums, symphony orchestras, ballet companies, and so forth. It must operate on the basis of a recognizable and definable policy. It must have resident personnel who stay with it for years at a time, shape its destiny and participate in the life of the community. At its core must be a resident acting company. The "roadhouses" that host touring companies are hotels; "one-shot" productions organized for profit in New York City are not the answer to our cultural needs. Their worth is always singular. Culture and tradition imply continuity. The resident theater, a creative unit in a group art, welded to the life of a community from whom it draws life and to whom it gives life, is the only hope for our future. The artist will benefit in the development of his craft; the audience will benefit from the increased quantity and quality of the art; and the nation itself will gain the dignity and self-respect these companies afford.

Production by the permanent company method is the normal, recognized, and organic method for theater, both historically and currently, in all countries of the world but ours. (This statement is true despite the fact that in many of the cities of Europe commercial theater exists side by side with repertory theater.) European theater has for centuries grown around the idea of permanent companies—Shakespeare and Molière wrote their great plays specifically for the troupes to which they belonged, and Stanislavsky did all of his important experimental work in acting methods with a company. France, England, the Soviet Union, Germany, Italy, Austria, all have several leading and revered acting companies. There is hardly a country in the world that does not boast its own national troupe.

America has inherited much of its talent from one such theater (short-lived though it was)—the Group Theatre. Beyond the Group, though, we have yet to develop one permanent theater company to represent American theatrical tradition or an American style of production.

Theater is a composite, collective art. It is practiced by people working together in creative association—the playwright, director, actor, designer, technician. The art develops as the people who create it develop, each in his own right and all together. A nation's theater is a part of its cultural tradition. It is part of the nation's social heritage—its folkways—as well as its art, education, and philosophy. A nation that values its traditions as a living force and that wishes to develop and build on them finds a way to nurture these traditions and to make them available to the people. It creates universities, schools, museums, churches. It creates permanent theater companies.

The American commercial theater, built on a pattern of the haphazard, discontinuous, isolated, sporadic, unrelated, for-profit production of a series of single shows, is an anomaly. It is un-historical and out of step with the times. Most tragically, it is in all ways at war with the highest potential of which theater is capable. For it destroys talent, makes impossible the accumulation of tradition, and is basically indifferent to the fact that it does either as long as it makes money. Unless we accept as inevitable the idea of a permanent theater company, the American theatrical muse will remain stymied.

The way to develop talent is to give it something to feed on, soil to sink its roots into, and time to mature. The Broadway commercial theater makes the artist begin work anew with each effort. The result is not only wearing and discouraging, it is profoundly uncreative. The individual artist needs a permanent base that allows for a continuity of experience to reach his peak powers. The permanent acting company is the actor's best friend.

It is also the audience's best friend. Those who were fortunate enough to see the Old Vic or La Comédie-Française or the Théâtre National Populaire on their recent visits to this country will understand, for they would have seen productions that were uniquely integrated, expressive, and perfect in every detail. They saw a coordination of text and performance and a refinement of skill uncommon, if not unknown, in the American theater.

According to Dr. Guthrie, only sustained ensemble work in a permanent company creates the feeling of intimate relationship between audience and actors. He locates this audience-actor intimacy in the feeling of loyalty, the sense of belonging to something larger than the sum of its individuals, that an acting company possesses and, so, projects from the stage. This collective esprit radiates and, with it, a sense of unity of purpose, all felt palpably by those who witness it.

Permanent repertory theaters can serve as living libraries. They present and so preserve the literature of the stage. A repertory is a "storehouse," a "collection," a "place for finding things." Nonprofit in structure, cultural and educational in aim, versatile in range, the permanent company can make a living force out of great classics, old and modern, and so provide a place for finding things of lasting, humanizing value.

On a national level, it continues to be a source of profound embarrassment that America has not a single repertory theater that can represent our theatrical culture abroad. (Finland, a tiny country with about four million in population, has thirty-two subsidized professional repertory houses.) "When the Old Vic comes to this country, what do we have to send to England in exchange?" Joseph Kramm, Pulitzer Prize–winning playwright, asked in 1954. "When Jean-Louis Barrault comes to this country, what do we have to send to Paris in exchange? When the Greek National Theatre comes to this country, what do we have to send to Athens in exchange?"

When Cecilio Madanes, director of the Caminito Theatre of Buenos Aires, visited Washington, the *Washington Post* reported his surprise that a city like Washington had so few theaters. "It is incredible—the Capital of the United States!" Mr. Madanes commented. "I cannot understand why the United States has not sent a theater group to Buenos Aires," he marveled, noting that nationally subsidized companies from France and Italy have regular seasons there. "Instead of giving away automobiles and refrigerators on television, why not give round-trip flights to South America for a theatrical company?" What Cecilio Madanes did not understand, and what one would regret to tell him, is that the round-trip tickets would be wasted, for we have no theatrical companies to send.

One theater does not make a theatrical renaissance. It will take a permanent company in Washington—and then, one hopes, others in Chicago, Los Angeles, Boston, Philadelphia, and all cities large enough to provide an audience—presenting a broad, humanizing repertory at the highest level of ensemble acting, to collectively add up to a national theater. Such companies could proudly be sent abroad as emissaries of American theatrical culture. Even more importantly, such companies would be part of the warp and woof of American life.

Excerpted from Zelda's position paper, "A Permanent Classical Repertory Theater in the Nation's Capital," June 1959. This paper, seventy-four typed pages long in its original, unedited form, is—with the exception of letters, reports, and a single speech—the first sustained writing in Zelda's lifetime of collected writings. It contains the seeds of nearly everything she would write and build over the next fifty-five years.

ACKNOWLEDGMENTS

The writing collected here was composed over fifty-two years in a nearly seventy-year career. During that time, countless people contributed in a variety of ways. Without Zelda's own list, it is impossible to identify all of them. Thankfully, some of Zelda's close friends and associates have helped assemble and check the most likely version of that list. If I've missed anyone, please know it's my oversight and not hers. Specifically, it would be impossible to thank all the members of Arena Stage and the NYU Graduate Acting communities who influenced Zelda's thinking, working methods, or writing. Her gratitude to all of them is everywhere in these pages. [T.L.]

First thanks go to Angie Moy, Zelda's longtime assistant, who was a full partner in the collecting, culling, cataloguing, envisioning, and making of this book. Zelda's most intimate collaborators share with her a legacy of vision and accomplishment, evident through her writing. They include Guy Bergquist, Allen Lee Hughes, Stephen Richard, Tazewell Thompson, Douglas C. Wager, Jaan Whitehead. Of these colleagues Laurence Maslon deserves special thanks, as he literally wrote the book on Arena Stage (*The Arena Adventure: The First 40 Years*) before continuing his collaboration with Zelda at NYU. Some of this inner circle are no longer living, but they are absolutely present in her words: Robert Alexander, Tom Fichandler, Peggy Laves, JoAnn Overholt, and Elspeth Udvarhelyi. Several others led to this book in one way or another, helping Zelda edit, gather, or think through the material. Thank you Christie Brown, Cynthia Burns Coogan, David B. Feiner, Ann Matthews, Ari Roth, E. Garland Scott, Hannah Smith. Extra gratitude goes to the late Jim O'Quinn, who edited all of Zelda's writing for *American Theatre*.

To the above thank yous on Zelda's behalf, I add my own: This same Jim O'Quinn, my late, great friend and mentor, is only one of numerous people who appears on both Zelda's gratitude list and mine. Also at the top of that shared list are Angie Moy, Tazewell Thompson, Jaan Whitehead, Laurence Maslon, and Guy Berquist. Thank you Mark and Hal Fichandler for trusting me with your mother's lifetime of writing. Thanks also to Alison Irvin, Edgar Dobie, Molly Smith, and Seema Sueko at Arena Stage; Space at Ryder Farm (Family Residency); and the Floyd U. Jones Family Endowed Chair at the University of Washington. I leaned on a lot of people for help over the years with Zelda's papers: Claudia Alick, Daniel Banks, Mia Barron, P. Carl, Brittney Falter and the team at the George Mason University Fenwick Library Special Collections Research Center, Ann Matthews, Jonathan Moscone, Jennifer Nelson, Terry Nemeth, Laura Penn, Mimi Santos, Kathy Sova, Douglas C. Wager, Rob Weinert-Kendt, and, especially, Mary B. Robinson. Thank you Nikkole Salter for your beautiful Foreword. And heartfelt thanks to the folks who in many ways over many decades brought Zelda and me together: Arthur Bartow, Christie Brown, Melissa Kievman, Jim Nicola, Lindy Zesch, and, in grateful memory, Alan Schneider, David Wheeler, and Peter Zeisler.

INDEX

Entries are alphabetized letter by letter; not word by word. For example, "Act II" will follow "acting companies." Regardless of how "theater" or "center" is spelled in an organization's name, these words are alphabetized as if they were spelled with "er," for ease of searchability.

Schall, Ekkehard, 8, 131

Schechner, Richard, 112–113, 133

Schiller, Friedrich, 202

Schlesinger, Arthur, Jr., 111

Schneider, Alan, 69, 75, 209, 260–263, 273

Schneider, Eugenie "Jeannie" Muckle, 260n1

Schoenfeld, Gerald, 234, 236

Scott, Hal, 177

Seagull, The (Chekhov), 81–82, 264

Seattle Repertory Theatre, 127

Seattle, Washington, xxiii–xxiv, 127

segregation, xx, xxvii, 154, 164, 173, 182, 226

self-doubt, 75

self-knowledge, 201–203

Serrano, Andres, 194

set design, 26–27, 275

700 Club, The, 232

Shakespeare Festival (Stratford, Ontario), 8

Shakespeare, William, xiv, 13, 28, 33, 59, 63, 81, 91, 133, 143, 166, 170–171, 200, 285, 300, 303

Shaw, George Bernard, 59, 91, 115, 251, 264, 300

She Stoops to Conquer (Goldsmith), 4

Sherin, Edwin, 264–265

Shubert Organization, 234

Sidel, Ruth, 90

Silva, De, Sanjit, 55n1

Silvera, Frank, 169

Singer, Isaac Bashevis, 197

Sisters Rosensweig, The (Wasserstein), 265

Six Characters in Search of an Author (Pirandello), 169, 275

Skin of Our Teeth, The (Wilder), 262

Sklar, George, 176

Skraastad, Danielle, 275n2

Slave, The (Jones), 164

Smith, Maggie, 131

social conscience, 265

society

  Alexander, Robert, and, 268–269

  Arena and, 141

  art and, 147, 192–194, 206, 218, 233, 293–300

  censorship and, 202–203

  cultural melding and, 224–226

  funding for arts and, 126, 142–143, 206, 217

  guilt and, 98–99

  nontraditional casting and, 162, 169–171

  social change and, 169–170, 174–175

  theater and, xv–xvii, xxviii, 13, 19, 42, 61, 63–65, 128–129, 167, 170–171, 181–182, 297, 304

  value of art in, 111, 237–238, 299

Solzhenitsyn, Aleksandr, 46–48

Sonia Shankman Orthogenic School, The, 42

South Africa, 168

Soviet Union, 44–48, 181, 219, 273, 285, 294–296, 303

Sovremennik Theatre, 47

space, 23–27, 69, 275–276

Spanbauer, Tom, 191

Spaso House, 46

staffing, 150, 176–178, 273–274

Stage Directors and Choreographers Foundation, 283n1

staging, 23–27. *see also* arena staging; platform staging; proscenium staging; three-quarter thrust staging

Stanislavsky, Konstantin, 45, 60, 84–85, 131, 303

Stephens, Robert, 131

Sternhagen, Frances, 262

Stevedore (Sklar), 176

Stevens, Roger, 192, 195

Stewart, Ellen, 125

Stickney, Phyllis Yvonne, xiv

Stone, Chuck, 159

United States Art Foundation, 292
University of California, 172
University of Chicago, 42
University of Washington, xxiii

Vance, Nina, xix, 119, 284n2
Venture, Richard, 169
Vietnam War, 29, 39, 132, 193
View from the Bridge, A (Miller), 275
Voice of America, 46
vulnerability, 52, 61

Waiting for Godot (Beckett), 280
Walden Club, 174
Ward, Douglas Turner, 139
Ward, Theodore, 176
Washington, DC
    Arena and, xiv, xv, 4–5, 142–143,
      148–149
    Black Americans and, 158, 164
    race relations in, 29, 181
    segregation in, xxvii, 35, 154
    theater in, 148, 180, 305
    youth and, 128, 181
Washington Square Park, xiii, 198–199
Watcher at the Gate, 202
Waterston, Sam, 88
wealth redistribution, 220–221
Weinberg, Joanna, 168
Western civilization, 225–226
white Americans, 159–165, 170,
  172–174, 179–180
Whitehead, Jaan, 240–245, 250, 252
white supremacy, xxvi–xxvii, 29, 168,
  225–226
Whitman, Walt, 104
"Why I Wrote *The Crucible*" (Miller),
  98
Wiest, Dianne, 274
Wild Duck, The (Ibsen), 86, 212
Wilde, Oscar, 187
Wilder, Thornton, 138, 179–181

Wildmon, Donald, 231
Williams, Tennessee, 102, 214, 278
Wilma Theater, 283n1
Wilson, August, 59, 64, 177, 203
Wines, Halo, 86
Winnicott, Donald, 70–71
Wolf, Dennie Palmer, 229–230
women, 56, 89–92, 170–171, 193,
  233, 265
Wordsworth, William, 34, 67, 116
World Trade Center, 68
World War II, xiv, 34

yahrzeit, 68
Yale Repertory Theatre, 177
Yates, Sidney, 194, 196, 215
Yeats, William Butler, 202
Yiddish, xiii, 94, 101, 103–104, 197.
  see also Jews
Yom Kippur War, 46
You Can't Take It with You (Kaufman
  and Hart), 138, 256
Young, Stark, 127
youth. *see also* childhood (and
  children)
    arts training and, 139, 270,
      293–294
    as audience, 132–133
    Fichandler, Zelda, and, xiii–xiv,
      xxii
    minority training and, 175–177
    poverty and, 34, 181
    theater and, 136–137, 218, 240
Yugoslavia, 34

zamissel, 79
Zavadsky, Yury, 125
Zeisler, Peter, 132, 277–280
Zelda Fichandler Award, xxviii,
  283–287
Zesch, Lindy, 278
Zizka, Blanka, 283n1

ZELDA FICHANDLER (1924–2016) dedicated her early career to the establishment of America's regional theater movement. In 1950 she founded Washington, DC's Arena Stage and in 1968 she produced *The Great White Hope*, which became the first production to transfer from a regional theater to Broadway, winning the Tony Award and the Pulitzer Prize, and launching the careers of James Earl Jones and Jane Alexander. Her production of *Inherit the Wind*, which toured Soviet St. Petersburg and Moscow and Arena Stage, was the first American theater company production sponsored by the State Department. Like many other regional theaters afterward, Arena Stage cultivated a resident company—always evolving—over the decades that included some of America's best actors: Robert Prosky, Frances Sternhagen, George Grizzard, Philip Bosco, Ned Beatty, Roy Scheider, Robert Foxworth, Jane Alexander, James Earl Jones, Melinda Dillon, Dianne Wiest, Max Wright, Marilyn Caskey, Harriet Sansom Harris, and Tom Hewitt. In 1975 Arena was the first regional theater to be recognized by the American Theatre Wing and the Broadway League with the Regional Theatre Tony Award for Outstanding Achievement. When Ms. Fichandler retired as producing artistic director of Arena Stage in 1990, she had achieved the longest tenure of any noncommercial producer in the annals of the American theater. Before her death in July 2016, Ms. Fichandler was chair emeritus of New York University's acclaimed Graduate Acting Program where she personally taught, guided, and inspired more than five hundred acting students, including Mahershala Ali, Billy Crudup, Danai Gurira, Marcia Gay Harden, André Holland, Rainn Wilson, Debra Messing, Peter Krause, and Michael C. Hall. Her honors include the SDC Foundation's "Mr. Abbott" Award, The Acting Company's John Houseman Award, the Margo Jones Award, and the National Medal of Arts, and in 1999 she became the first artistic leader outside of New York to be inducted into the Theater Hall of Fame.

TODD LONDON's books include *This Is Not My Memoir* (with André Gregory); *An Ideal Theater: Founding Visions for a New American Art*; *Outrageous Fortune: The Life and Times of the New American Play*; *The Importance of Staying Earnest*; *15 Actors, 20 Years*; and *The Artistic Home*. He is the author of two novels, *If You See Him, Let Me Know* and *The World's Room* (Milestone Award winner). Todd spent eighteen years as artistic director of New York's New Dramatists, which received a special Tony Honor under his leadership. In 2009 Todd became the first recipient of Theatre Communications Group's Visionary Leadership Award for "an individual who has gone above and beyond the call of duty to advance the theater field as a whole." A former executive director of the University of Washington School of Drama and head of MFA Playwriting at The New School, Todd won the prestigious George Jean Nathan Award for Dramatic Criticism and in 2016 received an honorary doctorate from DePaul University's schools of music and theater. He is the founding director of The Third Bohemia, a national interdisciplinary retreat for artists.

THEATRE COMMUNICATIONS GROUP would like to offer
our special thanks to Furthermore: a program of
the J. M. KAPLAN FUND for their generous support of
the publication of *The Long Revolution: Sixty Years on
the Frontlines of a New American Theater*,
essays by Zelda Fichandler, edited by Todd London

Furthermore:
a program of the J.M. Kaplan Fund

tcg